Road to
BAGHDAD

Road to
BAGHDAD

MARTIN STANTON

PRESIDIO
PRESS

BALLANTINE BOOKS • NEW YORK

A Presidio Press Book
Published by The Random House Publishing Group

Copyright © 2003 by Martin Stanton

All rights reserved under International and Pan-American Copyright
Conventions. Published in the United States by The Random House Publishing
Group, a division of Random House, Inc., New York, and simultaneously in
Canada by Random House of Canada Limited, Toronto.

Presidio Press and colophon are trademarks of Random House, Inc.

www.ballantinebooks.com

Library of Congress Cataloging-in-Publication Data is available from the
publisher upon request.

ISBN 0-89141-805-9

Book design by Susan Turner

Manufactured in the United States of America

First Edition: June 2003

10 9 8 7 6 5 4 3 2 1

This book is dedicated to the officers and men of OPM-SANG and their civilian contractor counterparts in the Vinnell Corporation, the Second Brigade (King Abdul Aziz) of the Saudi Arabian National Guard, and lastly, to all those who were held hostage in Iraq during the Gulf war of 1990–1991.

ACKNOWLEDGMENTS

Writing a book, even one that is a labor of love, is an exhausting undertaking. At the end you feel as if you've run a marathon. The difference is, of course, a marathon you run alone but a book you get all sorts of help on. I'd like to thank the people who provided me the encouragement to write this book, Maj. Gen. James B. Taylor (Ret.) and Col. John Noble (Ret.). I'd like to thank many people for their recollections, John McCollah, Manfred "Lo" Locher, Shoichi Hasegawa, John Noble, Rich Cassem, my mother Mary Jane Stanton and my sister Peggy to name but a few. A great debt of thanks I owe to my editor E. J. McCarthy for his professionalism, thoroughness, and helpful candor; an author was seldom, if ever, better served. Lastly I save my greatest thanks for my wife, Donna, whose patient support when I was strongly tempted to chuck the whole project helped me carry the day.

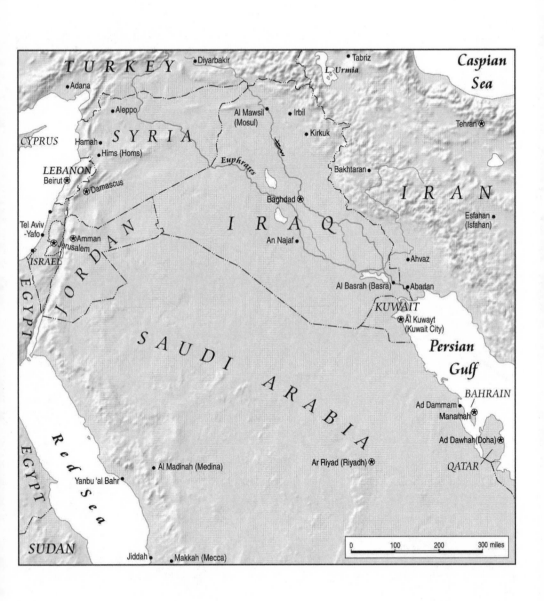

KUWAIT CITY

Jūn al Kuwayt

Map Legend

- **Major landmarks**
- **Neighborhoods** (KEIFAN)
- Major streets
- Motorways
- Built up areas

0 _____ 2 miles

Inset Map

IRAQ

KUWAIT

SAUDI ARABIA

- Umm Qasr
- Az Zawr
- Kuwait City
- Al Jahrah
- Al Funaytis
- Al Funayhil
- Mina Abd Allah
- Al Abdaliyah
- Al Wafrah
- Mina Said
- Al Khafji
- Ras Al Khafji

Neighborhoods and Landmarks

- SALMIYA
- RUMAITHIYA
- SALWA
- SABAH AL SALEM
- MISHRIF
- BAYAN
- EAST HAWALLI
- HAWALLI
- JABRIYA
- SHAAB
- DAIYA
- DASMA
- QADISYA
- NUZHA
- SURRA
- RAWDAH
- MANSOURIYA
- ABDULLAH AL SALEM
- FAIHA
- IDALIYA
- CORDOBA
- ABRAK KHEITAN
- SOUTH KHEITAN
- KUWAIT
- SHAMIYA
- KEIFAN
- KHALDIYA
- YARMUK
- OMARIYA
- SHUWAIKH
- INDUSTRIAL AREA
- RAY INDUSTRIAL AREA
- RABIAH
- JLEEB AL SHUYOUKH
- PORT AREA
- RIGGAE
- ARDIYA
- ANDULUS
- AIN BAGHZI
- GRANADA
- SULAIBIKHAT
- INDUSTRIAL AREA

Landmarks

- Mowarat Hospital
- Spring Continental Hotel
- Kuwait Towers
- Amiri Palace
- Amiri Hospital
- Sief Palace
- Sheraton Hotel
- Salam Palace
- Marriott Marina Hotel
- American School
- French School
- Kuwait University
- Holiday Inn
- Sewage Works
- Gama Abdul Sebah Hospital
- Maternity Hospital
- Kuwait University
- Container Terminal
- Farwaniya Hospital

Streets and Roads

- AL BLAJAT ST.
- BIDAA ROAD
- ARABIAN GULF STREET
- BAGHDAD ST.
- AMMAN ST.
- AL KHATTABI ST.
- ABDUL KARIM
- MASJID AL AQSA ST.
- FAHAHEEL EXPRESSWAY
- TUNIS STREET
- HAWALLI STREET
- BEIRUT
- AL WGHEERA ST.
- AL SAFR MOTORWAY
- CAIRO ROAD
- ISTIQLAL ST.
- RING ROAD
- FIRST
- SOOR STREET
- FOURTH RING ROAD
- FIFTH RING ROAD
- SIXTH RING ROAD
- SECOND RING ROAD
- THIRD RING ROAD
- KING FAISAL STREET
- AIRPORT ROAD
- GHAZALI STREET
- ARABIAN GULF STREET
- AIRPORT ROAD
- CANADA DRY STREET
- GHAZALI STREET
- NASSER STREET
- JAHRA ROAD
- FOURTH RING ROAD
- FIFTH RING ROAD
- SIXTH RING ROAD
- MOHAMMAD IBN KASSEM STREET
- ABU DHABI STREET

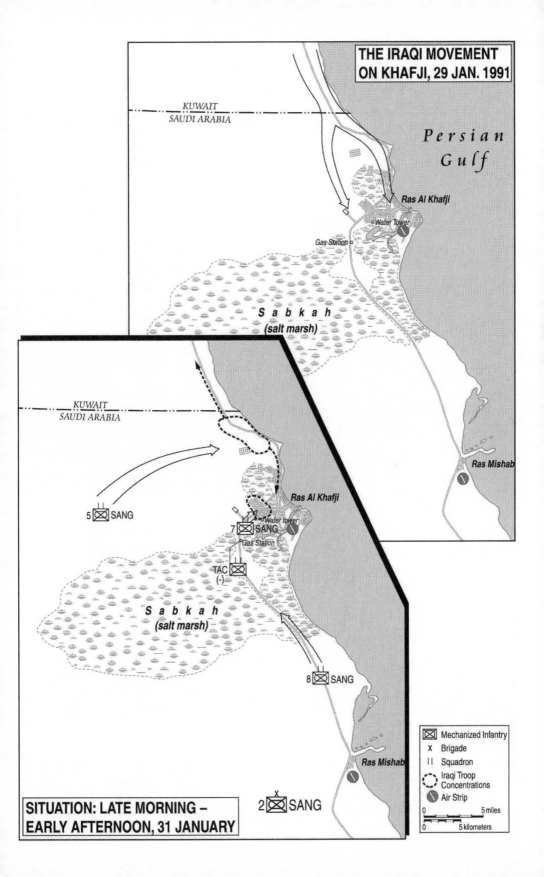

THE IRAQI MOVEMENT
ON KHAFJI, 29 JAN. 1991

KUWAIT
SAUDI ARABIA

P e r s i a n
G u l f

Ras Al Khafji

Water Tower

Gas Station

S a b k a h
(salt marsh)

Ras Mishab

KUWAIT
SAUDI ARABIA

5 ⊠ SANG

7 ⊠ SANG

Ras Al Khafji

Water tower

Gas Station

TAC (-) ⊠

S a b k a h
(salt marsh)

8 ⊠ SANG

Ras Mishab

2 ⊠ SANG
X

SITUATION: LATE MORNING –
EARLY AFTERNOON, 31 JANUARY

⊠ Mechanized Infantry
x Brigade
‖ Squadron
⬭ Iraqi Troop
  Concentrations
◉ Air Strip

0   5 miles
0   5 kilometers

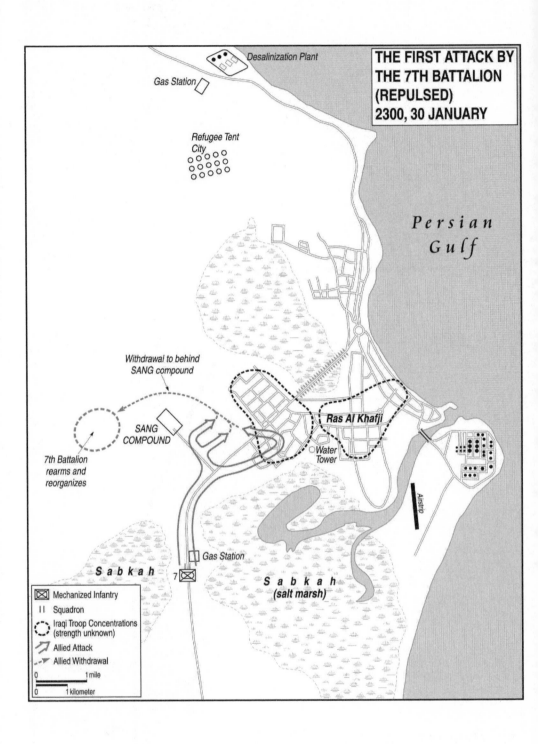

THE FIRST ATTACK BY
THE 7TH BATTALION
(REPULSED)
2300, 30 JANUARY

Desalinization Plant

Gas Station

Refugee Tent City

Persian Gulf

Withdrawal to behind SANG compound

SANG COMPOUND

Ras Al Khafji

7th Battalion rearms and reorganizes

Water Tower

Airstrip

Gas Station

Sabkah

7

Sabkah (salt marsh)

Mechanized Infantry

II Squadron

Iraqi Troop Concentrations (strength unknown)

Allied Attack

Allied Withdrawal

0   1 mile

0   1 kilometer

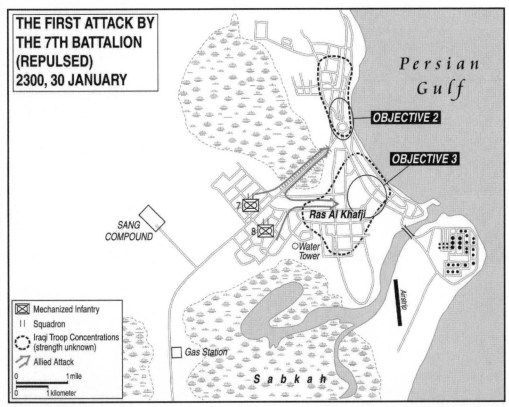

THE FIRST ATTACK BY
THE 7TH BATTALION
(REPULSED)
2300, 30 JANUARY

Persian
Gulf

OBJECTIVE 2

OBJECTIVE 3

SANG
COMPOUND

7

8

Ras Al Khafji

Water
Tower

Airstrip

Mechanized Infantry

Squadron

Iraqi Troop Concentrations
(strength unknown)

Allied Attack

0   1 mile
0   1 kilometer

Gas Station

Sabkah

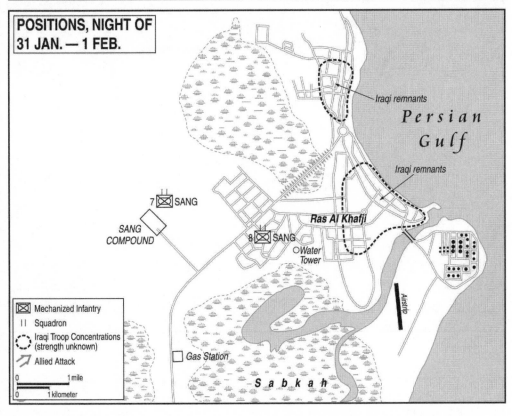

POSITIONS, NIGHT OF
31 JAN. — 1 FEB.

Iraqi remnants

Persian
Gulf

Iraqi remnants

7 SANG

SANG
COMPOUND

8 SANG

Ras Al Khafji

Water
Tower

Airstrip

Mechanized Infantry

Squadron

Iraqi Troop Concentrations
(strength unknown)

Allied Attack

0   1 mile
0   1 kilometer

Gas Station

Sabkah

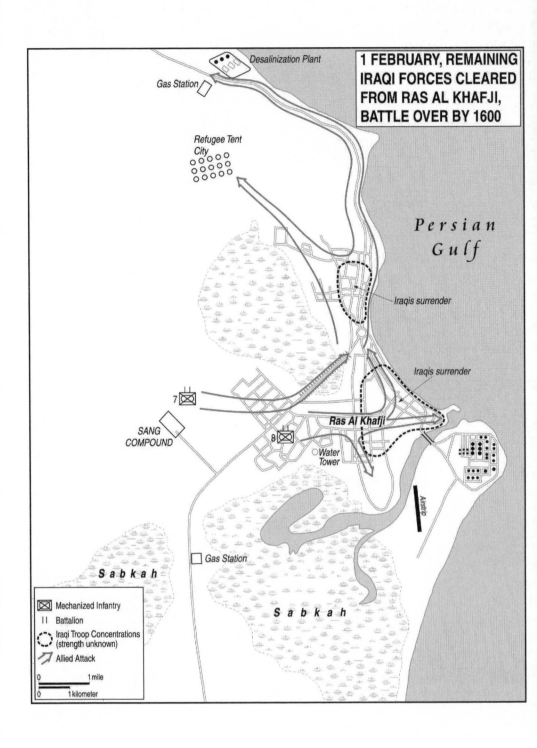

1 FEBRUARY, REMAINING IRAQI FORCES CLEARED FROM RAS AL KHAFJI, BATTLE OVER BY 1600

Desalinization Plant

Gas Station

Refugee Tent City

Persian Gulf

Iraqis surrender

Iraqis surrender

7

SANG COMPOUND

8

Ras Al Khafji

Water Tower

Airstrip

Gas Station

Sabkah

Sabkah

⊠ Mechanized Infantry

II Battalion

Iraqi Troop Concentrations (strength unknown)

Allied Attack

0   1 mile

0   1 kilometer

Road to
BAGHDAD

PROLOGUE

Fort Irwin, California,
Fall 1988

I SUPPOSE YOU COULD SAY the whole thing happened because of administrative error. I went before the promotion board for major in 1988 and didn't make it. The news reached me in the field at Fort Irwin, California, where I was assigned as an observer controller (a sort of umpire/trainer) in the large war games there. The news shocked me. I knew I wasn't the army's favorite son, but I couldn't figure out what I had done that was bad enough to deny me a promotion. Being passed over for major meant that I would have to get out of the army in another year or so.

As soon as we were out of the field, I flew to the army's personnel headquarters in Alexandria, Virginia, to look at my records and find out what had gone wrong. A quick look at my promotion review file revealed that it was missing an efficiency report and other key items. I requested and received a reconsideration for promotion based on administrative errors in the compilation of my promotion review file (oops, er . . . sorry, Captain. Let's look at that one again). Eventually I was informed that I had been reconsidered for promotion and selected for major. The whole nerve-racking process took about five months.

The trouble was, I had missed the assignments cycle. I was due to leave Fort Irwin in the summer of 1989 and still had no job. So I called my infantry branch management officer and asked him what was available.

Assignments officers are harried people who usually try to send officers where they want to go. Unfortunately there are far fewer good assignments than there are people who want them. (For example, Hawaii may have 1 percent of the major's slots in the U.S. Army, but

30 percent of the majors ask to go there.) An assignments officer spends a lot of time telling people what they don't want to hear, then trying to convince them that it's good for them. There is usually a small amount of negotiation involved, and you are given at least the illusion of choice in most cases. What it comes down to is that at any given time a certain amount of the slots in the army are due to come open and need to be filled.

The guy I got was artful. He began with a few clear nonstarters—recruiting in Lansing, Michigan, and reserve components instructor to the Massachusetts National Guard—stuff that no normal infantry officer would volunteer for. By declining these, I used up advantage. An officer can turn down only so many offers before he gets stuck with something. I could tell that this guy was maneuvering me into position for something he had in mind; he just wasn't ready to spring it on me yet. I had the sudden clear mental image of a largemouth bass being teased by a lure. Trouble was, it was the only game in town.

There was a pause in the conversation; then it came. "Well," he said, "I see on your preference sheet that you have Middle East checked as an overseas preference." This was true; I had also checked Europe and Asia. "I happen to have something that would be just up your alley. How'd you like to go to Saudi Arabia?" He paused. "It's about the best I can offer right now."

There it was, out in the open. I admit I was surprised. I didn't even know we had anything in Saudi Arabia. "To do what?" I asked. His voice warmed, like a used car salesman moving in for the kill. "To be a brigade advisor, man! You'd be the senior advisor to an entire mechanized brigade of the Saudi National Guard, which is a regular full-time force, not like our National Guard. You're more than qualified for it." I guffawed at this last bit. "Other than the fact that I'm not an FAO [foreign area officer] and don't speak Arabic, what else recommends me for this?" I asked. He paused, debating with himself. Honesty won out. "Well, you're as qualified as anyone else that's available right now. You've got a lot of desert time in the NTC [National Training Center], and you're unmarried. A lot of wives go nuts over there. Besides, it's easier to move you than someone with a family." A pause. "Whatdya say?"

In truth, the thought of going to Saudi Arabia didn't bother me. It was definitely off the beaten track. Most infantry officers go to Germany and Korea, or maybe Panama. But Saudi Arabia? I didn't know anyone who had been there. There was the definite allure of adventure, of visiting a place that few American soldiers ever got to see (little did I know). I joined the army to see the world, and this would definitely expand my horizons. (So I'm a tourist; there's a little tourist in every soldier.) I told him I'd take the job. He let out a whoop and said I'd have my orders in a few days. And so, with that simple, lighthearted decision, I set into motion a whole series of strange events.

Part One

THE KINGDOM OF SAUDI ARABIA

1

RIYADH

FIVE MONTHS LATER I got off the plane in Riyadh. It was a Lufthansa flight, and I noticed how the businessmen had been pounding down drinks as if they were the last they'd get in some time (they were). Being a light drinker, I stayed sober and tried to relax. I mulled over in my mind everything I had learned about Saudi Arabia in the past few months. Once I'd received the assignment, I tried to learn as much as I could. I had even gotten Arabic language tapes and earned strange looks, as I drove across the country to leave my car in Florida, talking to myself and repeating the Arabic on the tapes. I picked up quite a few facts about Saudi Arabia.

- ◆ I learned that modern Saudi Arabia was founded by Ibn Saud Abdul Aziz in 1902 and that the Al Saud had been in charge of Saudi Arabia for less than a hundred years. This came as a surprise, because I had imagined a dynasty of Saudi monarchs leading back to the beginning of Islam itself. Actually, Saudi Arabia was a younger nation (in the western sense of the word) than the United States.

- ◆ I learned that most of the people in Saudi Arabia were Sunni Moslems who followed the sect known as Wahabism, which was the strictest sect in Sunni Islam. It was the interpretations of Islam by the Wahabists rather than the faith of Islam itself that made Saudi Arabia such a religiously strict place to live. The Wahabist Sunnis dominated the population and the royal family. The only major population of Shia Moslems in Saudi Arabia was in the eastern province. The Sunni often distrusted the Shia.

◆ I learned that the rulers of Saudi Arabia since the death of Abdul Aziz in 1953 had been his sons: first Saud, who was peacefully deposed by Faisel in the early 1960s, then Khalid, who replaced Faisel when he was assassinated in 1975, and finally Fahad, who replaced Khalid when he died in 1982.

◆ I learned that Faisel (whom most Americans remember negatively as one of the faces behind the Arab oil embargo of 1973–74) was actually a pro-western leader and the antithesis of the spoiled, thoughtless, playboy oil sheik. Rather he was a skillful leader who did more than anyone except Abdul Aziz himself to bring the Saudis into the twentieth century.

◆ I learned that the armed forces of Saudi Arabia were divided into two distinct elements: the Ministry of Defense and Aviation (MODA) forces, consisting of the regular army, the air force, and the navy; and the National Guard.

◆ I learned that women couldn't drive in Saudi Arabia but could own property, that slavery had been abolished in 1962, and that many Saudis were educated in the West.

Depending upon whom you read, the Saudis were either a totalitarian, repressive, oil-glutted monarchy whose ruling members led lives of wretched excess, or they were a responsibly conservative oligarchy trying to manage a new nation's headlong plunge into wealth and modernity as best it could. I hadn't read many books that agreed in their interpretation of the Saudis, so I didn't know what to think. The only two movies I'd ever seen about this part of the world were *Lawrence of Arabia* (the action took place mainly in northern Saudi Arabia and Jordan) and *John Goldfarb, Please Come Home* (a comedy about an off-course U2 pilot who lands in a fictional Arab country called Fawzia). I figured I would get off the plane and be greeted by either the thought police or a modern version of Omar Khayyam.

The desert beneath us was black and featureless, with only the occasional pool of electric lights from a small town or oil field to give any sign of human habitation. Eventually we got to a larger pool of lights in the blackness and landed at Riyadh a little after midnight.

I breezed through customs in a surprisingly short time, considering that my flight arrived at the same time as one carrying a planeload of Bangladeshi guest workers. My diplomatic passport helped.

To my surprise, my bags were not rifled for alcohol or pornography (two big no-no's). I got just a cursory look from a customs official with a wild, frizzy beard and a set of prayer beads. He nodded and waved me through. *"Shukran"* (thanks), I said. I'd heard that the Saudis liked it when you tried to speak Arabic to them, and I was eager to try out mine. He smiled slightly. "Not at all, my good man," he replied, sounding exactly like Robert Morely. "Enjoy your stay."

I was met by the guy I was replacing, Maj. Bob Sullivan, a big, friendly air defense officer several years senior to me with a Texas accent a mile wide. (I found out later that he was, in fact, from Oklahoma.) We threw my stuff in his truck and headed toward Riyadh. It was about 1:30 in the morning, so I didn't think there would be much going on. The Riyadh international airport is quite a distance from the city proper, connected by a well-lit, six-lane highway. Bob told me what was scheduled for the next few days and what my quarters would be like. I was only half listening, however, because I kept seeing groups of cars by the side of the road off in the desert. People were clustered around them and there were open fires, sort of like a Toyota pickup/BMW weenie roast. There were a few tents. Some people appeared to be sitting clustered around something that was glowing gently. My curiosity got the better of me and I asked Bob what they were doing.

He glanced over. "Oh, they're watching television," he said, completely nonplussed, obviously an old Arab hand. "They do it all the time—get the family together, drive out into the desert, have a picnic, and watch TV." Studying each little group more closely as we passed them, I could see that they all had TVs. Perplexed, I asked him where the power for the TVs came from. He looked at me with a sort of benevolent patience, like a master addressing a new apprentice. "They've all got portable generators. You won't see a Bedouin tent without some sort of TV antenna sticking up from it." He paused, noting my bewilderment. "Looks kinda crazy, doesn't it?" It did: odd and definitely out of place. I spent the rest of the drive listening to Bob and wondering what Lawrence of Arabia would have thought.

Bob dropped me off at my quarters and told me to sleep in, that he would be by to get me around noon. My house was huge for a bachelor officer's quarters, two bedrooms, a den, a large living room, a dining room, and a palatial kitchen. Whatever else this job had in store for me, there wasn't anything wrong with the digs. I spent about fifteen minutes exploring the house, then went up onto the roof. I had an excellent view of Riyadh, alien and sleeping. I felt a little out of place. (There's nothing like dropping in on a different culture at 2 A.M. to make you feel like a lost kid.) I called my family in the States to tell them I had made it to Riyadh, then I went down to the bedroom. There was a note from Bob Sullivan on the bed: "If you hear a lot of hollering and screaming at 5 A.M., don't worry, it's just prayer call." Armed with this helpful little hint, I lay down to rest, wondering just what I'd gotten myself into.

I spent the first day doing administrative in-processing. This included going to a Saudi clinic to get blood drawn in order to get a driver's license. The clinic was clean and modern, but the Saudis in their white robes and red-checkered headdresses looked out of place. Women would enter the clinic and quickly go through a door to the women's section. I thought it odd that I would have to get blood taken for a driver's license. Sullivan told me that Saudi citizens were required to give a pint of blood, but U.S. military advisors were excused from this. Later when I realized how many traffic accidents there were in Saudi Arabia, I came to see the sense in the pint-of-blood policy. For many people it was like a down payment. I got my license the next day. The in-processing schedule was leisurely, and I would not be going out to my brigade for about five days.

I borrowed a truck from the motor pool and spent the next few days familiarizing myself with Riyadh and its environs. The Saudi capital was a strange city to wander through. If I were writing travel brochures, I might be tempted to say something like, Riyadh is a city of contradictions, an exciting place where the old and the new collide. This, however, would have been gilding the lily. Riyadh was not a particularly exciting place, just strange. The old and the new did collide there, though. When I first saw Riyadh in the summer of 1989, modernization was still going on and a lot of the old souk area, with its traditional Arab open-stall markets, still existed. New public buildings (including several that looked like spaceships) rubbed elbows comfortably with the mud-and-block buildings and narrow, winding streets of an Indiana Jones movie. There were a few western-style shopping malls (where the merchandise was pricey) and a lot of souks. Some of the latter would take you right back to the Saturday afternoon serials of the 1930s: dark, cluttered alleys thronging with people, all manner of bartering and haggling going on around you, sinister faces peering out of shops as you—the outsider—wandered by. Actually, you could take this flight of fancy too far. No one comes out and grabs you and drags you into their store. Senor Ugate will not try to sell you the letters of transit (à la Casablanca), and that sinister face in the store is probably just wondering if he can off-load some of his cheaper "genuine Arab" (made in Poland) carpets on this gullible Ameriki. Oh yeah, just about everyone took MasterCard.

Most Saudi men wore the same thing: a *thobe*, which is like an ankle-length all-white nightshirt with a Nehru collar, and their traditional headdress, called a *gutrah*, which looks like a miniature checkered tablecloth from an Italian restaurant. A few of the more rebellious-looking teenagers cruising Hardees and Baskin-Robbins wore Pirate-label blue jeans and Fido Dido T-shirts. (I never did figure out what Fido Dido was.) For the most part, though, it was mostly *thobes* and *gutrahs*. You were supposed to be able to tell whether or not a man was rich by the quality of his *thobe*. I never could. I could, however, deduce that the man in the white *thobe* who was getting into the brand-new Jaguar was probably richer than I was.

Women were another matter entirely. All Saudi women wore the *abayah*, which humorist P. J. O'Rourke once called a "one-girl pup tent." It's as good a description as any. The *abayah* is a complete, head-to-toe black body covering that is supposed to hide a woman's every feature. There were slight variations: a sort of racier version with a vision slit for the eyes that would let a woman actually see. Other versions had a muslin veil that covered the entire face and left its wearer in a state of perpetual overcast. The Saudi women wore their *abayahs* whenever they left their house. The first time I saw them, I thought they looked like the ghosts from Pac-Man gliding down the sidewalk. It was strange to see them in stores. They sort of hovered over the merchandise they were interested in. Then a hand snaked out from under the *abayah*, picked up the item, and took it under the veil for closer perusal. Another technique was to lift the veil over the item like a Civil War photographer with his big camera on a tripod. Walking into a department store full of women shoppers was like watching feeding outer-space black jellyfish being photographed by a bunch of miniature Matthew Bradys. Some of the more conservative women even wore gloves so they would not have to expose any skin when they reached out from under their veils.

This face-covering practice applied only to Saudi women. Western women in Riyadh were allowed more leeway. They could wear either extremely conservative, skin-covering western clothes (for that schoolmarm-from-hell look) or an *abayah* that covered everything but their head. As a result, most western women in Riyadh looked like your mean aunt Sophie or as though they got lost on the way to commencement.

I wondered how the Saudi women could travel around without bumping into things. The truth was, sometimes they didn't. I learned later that if you sat in the Al-Kariyah mall long enough, you'd eventually see one fall on the escalator or misjudge and walk into a post. I suspected that there was a small percentage of Saudi women who never got the knack of seeing through the veil and as a result had multiple bruises and flattened noses.

What was unsettling to me in those first few days was that a society could choose such a bizarre way to dress and act. I could well imagine the women seething beneath their veils. I was at a loss as to why they put up with it. I later found out that I couldn't have been more mistaken. Talking to expatriate nurses who worked in various hospitals in Riyadh, I discovered that most Saudi women positively clung to their veils. In fact, they would wear them into their hospital beds and sometimes into the delivery room. Whenever just women were around, they would pull up the veils and chatter away, but as soon as a man came into the room the women would pull down the veils instantly. I was told that to be veiled at all times in public was their show of respectability, and only a tramp would let the world in general see her face.

Most of the stores in the souks were basically the same. Seemingly hundreds of rug stores all sold attractive, Arab-pattern rugs that were usually machine made in Eastern Europe. Genuine handwoven Arab or Persian rugs of much finer quality were also available but very expensive. I later found out that the Saudis used the mass-produced rugs in much the same way as we use indoor-outdoor carpeting. Every tent had a floor made up of rugs laid down and interlaced with one another. Open-air wedding parties would have several hundred rugs covering a football field–sized area, along with dozens of couches and chairs all arranged in a square facing inward. The other big seller in rugs was the Afghan "war rug." Some of the more expensive ones were authentic Afghan rugs with little Russian tanks, helicopters, grenades, and AK-47s woven into them. Most were imitations made in Eastern Europe.

The souk had hundreds of stores and spread for hundreds of meters in every direction. There were a lot of clothing stores, including many women's fashion shops with the latest expensive designs from Europe. I guess it's important to look your best under your black bag. I had read somewhere that women dress to impress other women; here was proof. As for the men, I suppose they wore western business suits when they traveled abroad. There were a great many variety stores; sort of one-man K-Marts, with the same brightly colored plastic housewares piled everywhere. Another standard item was a set of aluminum cauldrons ranging from two liters to literally bathtub size that fit inside one another. There were pet stores and stores that sold bolts of cloth, perfume and incense stores, and wild honey stores. There were also many stores selling candies and sweets (the Saudis have a national sweet tooth) as well as bakeries, all jammed next to one another almost as far as the eye could see. There were several souk areas like this throughout Riyadh, and in those first few days I spent most of my time wandering around them trying to take it all in.

The capper in Riyadh, though, was the gold souk. This was a huge market area near the Musmak fort (where Abdul Aziz killed Al Rashid, governor of Riyadh in 1902, and thus became the emir of what would become Saudi Arabia). From the outside, the gold souk looked like any other souk except that there seemed to be more gold there than in Fort Knox. The individual shops weren't much different from those in the other souks except that instead of plasticware and household goods they sold gold, lots and lots of gold (all eighteen karat or better; no cheapjack fourteen-karat stuff there, no sir). The sheer volume of the gold was mind numbing. A finely inlaid and intricately crafted twenty-four-karat-gold bracelet was impressive to see, although taken from a blue plastic garbage *bin* full of the same type of bracelet, it sort of lost something. Each store had bins such as these as well as countless display cases stuffed to the brim with every conceivable type of gold jewelry. Interestingly, there was almost no security, just a few beat cops walking around the way they did everywhere else I had been.

On my third day in Riyadh I was issued a new vehicle and my field equipment. I was impressed by the truck assigned to me: a 1989 GMC Jimmy with extra large fuel tanks, extra gas cans, and two spare tires. The vehicle also had other desert survival equipment, such as sand ladders, a winch, brackets for extra water cans, and its own tent/sunshade. Best of all, it had a high-frequency and a normal citizens band radio and a loran position-locating device. This was a vehicle meant for serious out-in-the-boonies desert driving. The equipment just kept on coming: a two-burner stove, two Coleman coolers, a lantern, a big water jug to put on the seat next to me, tool sets—you name it. If the NCO issuing the equipment had told me that the truck had an ejection seat, I wouldn't have been surprised. I also drew a little booklet of blue tickets that allowed me to get free gas at most gas stations (not really surprising, this being Saudi Arabia, but still a nice touch). It definitely wasn't your normal military vehicle, and it must have cost the Saudi government a small fortune to procure a fleet of them for the OPM-SANG (Office of the Project Manager, Saudi Arabian National Guard) advisory group. Clearly OPM-SANG was an organization that went first class in equipment.

They went first class in everything else too. I had assumed that the house Bob Sullivan put me in was just a guest house that I would be using until my smaller quarters were ready. After all, I wasn't married, and this two-bedroom house was easily 1,600 square feet. I was surprised to learn that this was my *little* house, and the one I would have in Al Hofuf was much bigger. I was actually in the smallest set of quarters that OPM-SANG owned in Riyadh. The married people on the other compound had much nicer houses. I looked at my two bedrooms, huge living room, and big kitchen and thought of the little bachelor officers' quarters I had just left in Fort Irwin. Bob Sullivan apologized that they had to put me in the smallest digs because I was the junior major. It was hard for me to be deadpan, but I told him I'd make do.

Bob also showed me around the other compounds in OPM-SANG. The main one (called the Oasis) held most of the married families with children. It was a big, shady place with large houses and a recreation center in the middle of the compound. The recreation center had a pool and a complete gym as well as a library, video library, and crafts shop. It also provided the satellite feed for the Armed Forces Television Network (AFN) from Italy to all of our houses. All in all, OPM-SANG was a very well kept secret in the army.

The other American service people in Riyadh lived well, but not as well. The only other major organization was the United States Military Training Mission (USMTM, pronounced "you-smit-em"). These soldiers were usually on one-year unaccompanied tours and lived on their own compound in apartments. They usually dealt only with the strict logistical functions of fielding new equipment systems to the Saudi MODA forces, as opposed to offering prolonged advisory services. The USMTM compound did have a good restaurant, as well as the only bar in all of Saudi Arabia—the Camel's Breath Saloon. Although technically illegal under Saudi law, the bar was overlooked by the Saudi authorities on the tacit understanding that it be kept low key and only U.S. servicemen and their western guests could drink there.

Each day during my in-processing and orientation, I went to briefings on the Saudi National Guard and OPM-SANG and their missions and organizations. What I learned confirmed to me that this was going to be a very unusual assignment.

The Saudi National Guard was made up of Saudi Bedouin tribesmen who were loyal to the house of Al Saud. The National Guard, headed by Crown Prince Abdullah, was the primary internal security force in Saudi Arabia. It had been formed by the founder of Saudi Arabia, Abdul Aziz, and originally went by the name "The White Army." It was unique in numerous ways. First, it was exclusive; you had to be a Sunni Moslem and a Saudi Bedouin to join. Second, it had various levels of organization, ranging from conventionally organized mechanized brigades to provincial battalions of light infantry to tribal levees complete with flowing robes, frizzy beards, bolt-action Mausers, and bandoliers across their chest. Although the National Guard had the mission of augmenting the MODA forces in the event of an external threat to the Kingdom, it was first and foremost an internal security force, responsible for the security at the two holy sites and the oil fields in the eastern province (which coincidentally had the biggest Shia population in Saudi Arabia). The positioning of the National Guard units was the clearest indicator of this. The units were stationed in the center of the country, with one mechanized brigade in Riyadh and one in Al Hofuf, near the eastern province oil fields, as well as light infantry battalions in the major population centers. The MODA forces, on the other hand, were positioned around the borders of the country, in King Khalid Military City, Tabuk, Kamis Musheyt, and other sites. The SANG were in effect the Praetorian Guard of the Saudi regime. The SANG had undergone foreign training and modernization by Jordanian and British officers in the 1950s and 1960s, but these military training missions were unsatisfactory to the Saudis. In 1973 the Saudi government negotiated with the U.S. government for a military training and modernization mission with the National Guard, and OPM-SANG was born.

OPM-SANG was a unique organization by anyone's standards. Although administered by Army Material Command, it was in fact the U.S. Army advisory group for the Saudi Arabian National Guard. Upon receiving orders for it, I had imagined that this was a relatively new organization. I was surprised to learn that, in fact, OPM-SANG had been in existence since 1974 and the initial memorandum of agreement (MOA) with the Saudi Arabian government had been signed in 1973. According to the MOA, the mission statement of OPM-SANG was as follows: "To provide technical and supervisory assistance to the government of Saudi Arabia in connection with preparation of a National Guard Modernization Plan to cover such functions as organization, training, procurement, construction, maintenance, supply and administrative support; development and administration of training programs, procurement of facilities, materials, equipment and services necessary to implement the Plan. Supervision of the design and construction of training, maintenance, supply and communication facilities and other facilities related thereto, as necessary to implement the plan. Management of the establishment and operation of training administrative and logistic support elements."

In turn, the Saudi government's responsibilities under the MOA were also clearly defined: "To be responsible for payment of all defense articles and services procured for the program, to be responsible for the necessary planning, programming, priority establishment, recruitment and selection processes which are required to provide qualified manpower and all other such supporting facilities and services required for this program; to give the modernization program priority over any other project for improvement of the National Guard."

The first sentence in this last part of the agreement was significant. Unlike many other foreign military assistance programs that the U.S. Army conducts in other parts of the world, this one was funded entirely by the Saudis. They footed the bill for virtually everything, including housing, vehicles, and reimbursing the U.S. government for our paychecks while we were there. Keeping Maj. Martin Stanton on active duty in Saudi Arabia for two years wasn't costing the U.S. government a cent. This was a source of great pride to the Saudis. They were happy for our military/technical advice and our training support but were determined to deal with us on an equal footing.

OPM-SANG was commanded by a one-star general who went by the title of project manager. The project manager when I arrived there was Brig. Gen. Waldo Freeman, who was replaced in July 1990 by Brig. Gen. James Taylor. OPM-SANG headquarters was broken down into an administration section, logistics directorate, and operations directorate. The logistics directorate, headed by a full colonel, coordinated all logistics and procurements with the National Guard and assisted them in all aspects of supply and support operations and policy. The operations directorate, the larger of the two main directorates, was responsible for the advisors to the National Guard staff and the National Guard military academy, which encompassed not only the training of officer cadets but all military skills schooling for National Guard soldiers. The operations directorate also controlled the advisors to the eastern and western provinces; the advisors and their small staffs were located in Dammam and Jeddah, respectively. In addition, the operations directorate was responsible for the advisory teams with the two Saudi National Guard mechanized brigades: the Imam bin Saud Brigade, located in Riyadh, and the King Abdul Aziz Brigade, located in Al Hofuf. I was to be the advisor to the King Abdul Aziz Brigade. In addition to everything else, the operations directorate was heavily involved in helping the Saudis select a follow-on fighting vehicle to the V-150 armored cars that they currently operated. Over the next year, I became involved in the design for this force structure and the organization of the brigade reconnaissance companies.

OPM-SANG was not a big organization. Only fifty to sixty U.S. Army soldiers (mostly officers and senior NCOs) were assigned to it prior to the war. The staff was augmented by Department of the Army civilians and by local hires, many of whom were the wives of servicemen stationed there. The staff performed many of the secretarial and administrative duties internal to the organization. However, the job of training the guard and assisting in the administration and execution of its modernization plans took hundreds of people. Most of these were contractors from the Vinnell Corporation. The Vinnell Corporation personnel (or "Vinnellis" as they were called) were made up mostly of retired NCOs, warrant officers, and officers. They did most of the "rubber meets the road" training under the direction of OPM-SANG staff. The Vinnellis were highly professional, and their contract administrator was a retired army general named Victor Hugo, who did not suffer fools and also got along well with the Saudis.

I was to work in the operations branch. My duties were split between Al Hofuf, where the King Abdul Aziz Brigade was, and Riyadh, where I had to report once a week for meetings. I would be doing a lot of driving in the eastern province, that's for sure. When I arrived, the operations branch was headed by Col. Early Smith, an easygoing and congenial army aviator. The brigade and province advisory teams were controlled by Lt. Col. Robert Brown. He was responsible for compiling evaluation sheets on the Vinnell contractors and, from these evaluations, awarding funds for contract performance. This made him sort of the bad guy in some of the Vinnell Corporation people's eyes, but he wasn't. Like anyone else with the unpopular job of enforcing standards, he was bound to make some people angry, but I never saw him do anything unfair. He had just extended his tour and would be my boss for the duration of my stay in Saudi Arabia, although as things turned out I spent most of my time outside of his supervision.

I had my interview with Brigadier General Freeman. In it we discussed the National Training Center and the tactics, techniques, and procedures I had learned there. Brigadier General Freeman was a highly decorated infantry officer from the Vietnam War. Judging from his interest and semi-wistful expression at my descriptions of the training that went on there, I suspected that he would much rather have been the commander at the NTC than the project manager of OPM-SANG. Nonetheless he had a thorough command of his job and the purpose of OPM-SANG. He welcomed me to the unit and cautioned me on two different subjects. The first was not to be impatient with the Saudis and to learn that they worked at their own speed. The key was to be there when they needed my help. The second was to ensure that my Vinnell contractors performed their duties to standard and to not get "Stockholm syndrome" (identifying with the adversaries) in dealing with the Saudis. We could work together and get along fine, but I was not to forget that I was ultimately the Saudis' evaluator. Armed with this advice, I thanked the general and went home to pack. The next day I would go to Al Hofuf and meet the Saudi guardsmen I was to advise.

Bob Sullivan and I left for Al Hofuf the next morning. We drove east down the Dhahran-Riyadh highway, passing National Guard headquarters and Camp Vinnell as we traveled. The built-up area of the city became more sparse, then abruptly halted as we climbed the escarpment east of the city and entered the desert. It was my first view of the Saudi desert, and it was impressive. I had imagined that I was an experienced desert dweller from my time at Fort Irwin. However, the California desert was a lot different from what I encountered here. The California desert had ridgelines and mountains to navigate by, and there were some plants, such as Joshua trees and creosote bushes. Although the California desert was inhospitable, it gave the impression that life existed there. The Saudi desert gave a different impression. It was flat and almost devoid of plant life. The wide, modern, six-lane highway seemed out of place on the alien landscape. There was little terrain relief, and I could see the horizon in every direction. About twenty miles outside of Riyadh, we stopped at a checkpoint on the highway and had our passports inspected. It was another indicator that I was in a different part of the world. Travel in Saudi Arabia was restricted, and a passport into the country didn't guarantee travel everywhere within the country. The policemen at the checkpoint were friendly, though, and recognized Bob; they let us through with a perfunctory wave.

We turned off the Dammam highway and went down the Khurais highway toward Al Hofuf. The Khurais road, a lot different from the Dammam highway, was a little, two-lane road that traveled through the dunes of the deep desert and the Khurais oil field. With the exception of the little town of Khurais itself, there was no civilization whatsoever along the road, just dunes and flat sand. The most disconcerting thing about the Khurais road was the number of wrecked cars and trucks along it. Bob Sullivan told me that the Saudis drove along the Khurais highway at breakneck speeds and often traveled the little road two or three abreast, so the oncoming traffic had to thread its way through opposing traffic. Bob cautioned me to "take to the desert" if it looked as though I couldn't get past oncoming vehicles. "You might get stuck, but it's better than having a head-on," he told me. I digested his warning for several minutes. The number of wrecks increased. It was clear to me that the Khurais road was a dangerous place. We drove on through the desert and saw a camel herd and some Bedouin with their goats, but for the most part we saw only sand and more sand.

We finally reached Al Hofuf after about three and a half hours of fast driving. We passed through some low, bare hills as we approached the town. It could see it in the distance, but we turned down a side road before entering town. Just past a low ridgeline we reached the 2d Brigade area. I wasn't supposed to meet the brigade commander for another hour, so Bob spent about an hour driving me through the various battalions and showing me the lay of the land. The 2d Brigade's area was huge. Three of the infantry battalions and the engineer company had separate camps along the main road; sharing a larger camp nearer to town were the field artillery, a 4th Infantry Battalion, the support battalion, and the air defense battery. The housing area for the brigade's families was huge, with hundreds of little houses along well-ordered streets. The motor pools and equipment warehouses were all well laid out, and the vehicles were neatly lined up. The first impression I had was a positive one. The brigade looked clean and orderly. We finally turned into the brigade headquarters and went to our own little trailer outside the main headquarters building to meet my Vinnell advisor team.

Bob Quinn was the chief Vinnell advisor, and I liked him from the start. He was a retired full colonel of infantry with multiple combat tours in Vietnam. Bob Sullivan had spoken highly of him, and after a few days with him I could see why. Our relationship could have been much more difficult than it was. After all, although I was a brand-new major, I was also his boss and contract evaluator. This was like putting a new high-school football coach in charge of Mike Ditka. But Bob wasn't a big-ego kind of guy. He knew exactly how good he was but also exactly what he was there for: to train the Saudis. I was his third regular army advisor and contract evaluator, and he brought me up to date on his team's activities thoroughly and professionally. He understood that we both had our functions in this relationship and the most important thing was to give the brigade the best training possible.

I met most of the Vinnell team that day, and they were real characters. All were retired officers, warrant officers, or NCOs of exceptionally long service. All were Vietnam veterans (Junior Stewart was even a Korea veteran), and all were long-service personnel with Vinnell who had been with the contract for more than three years. Some were saving all their money to buy homes or put their kids through school. Others were paying alimony to multiple ex-wives and lived for their biannual trips to Thailand. But all were thoroughly professional. Bob Quinn ran a tight team.

Around 10:30 P.M. I went to see the brigade commander, Meteb Jawal Al Anazi. I reported in to him, formally walking up to his desk and saluting. I thought I would use some of the Arabic I had learned from tapes, so I said, *"Marhaba Aqid Meteb Jawal, ana Raa-id Martin Stanton, Il Jaysh Ameriki, Kayf ha alek?"* (Hello, Colonel Meteb Jawal. I am Major Martin Stanton of the American Army. How are you?) His lean hawk face brightened and he replied jovially, "Hey . . . Schloanak!" I had no idea what it meant. (I learned later that it was slang—literally translated "What's your color?") So much for my Arabic introduction. Fortunately, Meteb Jawal spoke excellent English, so we conversed without difficulty.

He was a tall, lean, weather-beaten figure of a man, about fifty, with sharp features, thick black hair, and direct black eyes that looked right into mine. His demeanor was commanding but friendly in an expansive sort of way. I was reminded of Anthony Quinn in *Lawrence of Arabia*. Meteb welcomed me to the brigade and wished me a good stay in Saudi Arabia. We talked about my career and what I brought to the table. I could see that he was surprised at my youth, but I tried to put my best foot forward. Colonel Meteb spoke well of Bob Quinn, and it was clear they had developed a close relationship over the years. Meteb spoke about his passion for falcon hunting and promised to take me on a falcon hunt. We then went to lunch, where I met the rest of the brigade staff. They were an interesting group. Some were older guys who hadn't missed a meal lately; others were young and fit. I was to find that enthusiasm for and proficiency at their jobs varied from man to man. Most spoke some English, and a few were fluent in it. All of them regarded me with a detached, friendly curiosity. I wasn't the first American officer they had seen, so I wasn't a big event to them. They were fascinating to me. The lunch was my first experience of a traditional Arab meal, consisting of roast goat on a bed of rice. Everyone just reached in and yanked out a piece of meat with their bare hands. My hosts could see that I was a newbie at this, so they pulled out pieces and gave them to me. The hardest thing was eating rice with my hands. Then we washed our hands with detergent, and the Saudis went to prayer call. Bob Quinn, Bob Sullivan, and I went back to Quinn's office, where I promptly threw up from drinking warm milk in the heat. It was not an auspicious start.

The workday was from 7 A.M. until noon prayer call. Bob Sullivan and I spent the rest of the day getting settled into our quarters and exploring Al Hofuf. Our house was a typical Arab villa—huge in comparison to quarters that a major would normally have. The villa was three stories and had eight bedrooms, two separate living rooms, and a kitchen that could easily feed a platoon of troops. I had to re-mind myself that this was a house built for a guy with multiple wives and a dozen or so children. When Bob Sullivan left, I would have it to myself. The house was in the middle of a typical Saudi suburban neighborhood, and like every other house in Saudi Arabia was sur-rounded by a wall, behind which the women of the family could walk around unveiled. I was to find out over time that the house had all sorts of quirky imperfections: The counter cabinets opened on the top instead of the side. A drain in the master bathroom was actually at the highest point in the floor, so I would have to squeegee water up into it (someone was sleeping in architect class that day). There were sinks in the hallways for guests to wash their hands and feet. There was red crushed velvet carpeting that assaulted the eyes. All in all, it was the strangest quarters I had ever been given. But the air-conditioning worked, and it definitely wasn't cramped.

After dropping off our stuff, Bob took me for a tour of Al Hofuf. It was a much larger town than I expected, a small city in fact. It was situated on the largest oasis in the Arabian Desert; its date palm groves were reputed to make the best dates in the world. Al Hofuf dates constituted the only other export of Saudi Arabia besides pe-troleum products. The date groves lent an aspect of greenness and shade to Al Hofuf that mitigated (but did not eliminate) the harsh-ness of the desert.

Al Hofuf itself was a fascinating place. Most of the town was less modern than Riyadh, so it kept a larger portion of its *Arabian Nights* mystery. There was a large mud fort in the center of town similar to the Musmak fort in Riyadh. In addition, the low hills outside Al Hofuf were honeycombed with natural caves, which were a big tourist attraction. Driving through town after evening prayers, we went through several souks thronging with people. I was surprised to see women walking along conservatively dressed but unveiled. Bob Sullivan told me that they were Shia Muslims and that a large por-tion of Al-Hofuf's population was Shia. One of the major reasons the King Abdul Aziz Brigade was in Al Hofuf was to provide a security force against a possible Shia uprising. I didn't know how much of a threat this really was. (Later I got to know some of my neighbors—all Shia—and had the feeling that, left to their own devices, they might have changed some of the figures in local government, but they were hardly the flaming Shia radicals that I saw on TV during the Iranian hostage crisis.) There was a huge camel souk outside town that we walked through; it stank to high heaven. Most camels do not like westerners (something about the way we smell), so Bob and I were careful to keep our distance in order not to get nipped or spit on. He showed me the marketplace where the Thursday souk was held: a huge, open field with only a few vacant wooden stalls in it. Bob told me I wouldn't be disappointed if I went there, and I made a mental note to pay it a visit.

Bob Quinn and Bob Sullivan spent the next three days introducing me around the brigade and briefing me on the training planned for the next year. In truth it didn't seem as though we were doing much, just a brigade exercise in December, a live-fire density in February or March, and a couple of command post exercises. For a brigade-sized element, it was a leisurely schedule. I needed background as to why we weren't training more, so I asked Bob Quinn. He gave me a good rundown of the problems of training the Saudi National Guard. He had excellent insights, not only from working with the Saudi National Guard but from his tours in Vietnam and Germany as well. I was to learn a great deal from him in the upcoming months.

What Bob told me was that a nation's military establishment is a reflection of its culture. Culturally, the Saudis were very different from Americans. These differences manifested themselves in the characteristics of the Saudi military. These characteristics could be summarized as follows:

- ✦ The Saudis had an authoritative/centralized command and control ethos. They did not make decisions quickly and tended to make decisions by committee. Seldom would you find a "risk taker" who would stand up and take responsibility before he knew it was safe to.

- ✦ Junior leader initiative was not encouraged. Lieutenants learned by watching their risk-averse company commanders. As a result they became strictly executors of higher orders. If the tactical situation changed, they would still follow the last orders given. Officers did not become real decisionmakers until they achieved battalion command. Even then, their long apprenticeship in the unempowered junior officer ranks left them ill prepared to be decisive, tactical decisionmakers.

◆ Most of the soldiers in the National Guard were older than those in the U.S. Army. A higher percentage of the soldiers were in their mid-twenties to early thirties. There existed in the Saudi Guard "professional privates," who just drove armored cars or were rifle squad members.

◆ The Saudi enlisted men were not as well educated as their American counterparts. Illiteracy was being overcome, but most soldiers still had less than an eighth-grade education.

◆ The Saudi National Guard had no noncommissioned officer (NCO) corps. Sergeants were merely senior privates with little command authority. All tactical and administrative decisions were made by officers, even at the lower levels.

◆ The officer corps was better educated than the enlisted. Many officers were bilingual. Most had university degrees.

◆ The Saudi National Guard had a five-day workweek, Saturday through Wednesday. The typical workday had three to four hours of useful time: from roughly 6:30 A.M. to noon prayer call, with several tea breaks.

◆ In addition to the short workdays, the National Guard's field training exercise program was limited in scope. Units did only two to three overnight field exercises per year. None of these exercises lasted for more than a week. This was in stark contrast to my experience in the U.S. Army, when spending more than 150 days a year in the field was not uncommon.

◆ Most National Guard units deployed to live-fire-gunnery/ qualification density just once per year. Again this contrasted sharply with my experience in the U.S. Army, where units conducted multiple gunneries per year, and rarely a month went by without some sort of range or live fire.

◆ Saudi National Guard soldiers usually had sixty days per year leave (ninety days is not uncommon), as opposed to the maximum of thirty days in the U.S. military.

◆ There was no training during the Islamic holidays of
Ramadan/Eid Al Fitr. This caused the loss of an additional
thirty-five to forty-five days of training time.

Quinn explained that these characteristics/parameters would not
change. There was no use trying to get the Saudis to increase their
workday or do more overnight exercises. They were culturally incapable of doing so. They had no interest in radically altering their behavior, because that behavior and lifestyle suited them just fine. They
looked upon our past attempts to change them as uninformed at best
and rude at worst.

A perfect example of how Americans misunderstood the Saudis'
motivation was the issue of field training. Nothing exasperated many
U.S. military advisors more than the seeming unwillingness of the
Saudis to go to the field and train. On the other hand, the Saudis re-
sented the American insistence on this and the Americans' general ig-
norance of what the true problem was over increasing field-training
time. The biggest obstacle to increased field exercise time was the
National Guard soldier's family. The guard soldier going to the field
had to either arrange for a male family member (such as a brother,
father, or cousin) to come and live with his family for the duration of
his absence, or send his family to live with other family members. He
could not easily leave his wife and children alone. To American soldiers who routinely left their wives and children with the car, the
checkbook, and a power of attorney, the Saudi practice was difficult
to understand.

We had to remember that women do not drive in Saudi Arabia,
and their position in society was not the same as that of American
women. The care of soldiers' families was an extended family responsibility, and there were no unit community blocks or family assistance groups as in the U.S. Army. The dependence of the soldiers'
families and the restrictions that this placed on extended field time
had to be accepted as a given.

The bottom line was that an advisor needed to have patience in
dealing with the Saudis. There was no point in telling them that the
U.S. Army trained to a certain operational tempo, because the Saudis
were not Americans. An advisor just had to be aware of opportunities to train and follow up on what the Saudi soldiers were interested
in. It was pointless to be adamant about training on one area when

the guardsmen were interested only in something else. There was a lot of one-on-one persuasion and salesmanship involved in getting the Saudis to commit to training events. The training was definitely not U.S. Army style. Bob Sullivan and I went back to Riyadh after four days. I officially took over the Al Hofuf mission from him and brought him to the airport. He wished me luck and departed. On the long drive back into Riyadh, I thought about the brigade and wondered just what I had gotten into.

2

I SPENT A COUPLE OF DAYS in Riyadh before going back to Al Hofuf. Because it was the weekend, Maj. Jim Good, one of the other bachelors in my housing complex, took me around and showed me the sights. I was surprised to learn that there was a considerable social scene in Riyadh. You'd never believe it to drive around town, but there were a lot of single women in Riyadh. Most of them were western nurses who worked in the local hospitals, including King Faisel Specialist Hospital, King Fahad Hospital, and King Khalid Hospital. The social circles of these women were fairly limited, because they couldn't drive and didn't have access to many of life's amenities that the diplomats and military advisors did. In short, I discovered that I was in a bachelor's paradise. I went to several parties that weekend and visited the Camel's Breath Saloon. I was utterly amazed at the number of women and the wildness of some of the parties. I went back to Al Hofuf that Saturday in a distinctly improved frame of mind. Clearly, things were looking up socially.

THE LIFE OF AN ADVISOR

My duties were divided between Al Hofuf and Riyadh. I would spend three or four days in Al Hofuf and one workday in Riyadh. Usually I would spend my weekends in Riyadh as well, except when I felt like exploring in the eastern province. I spent most of the first few months just rubbernecking around the brigade, finding out where everything was and talking to people. Most of my first office calls were innocuous. You never jumped right into anything in Saudi Arabia; there was a strict social protocol that was maintained. The first few office calls were always getting-to-know-you affairs. You would talk about anything but work: where you grew up, your family if you had one (children only; you never talked about wives), your travels, sports interests, and so on. There were a few taboo subjects; Israel was never brought up because the Saudis were too well mannered to mention it. Nor was there any discussion on the comparative merits of Saudi Arabia and the United States (although a Saudi's travels in the States were always a good icebreaker for discussion). Many of the Saudis I talked with expressed shock that a man of thirty-three had never been married and chided me that a man my age should have at least four sons.

My job, which revolved mainly around training the brigade headquarters, was an uphill struggle. All of the former training efforts over the past sixteen years had been directed at building a modern infrastructure for the National Guard while forming and training battalions. The effort to train a brigade headquarters was only a few years old. Much progress had been made in that time. The Saudis had formed staff sections (S1, personnel; S2, intelligence; S3, operations, plans, and training; S4, logistics), and they performed their basic administrative functions in garrison well enough. The challenge was training the brigade tactical headquarters. The brigade command post was not organized well for twenty-four-hour operations, nor did it have the requisite tracking charts and radio nets. The Vinnellis and I were basically working from scratch to get the headquarters organized as an effective tactical command and control facility.

Although we made baby step progress, we had trouble getting any of the staff or the brigade commander interested in serious training. That would have involved taking the brigade headquarters out into the field for several different command post exercises, and moving the headquarters several times both in daylight and at night. Only by practicing could the men become proficient, putting up the headquarters and taking it down to a timed standard while maintaining communications. Unfortunately their previous experience of internal security missions called for them to deploy battalions to various sectors within the oil fields or a city (such as Mecca), then set up the brigade headquarters in some government building and use radios dismounted from their vehicles or commercial telephones for command and control. The men understood that they should have a brigade tactical command post, but they didn't think it was that big a deal; they would get to it eventually. So we had to get things done in little steps.

The officers most receptive to our training overtures were the younger ones who had been to British and American military schools and knew what "right" looked like. Over time I came to know many of these officers well. My best friends were in the S3 section. Captain Mohammed Al Gharni, who had been to the U.S. Army officer advanced course, was easily the most proactive and aggressive of the Saudi officers I worked with. He was always asking questions about brigade organization and how a brigade command post should be operated. He was also responsible for coordinating the training ranges and ammunition for the brigade. He was a humorous, friendly sort who was not politically connected by family but had made a place for himself by sheer competence. He could always be depended upon for a straight answer.

Captain Ayash was another highly competent officer and a favorite of Bob Quinn. He was not particularly happy being a staff officer and looked forward to being a company commander. The brigade's communications officer, Capt. Saud Aziz, spoke the best English and was technically very adept, although he expressed continual frustration with the British radio systems that the brigade was equipped with. He and my Vinnell communications advisor, Gerry Smith, were two happy wireheads who liked nothing better than talking communications and figuring out how things worked. Like any communications officer, Captain Aziz had the grim determination to make it work, no matter what. These officers kept the operations shop going.

The operations officer, Lieutenant Colonel Abdullah, was a jovial man who took little interest in the nuts and bolts operations of the brigade and was content to let his more eager subordinates do the work. The other staff sections were a mixed bag. The S2 (intelligence) section wasn't in any way proficient at being a tactical intelligence staff. It was focused instead on working with the eastern province police authorities in supporting the brigade's internal security role. The American advisors were purposefully excluded from this by the Saudis. The S1 section was competent on personnel matters but hampered somewhat by the low education level of some of the soldiers in it. (Personnel clerks with an eighth-grade education are not conducive to efficiency in an administration section.)

My Vinnell personnel specialist, Junior Stewart, had his work cut out for him, but he had the serene personality to deal with it. The best-organized staff was the S4 (logistics) section. Lieutenant Colonel Khalid, the S4, ran a tight ship. He and his Vinnell advisor, Tom Tracey, got along exceptionally well. Logistics and support was in many ways the brigade's strong suit. The men might have a way to go in tactical training and operations, but at least they wouldn't starve or run out of fuel while they were doing it.

We still got some training in, though. Gerry worked with Capt. Saud Aziz and the signal company, and I still had hopes of conducting a command post exercise. I don't know why I hung my hopes on this so much; the men were clearly not interested in it. But it was the right thing to do. Bob Quinn and I actually made some inroads into working with the staff sections, although it seemed that the Saudis were always getting distracted from training by some administrative requirement. Sometimes the distractions were more original. On one memorable occasion we were having a useful discussion on how the shifts for a command post were organized when a sergeant came running in speaking frantically. In an instant the entire room was a blur of activity, with officers making telephone calls and men running out to jump into their cars. I thought for a minute that it was some kind of alert, but the Saudis didn't seem upset; in fact, most of them were smiling and some were laughing.

I asked Mohammed Al Gharni what was going on. He grinned and told me that one of Colonel Meteb's falcons had escaped and the battalions were directed to send out soldiers to find it. It seemed a fool's errand. How can anyone catch a falcon from a truck by chasing it across the desert? Mohammed Al Gharni explained that the falcon hadn't gotten loose from its perch; rather it had flown off and was dragging the perch with it. He reasoned that it would get tired soon. I was impressed with the way the brigade's officers quickly set up a search, assigned sectors to different battalions, and monitored the progress of each unit. Here at last was a positive example of command and control. They were successful too. A truck found Fred the falcon resting in the desert before resuming his flight south toward Oman. The bird was captured after a short chase and was tired but uninjured. The finders brought the falcon back to Meteb Jawal, and members of the brigade returned to their respective motor pools. Training for the day was over, but the men had proven to me that they could move quickly if they had a mind to. It was also a good measure of the esteem in which they held Meteb Jawal that they would cheerfully execute such a mission for him without griping. Everyone in the brigade genuinely liked him. He ruled the brigade like a benevolent tribal chief and dealt with disagreements among staff officers and commanders firmly but in a manner that saved everyone's face. He had a good grasp of his internal security mission and could be a hard man when he had to be. But for the most part he was a genial sort.

On Wednesdays I would go to Riyadh and attend the weekly meetings of the operations department and make my reports on that week's training. (Wednesday was the "Friday" of the Middle East—hence the saying among expatriots: TAIW, thank Allah it's Wednesday.) Then I would get up early on Saturday to drive to Al Hofuf and be at brigade in time for work. On the weekends I would go to expatriate parties with my friend Jim Good or go to the "Hash," a British version of cross-country running that many of the expats participated in. Hundreds of expats would go out into the wadis west of Riyadh and chase up and down following trails left by the lead runners. It was a typically British affair (as the saying goes, mad dogs and Englishmen go out in the midday sun), but you could meet many people, and there were a lot of women. One weekend in October, I met an American nurse named Ann McElroy, who worked at King Faisel Hospital. She asked me if I could get her and some of her friends into the Camel's Breath Saloon (nonservice personnel had to be signed in by a serviceman). I wasn't doing anything else that weekend, and Ann was a good sort, so I said sure. I went to the USMTM compound that night, signed Ann and her friends into the club, and met my future wife.

One of Ann's friends was a tall, beautiful, dark-haired Canadian woman named Donna O'Shaughnessy, and we hit it off from the start. She and several of her friends had been working as nurses in London (Ontario) and seen an ad hiring nurses for King Faisel Hospital. They signed up in a spirit of adventure, and here they were. Donna told me that working at King Faisel Hospital was definitely a change of pace. She had to take cabs everywhere and be back by midnight or not be allowed back into her quarters. The nurses all liked coming to the U.S. military compounds because the Saudis granted us a lot of freedoms that other expatriates did not have. That night after the Camel's Breath Saloon closed down the nurses didn't want to go home, so I took them all to my place. The next day I left to drop off Ann at the hospital, and when I got back I found Donna and her two friends Elaine and Leah dressed in portions of my uniforms and going through my tapes. I thought for a second that this might be one of those "Dear Penthouse Forum" moments, but they were just drunk and kidding around. They looked so silly I had to laugh. We stayed up half the night drinking and talking. The whole thing seemed like a tipsy slumber party: three women in a strange place blowing off some steam after a long week's work. Finally I left them to sleep in my two bedrooms and I slept on the floor. I brought them home after breakfast the next morning. Donna said she'd love to see me again and would be free the following weekend. I dropped off the women in a place where the religious police wouldn't see them, then watched them walk through the hospital main gate. *That is much woman*, I remember thinking. Yessir, things were definitely looking up socially.

The month of November was spent in much the same pattern: weekdays in Al Hofuf and weekends in Riyadh. We didn't do any serious tactical training, and I began to feel as though I was not doing anything of import to help the Saudis. Much of an advisor's life is just being there to answer questions. It was definitely different from the high-speed-operations tempo of Fort Irwin. I did get to see Donna every other weekend, though, when she wasn't working.

The brigade's exercise tempo finally picked up in December, when the brigade began its first field training period of the year. The men went out to the field over a period of three weeks, two battalions at a time. I tried to encourage them to keep the brigade's tactical operations center out for the entire duration of the field training period, but this suggestion was not acted upon. As a result, the men took the brigade headquarters to the field, set it up for three days, then took it back down and went in. Not a rigorous headquarters training schedule, but better than nothing. I made a mental note to try to get them to plan a command post exercise for next year's training density. Maybe with enough prodding and planning, we could pull it off.

After the brigade headquarters training exercise, I went down to the battalions to see how they were faring. I was disappointed by the quality of tactical training I saw. The exercises consisted basically of driving around in the desert. There was no opposing force, and no one had any blank ammunition. The guardsmen did not dig in when they stopped in the defense. Nor did they move in overwatch formations with some armored vehicles stopped and covering the others as they advanced. Another distressing discovery was that all training stopped at night. There was so much that the men needed to do better that I

had to force myself to find something good about what they were doing. They did actually keep decent intervals in movement through
the desert. They might move in a gaggle, but at least they kept spread
out. Their vehicle load plans were adequate, and they could sustain
themselves. No one ran out of fuel, and broken vehicles were recovered quickly.

At night we would pull into tactical laagers in a kind of circle-the-
wagons formation. Then fires would be started and goats would be
slaughtered for the evening meal. Saudi rations consisted mainly of
goat and rice with vegetables and pita bread. After a few times out
with the men, I could usually tell how long an exercise was going to
last by the number of live goats in the mess trucks. Meals were consumed from the communal dish, with the roast goat in the center.
Officers had to be careful to not eat much, because the soldiers
would be waiting in the wings to eat whatever was left. Initially this
appalled me, because it was so different from the ethos of the U.S.
Army. No officer worth his salt would ever sit down to eat before
making sure his troops were fed. Unfortunately, the Saudis didn't op-
erate this way. I couldn't *not* eat with them, because mealtimes were
important social events in the day and were often when I would get
my best chance to offer advice on brigade operations.

After dinner we would sit around the campfire and talk. The conversation revolved mostly around happenings in the brigade or Saudi
internal matters. I was included in the conversation as the American
information center and was expected to be the know-all about the
United States of America. People asked me all sorts of things: What
are good places to visit and what is it like at one place or another.
Many asked about how to go to American military schools. A favorite
topic of discussion was American dating mores. This aspect of
American society fascinated the Saudis because it was so different
from the structured and inhibited society in which they grew up.
Many of them had never been to the States; their only exposure to
us was from movies. To them America was a land of wealth, violence,
and beautiful, lustful women who were after sex all the time. I tried
to dissuade them from some of their wilder misconceptions about
American women, but even when presented with the less-than-lurid
truth they were still wide eyed. Some of the more Islamicly strict
men would purse their lips in disapproval at my descriptions, but I
could see a lot of them doing fast mental arithmetic: Oooo boy, I
have to study up and pass my English test so I can go to America and

live this wild life. When I wasn't telling them about the not-so-wild life in America, I usually tried to steer the conversation to operations and training—sometimes with success, sometimes not.

The Saudis were always pleasant to me, and I was always welcome around their campfires. When I was out with one of the battalions on Christmas Day, every one of the officers I talked to made a point of wishing me Merry Christmas. So much for the stern, intolerant Wahabist Sunnis.

Meteb Jawal was in fine form on these exercises, sitting at the head of the feast in his large tent like the chieftain that he was. He was an exceptional desert navigator, and I accompanied him around from unit to unit. I was amazed that he seemed to follow a circuitous course but invariably ended up exactly where he wanted to go. His vehicle had no compass or position-location system of any type. He just navigated by the sun's position and by reading the dunes. He drove fast, too (his helpless enlisted driver sitting in the passenger seat as Meteb drove the vehicle), and accompanying him was always an experience. He would periodically stop and look into small holes near the scrub bushes. I was told that *dhabs* (large, scaly lizards) lived in these holes. Once he caught one and brought it back to camp, where he chased the Sudanese cook (who was scared of them) around with it.

The field training ended just before New Year's. I flew home on leave right after it, but my thoughts were with Donna. I had seen a lot of her and was getting to know and like her more and more. She had a droll, irrepressible sense of humor and told funny stories about working in various hospitals. Like Scheherazade in *A Thousand and One Nights*, she kept my attention.

There was hardly a weekend when something wasn't going on in our little row of bachelor quarters, and living in the communal gathering place was fun. The nurses made our small crowd of army bachelors their adjunct home away from home when they weren't at the hospital. Jim Good knew some of the men at the embassy, and one of them in particular, Maj. Rich Cassem, became a sort of honorary member of our group. Rich was frustrated because he was constantly up to his neck in administrative duties and wanted to get out into the country more. I offered to take him to Al Hofuf, but apparently because he was a defense attaché he couldn't drive just anywhere, as we could. His movements had to be announced and coordinated.

In February the brigade's live-fire training density started. It was often an uphill struggle. If there was one thing about the Saudi training program that drove me crazy, it was their reluctance to conduct live fires. In the U.S. Army, infantry, armor, and artillery units are constantly in the field conducting live-fire exercises. Doing so came naturally, and I had never worked in another army, so I assumed that everyone would be just like us. As mentioned previously, the Saudis conducted only one live-fire training density per year. This was no way to maintain proficiency except at a very basic level. OPM-SANG and the Vinnellis had been advising the Saudis to conduct quarterly or at least semiannual live fires for years, but the Saudis were adamant about one training density per year. The only good thing about our planned live fires was that at least we had a lot of ammunition, especially TOW missiles and 90mm main gun rounds. The Saudi guardsmen had an allocation of TOW missiles that was ten times the number an American unit would see in a year.

Bob Quinn, the Vinnellis, and I did our best to ensure that the Saudis got the best benefit from this annual live-fire training. The King Abdul Aziz Brigade's live-fire density was further complicated by the fact that it took place in the Kasmalan training area next to the National Guard base near Riyadh. This meant that each battalion would deploy to the ranges for two weeks, then redeploy to Al Hofuf. Although we had only one or two units there at a time, the entire density would take almost two months. I would be spending a lot of time on ranges. Still, it promised to be fun, and I was looking forward to it.

Kasmalan was a huge live-fire training area near the 1st Brigade camp and the National Guard military academy in Riyadh. It had ranges for every weapons system the National Guard had, including artillery. Each battalion came to Kasmalan once a year to do gunnery. Some of these exercises and ranges went well; others didn't. The 90mm gun armored car gunnery tables were straightforward, and the gun itself was a hoot to watch. The commander of the vehicle sat beside the driver on the front glacis and had to give fire commands from a position in which he actually saw less than the gunner. Still, they seemed to do OK. Other turreted weapons systems also had their battle runs. On the whole they did well, although I noticed that none of them was using a stopwatch to time the engagements. At least they were doing the gunnery according to the book in every other way. Their mortars were about the same—accurate but a bit slow. One particularly frustrating experience I had was with their platoon movement to contact live fire. The vehicles would move through the desert in proper formation and dismount their squads correctly, and the soldiers would then attack toward their objective, but I noticed that they were not using proper fire and movement techniques, and they seemed to stop frequently to pick up things. Intrigued, I asked the company commander through an interpreter what they were doing. "Oh," he said, "they are picking up the expended brass. All bullets have to be accounted for." I was dumbstruck. How could anyone possibly have a realistic live fire if they always stopped to pick up their brass? I learned that Saudi rules were strict on this. If the men turned in even one cartridge case short, they would have to come back and look for it. I encouraged the brigade headquarters in the strongest possible terms to discontinue this policy. Quinn just smiled and shook his head. He had been down this road before. National Guard headquarters was adamant about it and there was nothing brigade could do. It was galling to watch, however.

The gunnery training period at Kasmalan wasn't all frustration. Many of the ranges (such as the one for 84mm recoilless rifles) were being run to standard, and occasionally I was able to make a positive impact on the ones that needed improvement. I made my greatest contribution in TOW missile gunnery. When I first got to the range, I couldn't believe what I saw. The guardsmen were shooting their training practice missiles at old dumpsters that were about a thousand meters from the firing line. This was not good training for this weapons system. The TOW missile variant we possessed could hit a vehicle at 3,000 meters. Upon further investigation of the range, I saw a moving target that wasn't being used. I made inquiries and was told it "wasn't working." After the day's firing, I went to check it out. It hadn't been maintained but was in basically sound shape; it just needed a battery and some gas and oil. The target itself was a side panel of a tank that ran on an oval rail track at about ten miles per hour; the track was 2,700 meters from the firing points. This would be much better, I thought.

Initially I encountered a lot of resistance. The unspoken fear of the guardsmen was that if they missed the target, they would look silly. Eventually I managed to get them to shoot at it. The first man to go was the company's most junior private; if he missed, they wouldn't lose too much face. They all watched expectantly as the assistant gunner armed the launcher and tapped the private on the head. He fired almost immediately, and the missile leapt out of the tube and headed downrange. Two thousand seven hundred meters is a long way for the missile to fly, but all the gunner needs to do is keep the weapon's crosshairs on the target; the missile will correct itself onto the target. Of course the private hit the target. He had all the time in the world to get his crosshairs back on it. After this, others clamored to go next, and every subsequent missile punched cleanly through the target. I could see the men's enthusiasm building. At the end of the day there were 100 percent hits. From then on, all the companies fired at the moving target and achieved a greater than 90 percent hit rate. I felt proud of myself. Here was one tangible thing in which I clearly had a positive impact on the Saudis' combat readiness.

Soon after the range density, we stood down for the holy month of Ramadan. During Ramadan the brigade didn't do much; all the soldiers were fasting in accordance with Islamic custom. The fast of Ramadan meant that a Moslem could not eat, drink, smoke, or engage in sex (so they told me) during daylight hours. It was a holiday period based on the lunar schedule that shifted eleven days per year. During a winter Ramadan, the days were short and relatively cool. A summer Ramadan was a true test of faith. The only people you would find in the brigade were the odd duty officer who would offer you his sleepy greetings. Most Saudis sleep all day during Ramadan, rising just before dark for prayer. Once it got dark and the sunset cannon went off, Ramadan was an all-night party and gorge fest. Stores and restaurants would be open until two or three in the morning. Many Saudis would literally eat all night. It was an odd fact of life that many of them gained weight during this month of fasting.

The Saudis were buying Canadian light attack vehicles (LAVs), similar to the ones used by the U.S. Marines, to replace their V-150 armored cars. I was one of the officers in OPM-SANG on the committee to design the force structure for the new vehicle. I spent most of Ramadan in Riyadh helping design the new light attack vehicle battalion force structure. This suited me fine; I got to see Donna more often. We had grown very close over the months since our first meetings and spent all our free weekend time together. In truth I was smitten and was working up the nerve to ask her to marry me, but I didn't want to rush things. I remember this season of Ramadan most fondly. On nights when she was free, I rode down to the hospital and parked on the street. Our pick-up signals had some of the aspects of a John le Carré story. I looked around to see whether there were any Muttawin in the area, the kind who would make trouble for a western woman if she were in the car of a man she was not married to. If I saw a Muttawin, I put a red book on the dashboard, and Donna knew to walk by my truck and go to the alternate pick-up point. I drove around the block and she jumped in there. We went to dinner and she told me hilarious and strange stories about working in King Faisel Hospital. (Compared to her job, I only *thought* mine was strange.) We went to parties or ran on the Hash or just sat at home and watched movies. Every couple of weeks or so there was a "desert concert." Hundreds of expatriots and Saudis went out to a wadi west of Riyadh that formed a natural amphitheater whose acoustics were surprisingly good. A German expatriot named Hans and some of his friends rigged up generators to a huge stereo system with speakers that stood about six feet tall. They played selections of classical music that sounded haunting and beautiful under the desert stars. The concerts lasted for about three hours with from three to five selections depending on their length. There was a slight chill in the air and we snuggled up for warmth, the night air pleasantly tinged with the smell of grilling meat from the numerous hibachis. Life was good. In May, Donna and I took a trip to Thailand together and spent two weeks in Bangkok, Phuket, and Chaing Mai. Then it was back to Saudi Arabia and its blast furnace summer heat.

Soon after I got back from Thailand, the brigade changed command. This was an emotional event, because Meteb Jawal had been the original brigade commander from when the brigade was first formed and was loved and respected by all. His replacement, Turki Al Firm, came from a pedigreed Saudi family, but that was about all that recommended him. He was grossly overweight, and the first sight of him literally bursting out of his uniform made my heart sink. Morbid obesity in itself is not a detriment to higher command as long as the brain functions and the commander knows how to use his staff and takes care of his soldiers. There have been overweight commanders throughout history. Unfortunately, in most of the ways that mattered, Turki was the antithesis of what a commander should be. He had a continuous air of scheming furtiveness. He also didn't seem to get along well with the brigade headquarters. Officers were always visiting and talking with Meteb Jawal. The afterwork pool and talk sessions they had were always well attended. All this changed abruptly. I could feel the unease of the brigade headquarters. If Turki had come in barking orders and generally acting like the new broom, I would have put it down to just the normal change-of-commander grousing that any unit goes through. Unfortunately, Turki did virtually nothing in his first month of command. My Saudi friends were uneasy, although they never came out and said so. I mentioned this to Bob Quinn and he nodded in assent. He hadn't been impressed with Turki either. "We're going to have trouble with this guy," he said. Although we didn't know it at the time, this change of command was to have a profound effect on brigade operations during the war.

In June the brigade was put on a higher state of readiness in preparation for the Hadj. This is the period of pilgrimage in which millions of Moslems come from all over the world to visit the grand mosque in Mecca and perform the formal rituals of the pilgrimage. Every Moslem must perform the Hadj at least once in his or her lifetime. As a result the security forces in Saudi Arabia are always on a higher degree of readiness during this time. Training was limited to what could be done in the local area. Each battalion had vehicles at the ready to move. Although the training schedule was not stressful, I could see that the guardsmen were on alert status. Bob Quinn told me that in 1988 during the Hadj, thousands of Iranians had rioted in Mecca. From the descriptions the Saudi officers had given him, it sounded more like an armed insurrection. The King Abdul Aziz Brigade had been alerted and deployed to help put down the rioting, and the lead elements of the brigade had closed on Mecca within eighteen hours of notification, which was not bad by anyone's standards. Bob and the Vinnellis could not have gone with them, of course (people who are not of the Islamic faith are not allowed into Mecca), but they helped the brigade load out and organize the convoys. For the most part, though, it was a Saudi show. The result of that experience was that the Hadj in 1989 and 1990 was a period of alert lockdown for the guard. As it turned out, there were no riots, but sadly more than 1,400 pilgrims were killed in an overcrowded tunnel when the ventilation system broke down. The 1st Brigade was dispatched from Riyadh to help with the cleanup. Howard Swanson, the first brigadier advisor, told me later that many of the guardsmen who had worked that detail were deeply affected by it. I expressed my condolences to the Saudis, but Saud Aziz summed up their attitude succinctly by saying that the deaths had been God's will and there was nothing to be done about it but accept them.

OPM-SANG also went through several important leadership changes in June 1990. Brigadier General Freeman left in late June. He was replaced by Brig. Gen. James B. Taylor, another Vietnam veteran who had recently given up command of the 3d Armored Cavalry Regiment. He was an exceptionally tall, lanky figure with a pronounced Texas drawl and a no-nonsense air about him. He came out and visited me within a week of his taking command. We spent the evening discussing the capabilities of the National Guard and its training program. I was candid in pointing out the difficulties we often encountered in getting the Saudis to train at brigade operations, but he told me he had encountered similar problems as an advisor in Vietnam and just to drive on as I was.

The other new person in OPM-SANG was the chief of the operations division, Col. John Noble. He was an interesting character, a patrician southern gentleman of long service and a highly decorated veteran of multiple tours in Vietnam. He was an unlikely looking infantry officer, with a bulky, slouching frame and round face. But his demeanor belied his looks. He took over the operations section with the calm and competent air of a man who knew exactly what he was doing. Still, I initially put him down as just another senior colonel on his final tour. A nice enough guy to work for, but an old lion, comfortable with his place in the pride, about whom there was nothing particularly extraordinary. In this I was very much mistaken.

Lieutenant Colonel Howard Swanson (the Imam bin Saud brigade advisor) and I went back to the States in early July to attend LAV live fires and trials at Fort Bragg. The 82d Airborne was trying out LAVs on loan from the Marine Corps, and we went along to take a look at the LAV and make our recommendations for modification to the OPM-SANG staff. It was a fun temporary duty, and I was impressed with the LAV. Although not as capable a vehicle as the army's Bradley fighting vehicle, it was a simple, robust design that the Saudis could maintain and train with. The upcoming transition to LAVs over the next decade would leave the National Guard much more capable.

With Donna back in Saudi Arabia, I didn't want to spend any more time in the States than I had to, so I flew straight back without stopping to see my parents. I was later to bitterly regret this haste.

Donna and I made plans to go to London in mid-August. She was going to take a full month off and go home to visit her family for two weeks, then we would spend two weeks in London together. We had only a couple of weeks together before she went to Canada, and on our last night before she left I asked her to marry me. I hadn't intended to yet—I had meant to do it in London—but the moment seemed right. She paused and looked at me intently with her deep green eyes. "Big step," she said. She didn't say anything more, and I got worried. Then she said, "Do you mean it?" I told her I did, and she paused again. "Let me think on it," she said. "I'll give you an answer in London." I accepted this answer; it was in character. She would weigh it in her mind. I was pretty sure she would say yes, but I wasn't positive. We had fun together but had known each other less than a year. Maybe I had spoken too soon. I loved her, though, and it seemed the thing to do. Well, I had committed myself; there was nothing to do but wait for her answer. I brought her to the airport the next day.

With Donna gone, I had time to kill on weekends. Before she left, I had made plans to go exploring on the peninsula in her absence. OPM-SANG had a policy of allowing members to take two days in conjunction with a weekend to visit places in Saudi Arabia and neighboring countries. Brigadier Generals Freeman and Taylor encouraged this because it was good, professional development. Travel truly does broaden the mind. The last thing that OPM-SANG leaders wanted was people who stayed shut in their little-pieces-of-America compounds.

I had already visited Bahrain in September 1989 and made several trips within Saudi Arabia. I decided to travel abroad over the weekend of 2 to 5 August. I had originally intended to drive to the United Arab Emirates (UAE), but getting my passport stamped to go from Saudi Arabia to Qatar and Qatar to the UAE was too complicated. I decided instead to go to Kuwait. It was closer, and there was only one border post to go through. I got my passport stamped in the Kuwaiti embassy in Riyadh and made reservations in the Kuwait Sheraton.

There was news of increased Iraqi-Kuwaiti tensions and troops massing on the border. Before I left, I went to the embassy to talk to Rich Cassem about it, just to make sure. He said that the reports of Iraqi troops on the border were true, but the action was evaluated as just posturing for political leverage. The Iraqis wanted the Kuwaitis to forgive their debts incurred in the Iran-Iraq war, and there was some dispute about slant oil drilling under the border. Just business as usual in the Middle East, with a little overblown hyperbole thrown in. No doubt some accommodation would be reached once everyone was done posturing for the public. I left reassured and didn't cancel my trip. I figured if anyone would know, the embassy guys would. I didn't realize that the Riyadh embassy could be left out of the loop as easily as anyplace.

So on 1 August I drove to Kuwait City—a long drive even at high speeds. Once I was past Jubayl, the empty desert seemed to stretch forever. The bleakness was punctuated only by the occasional gas station and the turnoff to the trans-Arabian pipeline (TAPLINE) road. I drove for hours listening to my tapes—Steely Dan, the Rolling Stones, and Enya. I recommend Enya, especially for long, lonely stretches of desert. The slow, haunting songs bring an almost otherworldly quality to desolate terrain.

At about two o'clock I reached Khafji, near the Saudi-Kuwaiti border, and had lunch. Khafji was the first real-sized town I had seen since leaving Jubayl. It was a pleasant little place with seaside villas and a small oil refinery. I was tired of driving and did not look forward to the usual border delays at customs that one normally encounters going from one country to another in the Middle East. I had been told it would take two to three hours to get through Kuwaiti customs, and I almost decided to cancel my plans to go there. The Khafji Beach Hotel was right in front of me, and the impulse to check in and go swimming was strong. However, I chided myself for laziness and drove on. Looking at the map, I could see that Kuwait City was only an hour or so from the border. Even if I was delayed at the border, I would still be at the hotel by about 6 P.M. With renewed resolve, I drove up to the border crossing.

The pessimists had been wrong. It took me only about an hour to get through customs, and all of the Kuwaiti border officials were courteous. I had a good conversation with a pleasant customs official in his mid-twenties about where to go in the city and some of the good places to eat and shop. He gave me a map and pointed out a few places. He apologized that he wouldn't be able to show me personally, but he gave me the phone number of his brother. I left feeling relatively positive about Kuwait.

The drive to Kuwait City was a revelation. Whereas the roads in northern Saudi Arabia, although paved, were only two lanes wide, in Kuwait the road instantly went to a four-lane superhighway and I made excellent time. Everything I passed seemed newer and better constructed than in Saudi Arabia. It made sense: Kuwait was a richer country per capita than Saudi Arabia (or just about anyplace for that matter). That was evident from the spanking newness of much of the place. The city itself was very well laid out in a series of ring roads, and I easily found my way to the Sheraton, which was actually more than a mile from the main hotel district on the western side of town.

It wasn't a particularly tall hotel (about twelve stories), but it was taller than most of the other buildings around it and offered a good view of the entire western side of town. I did not appreciate any of these characteristics until later, of course. At the time, in late afternoon on 1 August, I was just congratulating myself on having persevered and made the drive in one day. Now I wouldn't have to waste time going through the border in the morning. With a feeling of accomplishment, I drove into the Sheraton's parking lot.

What a fool.

I checked into the Sheraton and went up to my room on the sixth floor. I had taken my binoculars and other items from the car because I didn't know whether Kuwait was as thief free as Saudi Arabia. After stowing my gear I went for a long walk around the city to stretch my legs. There were a lot of third country national (TCN) workers milling through the shops. In general it seemed like a normal evening in any of the Arab cities I had been in. A bit nicer though, and more modern. I found the gold souk, because I had resolved to get a present for Donna while I was in Kuwait. I ended up eating in a mediocre Chinese restaurant. After about four hours of rubbernecking around, I went back to my hotel room and took a shower. I went to bed at around 10:30. I would take a drive around town tomorrow and see the sights. I wondered vaguely what I would find, but I wasn't really excited about it. I expected only a mildly amusing weekend; that was all. Two weeks until I would see Donna again. Presently I fell asleep.

And while I was sleeping, the world changed.

Part Two

THE INVASION OF KUWAIT

3

I AWOKE TO GUNFIRE at about 4:15 on the morning of 2 August 1990. I was tired from my previous night's walk and had been in a very sound sleep, so it took a few moments for me to register what was happening. I lie there in bed and thought dreamily, *That sounds like shooting. . . . I wonder who could be shooting at this time of the morn— Shooting! Oh shit!* I dove out of bed and crawled to the sliding glass door to my balcony. Through the slats of the balcony railing I could see a lot of what was going on.

The first thing I saw of the invasion of Kuwait was that about a platoon of light infantry in uniforms I didn't recognize had secured the traffic circle to the southwest of the Sheraton. While I was watching, several buses, including one that looked like a Bluebird school bus, pulled up and started disgorging troops. That's how the Iraqis first invaded Kuwait City—on buses, getting off like workers at the gates of a factory. Several Toyota pickups with 14.5mm antiaircraft machine guns mounted on the back sped by. There was another flurry of firing from out of my field of vision, and all the soldiers I could see instantly took cover. A few of them started firing back down the street but were stopped by their officers after about a minute. The men stayed down for a few minutes, then gingerly picked themselves up and took up defensive positions around the traffic circle and the adjacent park, which was directly in front of the Sheraton. Soon another storm of small-arms fire erupted out of my field of vision to the south. But this time, although the troops had ducked down, as soon as they could see that the fire was not directed at them, they relaxed.

I was stunned. Clearly this was part of an invasion in strength. Most people had thought that Saddam Hussein had been just posturing. Rich Cassem had told me that, at the very most, Saddam might send troops into the northern oil fields of Kuwait, although he personally doubted that even this would happen. Apparently Saddam didn't know the script, because it looked as though he was going for the whole enchilada. Another triumph of U.S. intelligence.

Suddenly there was another burst of firing, and all the troops in the park went flat. A few of them started firing north into the parking lot that my car was in. Apparently a few armed Kuwaitis had fired at them from some government guard mount that they had overlooked, or maybe some of the local police were giving it their best effort. The Kuwaitis managed to keep the Iraqis in front of me pinned and crawling around for about five minutes. Then gradually the firing sputtered to a halt. I looked to see whether any of the Iraqis had been hit, but I couldn't tell. The fact that the city's lights continued to be on during all of this lent the firefight a surreal quality. I couldn't believe I was watching a real war.

It occurred to me suddenly that I should tell someone about this. I crawled back to my nightstand and grabbed the phone. I looked up the U.S. embassy and tried to dial in. All the lines were busy. I then did an international direct dial (God bless calling cards). I got the OPM-SANG operator and demanded to be connected with Brigadier General Taylor's house. He answered blearily but woke up fast when I informed him what was happening. He gave a low whistle when I described it to him, then asked me if I could positively identify Iraqis. I told him I could, because by then I could see the flags that some of their vehicles were flying. He told me to sit tight and keep reporting, then he hung up. In quick succession I called Colonel Noble and Rich Cassem. Noble was very quick on the uptake and asked only a few questions before going off to wake the rest of OPM-SANG's officers and men. Rich Cassem was incredulous. He reacted quickly, though, and told me to call him back in the defense attaché's office at the Riyadh embassy in about half an hour. Before he hung up, he hesitated and started to apologize for telling me that he hadn't thought the Iraqis would invade, but I cut him off. It wasn't his fault. He had simply believed the evaluations sent by intelligence people above him. The important thing was to stay in contact, so I told him to get to the embassy as fast as possible. Last I called Bob Quinn and told him to be prepared to help the Saudis roll the brigade, because I figured the call would come later that day (as it turned out, I was right). Bob took it like the pro he was, and I knew that my Vinnell team would be in there pitching. They were the least of my concerns. I told Bob that he had the reigns of the advisory effort until I got back or the army replaced me. He told me to take care of myself and not do anything stupid. I replied that I would be back as soon as I could and that I had already done something stupid: I had gone to Kuwait on pass. He laughed and wished me luck.

After hanging up, I felt desolate and alone. This was indeed a fine mess I had gotten myself into. I wondered how long the telephone would be in operation and resolved to call the Kuwait embassy again in a few minutes. Then I got the binoculars from my bag and crawled to the window for another look. More Iraqis had come into the circle and the park while I had been at the phone. They had set up two dismounted 106mm recoilless rifles, one apiece facing east and west on the main roads leading to the intersection. Each of the weapons had five ready rounds lying beside it; the crews were relaxed but ready at the weapons. There was firing in the town, but it was still out of my field of vision. More Toyota pickups with machine guns roared by. I could see what looked to be a battalion command group with officers and radiomen set up near a small, shaded structure in the park. I got my notebook and began to write down everything I observed and heard. I had the feeling it was going to be a very long day.

Vehicles continued to go through the traffic circle. I looked for armor because I was certain that tanks would show up soon. The light forces that had infiltrated Kuwait City would have to be backed up by additional forces and armor. However, the only other Iraqi forces I saw for the next hour or so were additional school buses that brought in even more dismounted troops to be disgorged by the traffic circle and more Toyota pickups with heavy machine guns mounted. There were periodic bursts of firing in the city. Now that the sun had risen I could see dense black smoke coming from the south and west in several places. Periodically shots made the troops below me duck, and occasionally bullets smacked into the hotel front. I stayed down on my belly and was careful not to be seen, lest the nervous Iraqis below me think I was a sniper and begin firing at me. Enough bullets were hitting the hotel as it was.

After a few more minutes of looking out, I tried to get through to the Kuwait City U.S. embassy. The line was busy initially, but to my amazement on the second try the phone rang and was immediately answered. I quickly identified myself and told the person in the embassy where I was. I then tried to give them as complete a picture of what was going on in my field of vision as I could: the infantry reaching the traffic circle, the school buses and the Toyotas with machine guns, the 106mm recoilless rifles, and the incidents of firing I had seen. The man on the phone related to me that the embassy was not in a good position to see any of this because it was surrounded by high-rises on three sides and was near the water on the fourth. I told him that I had seen at least a brigade's worth of light infantry and that more troops were coming in all the time. He seemed taken aback at this but confirmed to me that the troops were indeed Iraqis and this was the invasion that Saddam Hussein had been threatening. I told him to look for me because I would try to make it to the embassy after dark. (I had located it on my Kuwait City street map; it was about three kilometers from the Sheraton.) The man from the Kuwait embassy said that he understood but advised me to stay put for the time being because there was still a lot of shooting in the city.

After hanging up, I realized that I had been foolish in my initial reaction to the invasion. God only knew how long the water and phone systems would last. The phone I couldn't do anything about; I would use it until the system was disabled. The water situation I could help. I immediately went into the bathroom did a quick cleanup of the tub (hoping that the hotel staff had been thorough), then put in the stopper and filled the tub with water. I did the same with the sink. Then I took stock of the food in my room: a few cheese-and-cracker packets in my bag, my fruit bowl—courtesy of the hotel, two bottles of water, some packets of nuts in the little basket on the desk, and the mint from my pillow. That should sustain me for a couple of days. All in all my initial survival situation looked adequate. I went back to the window to take another look.

I got there just in time to see several helicopters fly past quickly, traveling north to Iraq. I didn't get a good look at the first two, but soon several others followed and I identified them as Russian MI-8 (HIP) troop carriers. Obviously they were traveling north after inserting troops somewhere in southern Kuwait. Several jets flew over at high altitude. I thought that this was another ill omen; clearly the Iraqis were using their air forces as well as ground forces in the invasion. Even at this early date, it was obvious that they were going for broke.

I tried to get through and update the Kuwait embassy on the helicopter movements I had just seen, but the lines were busy again. Then I remembered that I had promised to call Rich Cassem at the defense attaché's office in Riyadh. I was almost three hours late when I finally got through. I had to calm Rich and answer a few questions before I managed to finally convey to him that I was OK and still observing the situation. I gave him a brief update on everything I had seen and told him that in my opinion it was a full-scale invasion. There were some explosions close outside and Rich must have heard them because he asked what was going on. I crawled to the window and saw the infantry down on their stomachs and several of them firing down a road to the south. Several of them launched rocket-propelled grenades (RPGs), and they took a flurry of return fire from down the road. A few more bullets spanged off the hotel. I told Rich that there appeared to be Kuwaiti resistance still occurring in the city, but it was likely disorganized and in small groups based on the kind of firing I had heard. Rich then asked me for the manufacturer and date of the map I was using to see whether he could obtain a copy. Fortunately, it was the standard commercial Kuwait City street map that was available almost anywhere in the Gulf. Within an hour he had one, which made my reporting to him much easier. Colonel Fields, the defense attaché, came on line and told me to keep reporting; he was sending my spot reports directly back to Central Command (CENTCOM) and to the crisis action center in the Pentagon. Looking out the window at yet another battalion of troops getting off school buses and fanning out to the south, I numbly agreed to keep reporting. It wouldn't have occurred to me to stop in any case. At the moment at least, there wasn't much else I could do. Flight just wasn't possible.

I turned on the TV set; I figured I might as well listen to the news while I was watching what was going on outside. Sure enough, the BBC had interrupted normal programming and was giving what information it could about the "Iraqi invasion of Kuwait." Well, that made it official if nothing else did. Mainly the news said that the Iraqis had invaded Kuwait and were in Kuwait City (thanks a lot). There were a few telephone interviews with frightened people calling from different parts of town describing the firefights and military movements they had seen, but nothing of substance. While listening to the TV, I saw several large military trucks pull up in front of the hotel along with some Russian-type jeeps that had several radios mounted in them and were obviously used for some kind of command and control function. Iraqi soldiers dismounted and started carrying boxes and radio equipment into the hotel. This was not good.

Before this, the Iraqis had stayed outside the hotel. Now they appeared to be setting up some kind of headquarters in the lobby.

The phone was still working, so I called Brigadier General Taylor and gave him an update of what was going on. He promised to relay the information to the embassy, then he asked what my chances were of escape. I told him my Jimmy looked undamaged and I would try to reach it as soon as it got dark. Failing that, I would try to make it to the U.S. embassy or the West German embassy—which I could just see about a kilometer away to the west—or, if the opportunity presented itself, hot-wire a car and make for the Saudi border. Brigadier General Taylor was clearly appalled at the situation I was in and told me that as far as he was concerned I was free to use my own discretion and to be careful. I told him to get with Quinn and make sure the brigade was ready to roll. (A wasted effort as it turned out; Bob Quinn and my Vinnellis were already all over it.) I also asked the general to contact my parents and Donna and tell them not to worry. He solemnly promised he would.

I went back to the window and continued to watch Kuwait City being swallowed up. There were still a lot of sporadic flurries of firing as fugitive or enraged little groups of Kuwaitis kept bumping into the invaders. Most times I couldn't see the firing; it was out of my field of vision. Estimating specific direction and distance of gunshots in a city is difficult. The most I could tell was that the majority of the firefights appeared to be south of me. Several times, though, the troops in front of me reacted to sniper fire, and one of them was shot and wounded. He was promptly treated by a medic but then had to sit in the same location for several hours before someone put him on a truck and took him away. Oddly enough, once the immediate firing stopped the soldiers went back to their listless inactivity and poor security.

About the only thing the Iraqis seemed to be enthusiastic about was looting. They broke into food stores and at first took water, bread, meats, and fresh fruit; the latter seemed to be a particular favorite. Companies reacted differently. On one side of the traffic circle and park, soldiers looted indiscriminately and took what they pleased to feed themselves. The unit on the other side of the park seemed to have more discipline; a small grocery store was systemically stripped and its goods were moved into several trucks under the supervision of an officer. It was probably the unit supply officer, who was using this opportunity to stock up with food for the future. Once this company's soldiers had filled the supply trucks, the officer in charge of them had all the soldiers in the company take turns coming back a squad at a time to be issued some of the stolen food and bottled water. At the end of the hasty issue line was a large box containing bags of potato chips, and each soldier was given a bag of these as well. It was an interesting insight into the Iraqi army. Clearly some units were more disciplined than others, and some officers were more provident and forward thinking. It was sort of a looting version of the grasshopper-and-the-ant morality play. The Iraqis hadn't started going into jewelry or general merchandise shops yet; that would come later. Their number-one priority in the first flurry of looting was food. Maslow's hierarchy of needs at work.

It was now about 10 A.M., and I called the defense attaché's office at Riyadh to give them an update. Rich Cassem answered and took notes on everything I said. He asked whether I had seen anyone being taken away or summarily executed. I told him no, that if anything the Iraqis were fairly somnambulant invaders but there sure were a lot of them. I told him that as soon as it got dark I would try to move out of the hotel. He advised me to be careful and said he would relay my intent to Colonel Fields. Rich then told me that my spot reporting was "great" and everything I was sending in was being relayed directly to Washington. I was a little nervous, because the Iraqis in the lobby could be listening to the phones. But I was using direct dial to get through, so it was probably an automated switch. Mine was probably just another red phone-in-use light on the panel, if anything. This hotel must be full of people calling out.

I was worried that the switchboard would be cut off, so we tried to leave the phone open for as long as we could. After an hour or so the line disconnected itself. I had no idea why. Heart in my mouth I hung up, then dialed out again. To my relief I got straight through and Rich answered immediately. Still, we could never manage to leave the phone line open for more than half an hour or so without talking on it. I would just have to keep dialing out. I had no idea when I would lose phone communications, so I treated every phone call as though it were my last.

In the meantime, Iraqi units continued to pour into the city. Around noon an artillery battery of six 122mm D30 howitzers pulled into the park in front of the Sheraton and set up its guns facing the hotel. They managed to fit all six guns and their prime movers into the park, so the battery position itself was fairly tight. The in-

fantry unit that had gotten there earlier in the morning didn't want
to move, but after an argument between officers the men reluctantly
picked up their equipment and left the park. The artillerymen went
about their business, emplacing aiming stakes and placing ready ammunition by the guns (only six rounds each; they must not have expected to do any serious firing). Then they set up perimeter security
at the park fence, in spite of the fact that they were surrounded by
about a battalion of infantry. So far, the occupation of the battery position looked like a well-rehearsed battle drill. What I couldn't understand was their choice of location for the battery. The positioning
of their guns made little sense, because the Sheraton basically masked
their fire unless they super-elevated their gun tubes and lobbed shells
up at a better than seventy-degree angle. To do a large deflection
change and shoot south would require repositioning the battery. A
much better place would have been the park to the west or the parking lots to the north, both of which offered much more open terrain
for dispersion, better fields of fire, and no trees. No trees? All of a sudden the Iraqi artillery battery commander's reason for selecting his
position became apparent to me, and I could not suppress a laugh.
Shade was the primary consideration; they put their battery where
the men could get out of the sun. I had only to look at the artillerymen clustered around the trees to see that. Forget tactical considera-
tions; these guys were going to be comfortable if they had to sit
outside in the heat all day.

Around 1:30. P.M. the phone rang and the front desk demanded
that all guests report to the lobby. I had known that this would be in-
evitable but hadn't expected it so soon. I considered my options and
decided just to sit tight for the time being. Maybe they would not
take a room/head count. Soon I saw a group of about sixty men being led out of the hotel to the center of the grass traffic island in the
traffic circle. I could see no women or children with them, so I could
only assume that either the hotel held just men or that the women
and children had been purposefully segregated. Most of the men
seemed to be westerners; there were a few Asians and Arabs. All sat
in the direct sun on that blazingly hot afternoon under the guns of
their guards and suffered. I called this back to the defense attaché in
Riyadh, and he sounded alarmed. He asked me to get a specific count
of the men and try to determine their nationalities. (Yeah, right, I
thought, from 150 meters away and six stories up.) The attaché
wanted details of any physical abuse or possible questioning. I was in-

structed to watch these captives like a hawk and report any change of their status.

I set to work counting them, which was difficult because they kept shifting and overlapping one another. I counted three times and came up with a different number each time. I sent in the average, fifty-eight. I watched for any abuse, but other than sitting a bunch of out-of-shape businessmen in the hot sun, none occurred. After about two hours an officer came out of the hotel and the men were led back inside. I found out later that they were told to return to their rooms. I immediately tried to report this to Riyadh, but the defense attaché's line was busy. So I called Colonel Noble and reported it through him. While I was talking to the colonel, there was a series of seven large explosions to the west, and MI-8 helicopters flew by again. I had no idea whether the two events were connected and told this to Colonel Noble. He was very calm and friendly. Just the kind of reassuring voice I needed to hear. He told me to stay calm and hang in there. He promised to send my reports to the defense attaché. I asked him whether there was any U.S. military reaction as yet. Were we fighting? Noble said no, but the State Department was going to issue a statement soon. That was all he knew.

I turned on the TV to see whether any U.S. position was being put forth yet. (As a soldier, it's always good to know whether or not you are at war.) But so far the reporting was the same—the Iraqis had invaded Kuwait—and there was the occasional frightened-person telephone interview.

Iraqi armor didn't show up in front of the Sheraton until about four that afternoon. I heard the armored column before I actually saw it: a rumbling in the distance that grew gradually louder until the first T-72 pulled into sight. I was amazed at how small the Russian tanks were, never having seen one. They were dinky—about two-thirds the size of one of our M1s. The guns on the T-72s were huge, though, and there were a lot of tanks. At least a battalion of them passed right in front of the hotel, and I got a good look. The tanks were not buttoned up, and the driver's compartments were open, as were all turret hatches. I could see all three crewmen exposed in their hatches, with the two in the turret (tank commander and gunner) often sitting outside the turret on the tank roof beside their open hatches. Sloppy, especially because sporadic firing was still going on all over the city. Keeping the hatches open made sense in the heat, but sitting on top of the tank in this urban environment meant that the crews were vulnerable to sudden sniper fire. Two things surprised me about the armored column. First, three tanks were being towed by other tanks with tow bars. In the U.S. Army, broken vehicles such as those would be left for unit recovery teams in special armored recovery vehicles (called M88s). Here it seemed that if a vehicle was a mechanical failure, they just pulled it along. I noticed that each tank carried a set of tow bars. It made me wonder about their support echelons. The second thing I noticed was that each tank had crates of fruit and other food on top of the turret and back deck, and the crewmen appeared to be stuffing their faces as fast as they could. Obviously they had stopped to loot a supermarket and were now chowing down their stolen goods. They seemed oblivious to the fact that in these urban surroundings, only a few Kuwaitis with rifles and RPGs could inflict tremendous damage among them. The tanks chugged unmolested past the hotel and out of sight, however. A few of them had loose track flopping and folding under the drive sprocket, another sign of poor maintenance.

Eight tanks parked within my field of vision, and soon their crews were dismounting and wandering into stores that had been looted previously by the infantry. In many of the tanks, I observed three people dismount (a T-72 has three crewmen) and go on little local looting expeditions. There was still fighting going on in parts of town, and these guys were basically abandoning their vehicles to go foraging. A few tanks would have one crewman remain on the vehicle, but most tanks sat abandoned. I could only wonder what would happen if they were called upon to react to a sudden crisis. At first I wondered why their company commander would let them go off like that. Then I realized he was probably the first one into the stores for loot—yessir, lead by example.

I again updated Rich Cassem in Riyadh. He asked whether I could get a better idea of what was happening in other parts of the city. Apparently there was a dearth of reporting, because no one in the Kuwait City embassy could see what was happening. I thought of the stairwell on the side of the building and its long glass windows. It was worth a try. The Iraqis might grab me, but I doubted whether they had men on every floor yet. I told Rich to stand by. I gingerly stuck my head out the door of my room. There was no one in the hallway, so I took my binoculars and notebook and went to the stairwell.

I climbed to the top of the building and had an excellent view of the city. I began taking notes. Fires were easy enough to spot, with their long columns of black smoke. It was harder to tell what was going on, even with binoculars. There was still sporadic firing, but only rarely did I see Iraqi troops actually engaging something with their weapons. I never saw the Kuwaitis they were firing at. I saw three Iraqi soldiers cross a street under fire, and one of them was hit. The man lay in the street, and none of his compatriots made a move to assist him or even check to see whether he was alive. Unlike in the movies, most gunshot wounds are not immediately fatal. Unless a man had his head blown off, I couldn't tell from a distance whether he was dead or just unconscious. The pathetic thing was that there were tanks nearby, and it would have been a fairly simple matter to obtain one to use in the street as a shield for medics and drag off the casualty. I stayed in the stairwell for about thirty minutes after seeing this, and in that time no one came to help. In spite of the fact that the man was an invader (and, I suspected, an enemy), the lack of concern shown for this one poor soldier enraged me. I found myself wondering about the Iraqis. The failure to succor their wounded was shockingly unprofessional; worse, it was downright immoral. I watched that poor guy probably longer than I should have, hoping that someone would at least drag him out of the sun and check him out. No one came near him even when the firing subsided.

I found it difficult to make out the strength of units, because I couldn't see the pieces of them that were hidden behind walls or buildings. So I confined my observations to straight counting of systems. So many tanks here, artillery pieces here, antiaircraft systems there, infantry locations, trucks in convoy, approximate locations of firing, observations of looting: I wrote it all in my little notebook. I sat there in my vantage point at the top of that hot stairwell and soaked it up like a sponge.

Rich Cassem was pleased with it all, of course, and he told me to go back into the stairwell every hour and record my observations. I told him I'd be happy to one more time, but after that it would be getting dark and I was going to get out of there as soon as I saw an opportunity. He balked at this. "Just a minute, Marty," he said. So I waited. The next voice I heard was the defense attaché's (Colonel Fields), and he did not have good news. My reports were about the only blow-by-blow, in-house picture of what was happening in Kuwait City, and the National Security Council wanted me to continue reporting. I couldn't believe my ears and asked Colonel Fields to repeat himself. "Marty, your instructions are to remain in place and continue to report as long as you are physically able." He paused, then said, "I'm sorry, but escape is a no-go for the time being." I acknowledged his instructions and sat down on the bed. I was numb.

That's when the realization hit me. It had been in the back of my mind as a possibility before, but now it came home full force as a certainty. *I wasn't going to make it out of Kuwait City.* I was going to be captured (at best) by the Iraqis. The thought of it sent a chill through me, and I had a long, frozen moment.

There are moments in your life that you experience true self-revelation, and this was one of them. After all those years wondering how I would be in a crisis, it was daunting to discover that when all was said and done, I was not nearly as brave as I had expected. The thought of being captured was frightening, and for a moment it paralyzed me completely. Then several large explosions went off in the distance, and I walked to the window to see whether I could find their locations. They were to the west, past the German embassy. I noted the time and activity in my notebook for the next report I would call in to Riyadh. There was also a spattering of small-arms firing from that direction, and I guessed that another small group of Kuwaitis was still trying to take its toll of the invaders. I found the activity of recording the actions around me somewhat soothing and was soon over my momentary panic. I went back into the stairwell and continued to observe the events in the town, taking notes until it got dark. Then I called back and relayed my observations to Rich in Riyadh.

I wasn't being brave. If I had thought that running in circles and beseeching God would have gotten me out of there, I would have done it in a heartbeat. But I probably wouldn't have made it past the swarms of Iraqis. I didn't have any good options. I kept up my observing and reporting because there was nothing else I could do. That was the other self-revelation of the day, although unlike the first I didn't come to realize it until much later. If I wasn't nearly as brave as I had thought I would be, I was also more fatalistic than I would have ever believed possible. It tended to balance things out.

After I finished updating Rich on my observations, he made a suggestion that was so absurd I just laughed. "Marty, why don't you see what's going on in the lobby?" Well, Rich, let me see, maybe because I saw soldiers enter the lobby and not leave and it looked as though they were setting up some kind of headquarters there. Maybe because they would *capture* me, and you guys would lose the little observation post that you seem to like so much. Why on Earth do you want me to take that chance? Rich politely listened to my rant, then gave me his rationale. His thought was that the Iraqis didn't know me from Adam, and the hotel had to be full of stranded businessmen. "You'd be just another dweeb rubbernecking down there to see what was going on." That was an unflattering way of putting it but not an especially inaccurate one. I thought about it for a moment, then said okay. I looked out the window; nothing was happening, and many of the soldiers seemed to be bedding down for the night in spite of the fact that the sun had only recently set. Firing had declined to occasional single shots, and there didn't seem to be much action. So why not? It would give me something different to do. I told Rich I'd go down to the lobby in about five minutes and if he didn't hear from me again, his great idea wasn't so great after all. I took a quick bath with a facecloth, then put on a fresh pair of pants and a shirt. Thus fortified, and trying to look as presentable as possible, I walked to the elevator and pressed L. I had the elevator to myself. It was a very long six floors to the lobby.

The door opened to an empty hallway and I gingerly walked out. I was half expecting to be grabbed at any moment. Some people in civilian clothes stood at the end of the hallway near the lobby, and I walked toward them. I saw my first soldiers up close in the lobby. The Iraqis had indeed set up what looked like an infantry battalion headquarters, and there were about twenty soldiers present. Incredibly, the hotel staff was still manning the desk, and I went over to one of them and inquired about what was going on. The clerk was a nice young man who later explained that he was Egyptian and really admired Prince Charles (I forget how this came up in conversation). He told me that the Iraqis were operating out of the lobby because it was cooler than outdoors, but I was not to worry. He said that the Iraqi commander had explained to him that our being asked to go outside was a misunderstanding, and now he wanted us to stay in the hotel for our own safety. I looked beyond my helpful desk clerk at the Iraqis. They had remoted some radios out of the hotel and looked as though they had a map set up on a table. Several of them were snoozing on the big couches in the lobby. I could make out the rank of a major and two captains. It looked like a battalion headquarters all right.

The clerk then told me that although room service had been temporarily discontinued, I could eat in the dining room at the buffet that had been set up "free of charge." I looked at the clerk to see whether he was putting me on, but he was serious. This was getting weirder by the minute. Some western businessmen walked by us toward the dining room. I decided to head there too so I could add to the supplies I had squirreled away in my room. I followed the businessmen across the lobby. The Iraqis in the little headquarters seemed to take no notice of us.

The dining room was dark and crowded. When my eyes adjusted I could see that most of the tables were taken by hotel guests and Iraqi officers. I went through the buffet line between a German businessman and an Iraqi colonel who informed me in good English that "The potatoes were very delicious." I sat down at a table with two other people: an American named Steve and a Brit whose name I have since lost. Both were perplexed by the turn of events but neither seemed overly worried. They both recognized the basic powerlessness of their situation and were waiting to see what developed. Steve, a pleasant man in his late forties, represented some company; he looked like a senior executive. Both men were interested that I was in the army but were disappointed upon learning that I was just another unfortunate caught up in the hotel. We talked for a few minutes and I watched the crowd. It was like the bar scene in *Star Wars:* Iraqis of every rank in different types of camouflage mixing with waiters and hotel guests of many nationalities and ethnic backgrounds. There were even a couple of captured Kuwaiti policemen sitting down and eating their buffet like everyone else. Weapons were scattered about the place, and I was concerned that somebody would have an accidental discharge. Occasionally there were sounds of gunfire in the distance, and once a few shots were fired from right outside the hotel. That stopped conversation for a few moments, but when the firing didn't continue everyone went back to chatting away. I watched it all, amazed at its apparent normalcy. I had to give the Sheraton high marks for service. It would take more than a little invasion to shut down its dining room. There were no limits on any of the food, and the waiters kept bringing it out. Iraqis and many hotel guests went back for thirds and fourths. Soldiers kept trickling in and out.

I was just about to get up and wander around when I noticed a man and woman come into the dining room and walk onto the little stage upon which a microphone had been placed. The man sat on a stool and began tuning a guitar. The woman cleared her throat nervously. The talk in the room continued, although a few people noticed them. The man began to play a tune that was familiar to me; then the woman began singing, "Juan Tana Mera, Whajeela Juan Tana Mera." Hey, just because there's an invasion doesn't mean that the guests should forgo a little light music while dining. So I sat there and listened to her sing surrounded by Iraqi soldiers and confused hotel guests while the occasional shot barked outside in the distance. I thought to myself, treasure this moment, Marty; it's not often that one gets to experience the truly surreal. What you are watching right now is absolutely, positively, as weird as it can get.

Of course I was wrong about this; I just didn't know it at the time.

After filling my pockets with rolls and crackers, I went back to the lobby and decided to see whether I could walk out of the hotel without anyone stopping me. Unfortunately, all the exits had guards at them, and they all stopped me or motioned me back when I would approach their door. Apparently, we had the run of the lobby and the other floors, but that was it.

I was unfortunate in that I was in one of the few places in Kuwait where the Iraqi Army restricted people in their movements. I was to find out later that the rest of the town was in mass confusion. Many expats were to make good their escape in this confusion. Others were to make it to their embassies. The small group of US Army advisors in Kuwait (mainly Hawk Missile personnel) all made it to the embassy in the first day's confusion. A few of their number, led by a ballsy warrant officer made several other trips into the town over the next day to retrieve equipment and supplies before the Iraqis sealed them into the embassy grounds. A lot was possible in those first 24 hours, I was just in the wrong place.

The streetlights were on, and Iraqi soldiers were shuttling into the hotel to eat or bed down for the night. I looked at my watch; it was almost nine o'clock. This had been a long day. I went back upstairs and phoned Rich. He was tickled pink that I had been down there among the Iraqis and had escaped specific notice. I wasn't able to tell him much in terms of useful military information. The presence of a battalion-level headquarters in the lobby wasn't that big a deal. The guys in the Riyadh embassy were more interested in the behavior of the Iraqi soldiers themselves. Had I witnessed any random shootings or beatings or any similar atrocity? I had to answer this in the negative. Except for the looting of food and strong-arming the hotel out of a bunch of buffet dinners, the Iraqis' behavior was for the most part correct and, in fact, somewhat laid back. I did not have a high opinion of them as a military force from my day's observations, and I went into some detail about why I thought that way. It was subjective opinion based on only a single day's worth of observations, but they seemed eager to hear anything I had to say. I asked them whether I might possibly leave now, but they said I was doing great and it was imperative that I keep reporting. I reflected for a minute that maybe if my reports were less useful they would let me go, but it was too late now. Oh well, that's what you get for being an eager beaver. I should have just run like hell from the get-go.

I went back to the stairwell again and climbed to the top of the building. There didn't appear to be anyone on the roof, but I didn't want to go out there and check. If someone was out there and I didn't see him at first, my binoculars and notebook would need explaining. Even if no one was out there, someone in the street might take me for a sniper and start shooting. There was still occasional fighting that first night as small groups of Kuwaitis continued to contest the now-completed occupation of Kuwait City. All in all it was safer to stay at the top of the stairwell. I could see almost as much and be hidden from observation while I took notes at leisure.

The power was still on in most of the city that I could observe, and this lent an odd normalcy to the scene. I could see a few fires in town, and their smoke plumes showed up as slightly darker spots in the night sky. The only vehicle traffic seemed to belong to the Iraqi military. No civilian vehicles were moving. Even military traffic was light, and I could see no additional units coming into the city. I watched for half an hour to make sure I made a good sweep of the city. I looked back to where I had seen the Iraqi soldier get hit; he was gone. I found myself hoping that he made it, if only to be able to curse his squad mates and platoon leader for the worthless souls they undoubtedly were.

I reported to Rich Cassem and updated him on everything I had seen. Then I told him that there seemed to be a lull in the action and I was "going down" (sleeping) for a few hours. I then called Brigadier General Taylor and Colonel Noble and updated them on everything that was happening. Brigadier General Taylor informed me that the 2d Brigade would deploy for the border first thing in the morning. The news was like a body blow. The brigade that I was responsible for advising was moving out to the border, and here I was stuck in a hotel in the middle of what seemed like half the Iraqi army. I mentioned this to Brigadier General Taylor, and he told me to just concentrate on not being shot and to keep reporting. Colonel Noble had talked to my parents and told them I was fine and not to worry. I was grateful to him for that. The worry that my family must be going through was a great concern to me.

I turned on the TV and switched to the BBC. President George H. W. Bush was using fairly blunt language to denounce the "Iraqi aggression," and called upon Iraq to immediately withdraw to her preinvasion borders, or words to that effect. Every channel carried pretty much the same news. The world was almost universal in its condemnation of the Iraqi move, and the UN Security Council was meeting. British prime minister Margaret Thatcher was on the TV as well, and she sounded as tough as Bush. Other news reports indicated that the ruler of Kuwait, Sheik Al Sabah, had indeed escaped the Iraqi invasion, as had most of the Kuwaiti royal family, but there were reports of one prince—the head of their Olympic committee—being killed in a shootout at the palace. There were other reports of a massive refugee flow toward the Saudi border. Godspeed, guys, I thought. I wish it were me. I turned off the TV and the reading light, darkening my room completely so I could see outside. I pulled a chair up to the window and sat down with my binoculars, waiting for my eyes to adjust. Although I had told Rich I was going to bed, I was too keyed up to sleep. So I sat and watched the Iraqi troops below me.

They weren't doing much. Most were sleeping, and only a few were on actual guard duty. Others sat and ate—probably the food they had looted earlier. Their security in general seemed lax, and I didn't once see anything that looked like an officer or a sergeant walking around and checking on the perimeter. I felt a recurrent surge of professional disapproval. In my formative years as a lieutenant, all of my commanders and sergeants were Vietnam veterans, and they had beaten into me the necessity for constant security. Never set down anywhere without first checking your surroundings and posting adequate guards and outposts. The Iraqis acted as though they didn't have a care in the world. A squad with just rifles could have eaten their lunch.

I watched as one of them got up off his blanket roll, walked about twenty feet to the nearest bush, pulled down his pants, and defecated. There was a hotel with bathrooms literally right across the street and these guys were relieving themselves inside their perimeter. It wouldn't be pleasant in the heat of the day. They had better hope that they would move to a new location. I shook my head incredulously. This was amateur night. I was surrounded by the gang who couldn't shoot straight. Terrific.

A few shots rang out to the west, and a bullet chipped off the hotel near my window. I drew back hastily. I was relatively sure that no one could see me in the darkened room; it was just random fire. Still, the bullets with "to whom it may concern" on them can kill you just as dead, so I decided to sleep on the floor behind the bed. I stripped the sheets and comforter and made a bedroll behind the mattress. I surveyed my little nest. I was reasonably safe from stray small-arms fire, as safe as I could get anyway. I looked at my watch, almost midnight. I set my travel alarm for 4 o'clock and lay down. I was asleep almost instantly. Thus ended the first day.

My alarm went off right at four and I got up blearily. Four hours wasn't enough rest, but I was afraid to sleep any longer lest I miss something. I went to the window and looked out. The Iraqis were still sleeping, and only a few guards walked listlessly about. As far as I could tell, no additional units had come into the park/traffic circle area in the short time I had been asleep. Good. I went to see whether the plumbing was still working. Finding that it was, I washed up in the sink in a long and thorough sponge bath followed by a shave. Feeling much better, I put on fresh clothes and picked up my binoculars and notebook. A quick peek into the hallway revealed no one at all, and I went up to my observation post in the stairwell.

Kuwait City was quiet, although in the hour that I sat there a few shots rang out now and again. Maybe Kuwaiti snipers, but probably nervous sentries or some bored Iraqi troop shooting out streetlights for the heck of it. Most of the fires I had observed the previous day were out, although a few still burned. Single military vehicles came into view periodically, but I saw no convoys or major troop movements. I also saw a few cars and four-wheel-drive civilian vehicles making their way gingerly down side streets, avoiding Iraqi checkpoints. The cars' lights were out, and I noticed their movement only in the glare of the streetlights that they sought to avoid. I realized that I was watching people trying to escape from town. This again raised a lump in my throat. The Iraqis were clearly not alert now. I could sneak past their sleeping guards and get to my Jimmy and sneak out of town. Once I got to the open desert, no one would catch me. With my loran and compass I could head for an unpopulated part of the border away from the oil fields and cross into Saudi Arabia. If

Fort Irwin had done nothing else for me, it had given me an ability to navigate and drive in the desert at night without lights. I had enough gas in the car. The temptation to make a run for the border was overwhelming.

I steadied myself and fought these thoughts. My instructions to stay in place and report left no room for interpretation or discretion. If I abandoned my observation duties now, I would be disobeying orders. I did not especially care for my present role, but it was the one that had fallen to me. There was nothing for me to do but keep up my reports. Maybe I could get permission to leave soon. I understood that my window of opportunity for successful escape became smaller every minute. I resolved to ask for permission to escape again when I made my next report.

I wondered whether the phone still worked. When I picked it up and direct-dialed, I got straight through to the embassy in Riyadh. Rich Cassem was asleep, but the sergeant woke him as soon as I called. It had been a long night for him also. He took my report, then filled me in on the situation. There was a concern that the Iraqis might keep coming south once they consolidated their gains in Kuwait and took an operational pause. The Saudis were deploying their entire army to the border as soon as they could, but this would probably take some days to accomplish. My brigade was also going to the border and would probably be the first ones there. The United States was sending aircraft carriers toward the Gulf, and probably air and ground forces would soon follow. I swallowed hard. This sounded as though the invasion of Kuwait might be just the first act. I thought of the Saudis. At least my guys in the King Abdul Aziz Brigade were more proficient than the Iraqis I had been observing, but there sure were a lot of Iraqis. If they pushed south with resolution, my guys could well be swamped. I felt even worse for not being with my brigade. I asked Rich again if I could evacuate my little observation post and escape to Kuwait. He answered in the negative. He told me that both Brigadier General Taylor and Colonel Fields had recommended that I be allowed to escape if the opportunity presented itself, but that staff members in Washington had declared my reporting "too valuable" and directed that I remain in place for the time being. "I'm really sorry, Marty," Rich said. I told him straight up that I thought I had a chance if I ran now, but the longer I waited the poorer my chances. He assented grimly to my estimation. He instructed me to identify myself as a U.S. Army officer and a diplomatic passport holder "when I was taken." I told him that I really appreciated the "when." He said that the plan currently was to try to get all Americans out before hostilities commenced if it were at all possible. Maybe I would be taken out through Baghdad. "You're just going to have to wait on this one, Marty," he said. "No one knows what's going to happen yet." It wasn't a very comforting assessment, but it was an honest one. I told Rich I would call him back in a couple of hours.

The sun was just coming up, so this night was lost to me for escape anyway. Damn. I thought about captivity, and the mental image of cells or prison food was not appealing. I made a quick glancing inventory of all that I possessed: an overnight bag and some shirts, my sneakers, one pair of pants, one pair of shorts, underwear, socks, shaving kit. It was to have been a weekend trip. One normally doesn't pack to be in a survival situation. I would have to look around to see what I could steal from the hotel. I sat and looked out the window with a sense of the ominous. What Rich had told me left me little room for optimism.

I called Brigadier General Taylor and Colonel Noble and checked in with them. Noble would be leaving to link up with the brigade on its way to the border. The brigade would be moving out right about now, at dawn. Brigadier General Taylor would be coordinating the effort supporting the SANG from Riyadh. Taylor and Noble reiterated for me to just take care of myself and not worry about my family. Brigadier General Taylor had called my parents twice so far and given them updates. I asked him to have someone stay close to Donna and keep her in the loop as to what was happening to me, and he promised he would. I hung up feeling a little better. I was in trouble, that was for sure. But at least the people I loved were being taken care of.

The TV had only last night's news, so there wasn't much new. The BBC had information on a British Air flight that had been trapped at Kuwait airport while stopping to pick up passengers. CNN showed footage of the UN Security Council, and everyone agreed as to what a bad thing the invasion was. But nothing new came out of Kuwait City itself. The newspeople were hard pressed to fill their allotted time because there was a dearth of video images available. The Iraqi army obviously didn't allow reporters to go with it, and no independently taken video had escaped the country as of yet. I suddenly wished that I had my camera but then dismissed this thought as silly. As if any Iraqis would allow me to keep the camera or any film I took during the invasion if I were captured.

At around 7 A.M., Iraqi convoys started moving into the traffic circle. I spent most of the next hour counting vehicles and recording the weapons systems and units I saw drive past. More armor came into the city: tanks and armored personnel carriers of Russian and Chinese origin. I called in more spot reports to Riyadh, because I didn't think I could wait to hold the information I was gathering for the allotted time. I ran to my place in the stairwell and looked out over the city. There was a renewed movement of Iraqis everywhere I looked. There were a lot of convoys toward the south on the third ring road, and others that were not there previously were parked along the second ring. More infantry soldiers walked the streets, and a few shots rang out as these newcomers encountered Kuwaiti pockets. I watched one Iraqi infantry unit move down a street to the southwest. Its commander was clearly discernible because he carried a map that he referenced occasionally, carried no rucksack, and had only a pistol for a weapon. He was surrounded by radiomen, who made no attempt to hide their radios in rucksacks. One of the radio antennas even carried a small pennant. Amateur night. Those guys would be dead meat for even the most unobservant sniper.

A few of the larger fires still burned, but no new ones had been started. I surmised that the Iraqis had seized and consolidated their hold on all the key objectives they had designated in the town on the first day, and now these forces were moving in to eliminate the pockets of Kuwaiti resistance from the rest of the town. This showed good sense. Although the Iraqis at lower echelons had so far shown themselves to be something of a soup sandwich, their overall dispositions seemed to indicate that they had a plan.

Returning to my room, I was disconcerted to look out the window and see a mass of Iraqi armored command vehicles and trucks stopped in front of the hotel. With my binoculars I could clearly make out the insignia on the side of their vehicles. It was a red symbol with what looked like a falcon's head on an inverted shield. When I described this to Rich Cassem, he told me it was a Republican Guard symbol and asked if I was sure of my description. I started reading off the bumper numbers of the vehicles. I watched as the Iraqis backed up several of the command vehicles (Russian MTLBs) to the window of a conference room directly below me. They appeared to be remoting radios from the vehicles into the conference room. More soldiers took boxes and map boards from trucks and brought them inside. There were a lot of Iraqi colonels and lieutenant colonels around, and I realized that I was watching a major tactical headquarters in the process of off-loading and setting up operations on the ground floor of the hotel. Over the course of the next hour, the Iraqis off-loaded ten trucks and several more armored command vehicles. Around 10 A.M. a command car with a security entourage came to the front of the hotel, and I observed several general officers get out of the vehicle. They were unmistakable with their huge red shoulder boards with gold swords on them. I was too far away to make out what kind of generals they were, but there could be no doubt that they were generals. The headquarters on the bottom floor had to be at least division echelon.

I called this back to Riyadh, and they just about drove me crazy asking for every last little detail of what kind of vehicles and what did I see carried into the hotel and how many generals, colonels, and others I saw. They were quite excited with the news. I for the life of me couldn't see what a big deal it was. Logic followed that the headquarters elements would follow their troops. The city appeared to be, for all intents and purposes, secure. So why wouldn't they displace forward? Rich explained that some analysts persisted in the belief that this might still be just a "raid" and that, after invading Kuwait, Saddam might withdraw to the north of Kuwait City and merely retain the Rumaliah oil fields. My observation seemed to knock a hole in that theory. Well . . . duh. Iraqis were swarming over Kuwait City like the Goths taking Rome and somebody somewhere still thought it might be just a show of force? I told Rich that in my opinion whoever thought that was just plain crazy, and I reiterated to him all of the troop dispositions I had seen. He listened to my rant and soothed me as best he could, explaining that no one agreed with that assessment and they were grateful for the confirming evidence. Then, "By the way, Marty, do you think you could pop down to the lobby for a look-see?"

At first I thought he'd lost his mind. A sleepy battalion headquarters set up in the lobby was one thing. But a division-level headquarters was something else. It would have dedicated security guards and access control. No one without authorization could get near a division operations center in the U.S. Army. I stopped myself right there. In the U.S. Army. But these guys weren't the U.S. Army. It was worth a shot.

I told Rich that I wanted to give the Iraqis at least a few more hours to get set up before I went down there. That way I could act like any other hotel guest going to the dining hall for lunch. He thought about it for a second, then agreed. In the meantime I would make one last observation of the Iraqis from my window and the stairwell in case I got grabbed in the lobby. I told Rich to make sure the State Department people were ready to ask about my status if I didn't report back in. He said that the Riyadh embassy was already working on that but no one would take action until I was captured because they didn't want to tip off the Iraqis that I was there.

After hanging up I went back to the window. I didn't bother staying hidden because no one was looking at the windows anyway. I sat down in my chair and gazed at the troops below me with something approaching leisure. I was looking for general indicators of professionalism: troops conducting maintenance on vehicles or cleaning weapons, troops on guard, officers and sergeants inspecting equipment, troops repacking equipment—those kinds of things.

The guys in the artillery battery weren't doing much of anything. Mostly they were sitting in the shade near their guns trying to keep cool. With their lax latrine discipline I wondered how it smelled down there now that it was getting really hot. No one was doing any kind of work on the vehicles and equipment that I could see, and their rifles remained stacked by the cannons. Their ammunition trucks were pulled up behind the guns in close proximity to one another. If one truck blew up, they all would, and a nice crater they'd make too (not to mention destroy the front of the hotel that I was in, at which thought I laughed a little less enthusiastically). They had not fired a mission since occupation; come to think of it, they hadn't even fired registration. Most artillerymen prefer to register their guns by firing a few rounds to confirm their gun's lay after occupation. These guys had forgone even that. I didn't envy anyone they would be shooting support missions for, especially if those missions were "danger close" (inside three hundred meters). I also wondered what the general in the hotel would say if the artillerymen fired their guns and shattered the windows of the hotel. All in all the artillery battery was unimpressive.

The tanks were not any better. The T-72s hadn't moved for almost a day. Their crews sat by them, finding what shade they could. Armored vehicles, especially tanks, require a lot of maintenance. After making an overland road march from the Kuwaiti border, a well-trained tank crew would give their mounts a thorough going-over once they halted for any period of time. The crews should have been checking and tightening track tension, checking engine fluid levels, lubricating road wheels, repacking personal equipment, and in general taking care of their vehicles. None of this occurred, at least in my observation. The crews seemed to be more interested in staying cool. I remembered the other tanks I had seen moving past and how loose some of their tracks were. Everything I had seen indicated sloppy maintenance and poor training on the part of the tank crews. Interesting.

About the only activity I did notice while I was waiting to go downstairs was another indicator of discipline, or lack of it. Soldiers walked into my field of vision from around the eastern side of the hotel carrying merchandise evidently looted from nearby stores. A few carried suitcases filled with goods. Some had TV sets; others had boxes with stereos or other electrical appliances. One soldier carrying a large umbrella was stopped and upbraided by an officer and forced to throw it away. (Moral of the story: You can loot, but don't walk around with an umbrella like some pansy.)

The evidence of looting made me go into the stairwell again to get a better look at what was going on. I had a good view of a whole line of stores, and looting was taking place on a massive scale. Dozens of soldiers were in each store jostling past one another to get in or to leave the store with loot they had already acquired. This was not looting for food as I had seen the first day. Nor was it an isolated incident of indiscipline; it was too big for that. No, what I was watching was a sanctioned event. The Iraqi army command knew about this—it had to—and it approved or at least acquiesced to it. I realized that I was watching something from previous centuries: a conquering army despoiling a city that it had taken for plunder. It was an ugly sight—windows smashed and unwanted goods strewn about the road in the sun. What they couldn't carry off they vandalized. I sat there and watched it for a long time, dumbfounded by what I was seeing.

Eventually I managed to tear my eyes away from the looting and make a thorough scan of the rest of the city within my vision. The Iraqis were clearly beginning to mount sweep operations through neighborhoods in order to check out individual houses and find Kuwaiti holdouts. This was a tedious job, and I got to watch several companies at work. Some were better than others. One unit looked as though it had the drill down pretty well, with some soldiers covering the house from the outside, ready to shoot, while others entered the house in disciplined teams. Kuwaitis were brought outside while the house was searched but were quickly released once the soldiers came out. One of the soldiers marked the house with spray paint, then they moved on to the next house. I nodded in mental approval. At least someone in the Iraqi army appeared to take his business seriously. In other places the Iraqis were not as thorough, and I watched them skip several houses on what should have been a house-to-house search. In one hilarious incident I saw a soldier who was swinging his rifle around carelessly by the pistol grip have an accidental discharge. The man next to him, not seeing this, immediately assumed that the first guy had observed something and began firing at a house across the street. Others in his squad joined in. Sad Sack himself just shrank back against the wall and didn't try to stop his squad mates, who were by now all whaling away at the side of the building, shattering its windows and causing a lot of other damage. It took an officer running up about half a minute later to get them to stop firing. I could almost hear him yelling at them as far away as I was. They walked off sheepishly. One of them kicked the guy who'd had the accidental discharge.

After about two hours I went back to the phone and called in a detailed report to Rich Cassem. He was surprised by my observations of the Iraqi army but was most interested in the extent and depth of looting that was taking place. I could tell him only that in my observation every commercial establishment in sight was fair game, but I couldn't confirm whether the apparent license to loot had been extended to private residences. It was almost one o'clock, so I told Rich that I was going down to the lobby. I informed him that if I didn't call back in three hours, he was to consider that I had been taken prisoner. Then I walked down the long, empty hallway to the elevator. I felt strange. Not frightened really, but apprehensive, as though I was about to perform a practical joke that might not work.

4

I STILL HAD THE FEELING that I might be grabbed the second I came out of the elevator, but again nothing happened. There were a lot of Iraqi soldiers and officers in the hallway leading to the lobby, and off to the right was a large meeting room that appeared to be at least part of a major headquarters. The double doors to the room were open, and I got a look at tables with radios on them and a mass of radio and power cables taped to the floor. There were charts, which were obviously used to track unit status, and several large maps of Kuwait and Kuwait City. Surprisingly no guards were at the door, and as I stopped to look in no one took the slightest notice of me. As I watched, more soldiers brought up a large map of Kuwait City on a board, and a captain directed them in placing it on an easel near the door across from some desks. The captain looked over and saw me looking in. Uh-oh, I thought as he walked up to me. I considered walking away swiftly for about a millisecond but decided against it. Any flight now would definitely look suspicious. The only thing to do was brazen it out.

The captain smiled and said, "Please do not worry. The situation is under control. Everything will be all right." I thanked him and asked where lunch was being served. He laughed and told me that it was around the corner across the lobby. I left, mentally calculating where I should stand when I returned from lunch in order to see as much as possible.

Lunch was a high-ranking-officer affair. All enlisted and low-ranking officer riffraff had been banished from the dining room, unlike the previous evening. (The little battalion headquarters had been sent packing from the hotel lobby as well.) I was surprised at the number of colonels and lieutenant colonels around me. Most divisions didn't have this many of those ranks for staff officers. Then a couple of generals came in and I noticed that one wore an insignia with two stars, swords, and a crown. I could see that he was the big guy by the way everyone deferred to him. I realized with a jolt that this wasn't a division headquarters at all. It was more probably a corps headquarters and this guy was a corps commander in charge of multiple divisions. I tried to listen in on conversations, but my Arabic was too rudimentary and they were not saying "Good morning. It is such a fine day" as in the taped Arabic lessons I had listened to. Nor was there a lot of conversation among the officers and the hotel guests. The officers sat at their tables and kept to themselves, unlike the previous evening. I envisioned that in a day or so we would be fed in a different area. After about an hour of watching and listening, lunch ended and I decided to head back toward my room.

I stood in the hall and looked into the Iraqi's operations center for about five minutes—as long as I dared. How the Iraqis didn't notice the big white guy who was sweating through his shirt in the air-conditioning is still a mystery to me, but they didn't. The map they had placed by the door was an operations map, and I could see the locations of many of their units by just reading the military symbology (a universal language of geometric graphics as opposed to writing). My mind raced to remember as much as I could when I broke off to return to my room. As soon as I got in the door, I frantically drew on my map all the symbols I had memorized: an infantry battalion there, a headquarters here. I put about ten symbols on the map. Then I called Riyadh.

Rich Cassem gave a low whistle when I told him about the general with his swords, crowns, and stars. He agreed with me that that kind of guy usually commands a corps, not a division. "You didn't catch his name, did you?" Rich asked.

These intelligence guys are never satisfied.

I then began to read to Rich the locations of the units I had taken down: infantry armor, air defense, headquarters. When I was done, Rich asked, "Marty, how are you getting all this information?" I told him I was reading their graphics, and there was a *long* pause. Then Rich said, "Really?" So I told him about the double doors and the map boards and being told "not to worry" and the fact that I had stood there for five minutes and no one had said "boo" to me. Rich considered this for a minute, then said, "I'll be goddamned." Pause. "Do you think you can go down there and look at it again?" I told him sure, when I went down for dinner in a few hours. If I started hanging around too much, the Iraqis might actually get wise, even as slow as they were.

About half an hour later I called Riyadh again. The Iraqis had moved in some SA-9 antiaircraft missile launchers to firing positions on the road near the water. I could just see them from where I was. Rich Cassem and Colonel Fields were both out of the room when I called, and I talked to someone I didn't know. He was suspicious. "How do I know you're Major Stanton?" he asked. I was exasperated. Who else would be calling? I told him about OPM and whom I worked for. He remained unconvinced.

"What's your wife's name?"

I told him I wasn't married.

"What's your mother's name?"

At this point I lost it. "Hell, *you* don't know my mother's name, so what difference does it make? My girlfriend's name is Donna O'Shaughnessy and she's Canadian. Find Rich Cassem, will you please?" A few seconds later Rich came on the phone. I had a short discussion with him about people who thought they were in some kind of James Bond movie, then I passed the information about the antiaircraft missiles to him. I asked whether there was any chance of me being given permission to slip out of the city tonight. Rich said no but promised that Colonel Fields and Brigadier General Taylor would ask Washington again. That was all he could do.

I called Brigadier General Taylor, but he wasn't in. I left a message saying that in my opinion I should be allowed to leave tonight; otherwise, my chances of avoiding capture would be poor indeed. I found out later that Brigadier General Taylor had interceded as far as he could for me and, in fact, had been pointedly told not to bring up the subject again. My little stint of observer duty would continue until further notice.

Nothing was happening outside, so I watched the news before I went back into the stairwell. For the first time I saw the matter of U.S. citizens trapped in Kuwait being discussed. The State Department spokesman was issuing statements that Iraq was being held "responsible for their safety." Great—that's just who I want responsible for my safety, I thought. The newsman said that Iraqi troops had reached the Kuwaiti border with Saudi Arabia and that Saudi forces were rushing to the border to confront them. So far there were no reported Iraqi incursions into Saudi Arabia. Well, that was something anyway. The news also had a few callers from Kuwait City giving their account of what was going on in the occupied city. This bothered me. Television broadcasts such as this would increase the speed with which the Iraqis became wise to people calling out of Kuwait City. A few more newscasts with some hysteric describing Iraqi looting and there might be an order to pull the plug on the telephone exchanges and communications satellite dishes in the country. I was surprised that it hadn't happened already.

I turned off the TV and went back into the stairwell. It was not air conditioned and I suddenly noticed how hot it was. Odd that I hadn't noticed it before. I was sweating profusely by the time I reached the top and had to keep wiping the perspiration out of my eyes with my T-shirt. For what seemed like the hundredth time, I looked out over the city.

All the fires I had seen previously were now out. The city looked undamaged at first glance. A closer look at commercial areas showed soldiers still looting, however, with multiple trucks pulled up to stores and soldiers using dollies to bring merchandise onto the trucks. Other trucks stood in line waiting their turn to load. Looting in bulk had commenced. Clearly this was a matter of established policy.

There was no traffic save for military vehicles. A few civilian cars could be seen moving around, but closer inspection revealed that Iraqi soldiers occupied them. It stood to reason that cars would be looted as well. I just hoped that no one would get to mine. Ominously, there was no firing. For the first time since the invasion started, I heard no gunshots. I figured that the Kuwaitis doing the shooting had escaped or gone to ground. Kuwait City was prostrate and in the grip of the invader. Iraqi control of the city was complete.

Suddenly the door opened in the stairwell above me and I heard men speaking in Arabic. Iraqi soldiers. I sat very still, afraid to breathe. Then I heard a noise below me as well. There were soldiers on the roof and soldiers coming up the stairwell. Damn. I was above the top guest room floor by one story. I wondered how far below me the men I'd heard were. I had to move, I was sure of that. The men above me would start coming down any second. If they hadn't stopped to talk with the door half open, they would be on me now. As quietly as I could, I went down a floor, opened the fire exit door, and peeked through it. Good—no one there. I slipped in the door and closed it behind me. Not waiting to see whether the Iraqis came up (or down) the stairwell, I ran down the empty hallway to the elevator. I pressed the button and waited interminable seconds for the elevator to reach the top floor. Then I went to the sixth floor and walked back to my room, trying to look as innocent as I could while covered with sweat and carrying a pair of binoculars. I shut the door, stripped off my shirt, and took a long drink of water. Toweling myself off, I reflected that this observer duty was getting less fun all the time.

At about five o'clock I went back down to the lobby, stopping for my second look into the Iraqi headquarters. They had made several improvements: better status charts, map boards for all their maps, and more radios and telephones. There seemed to be an air of permanence about the thing. I could see plush chairs being brought from other parts of the hotel. Clearly the Iraqis meant to stay awhile. I got more unit locations from their map near the door, then moved into the lobby. The Prince Charles admirer at the desk informed me that dinner would not be until six, so I went back upstairs after another brief look at the map. Iraqi soldiers actually had to jostle past me to get in the double doors, yet no one said a word to me. I memorized the symbols for a different part of town this time, then I went up to my room.

Before I called Riyadh, I marked the symbols on my map so I did not forget anything. Once I was satisfied that I had done a good memory dump onto my map, I went to the window for a final look. The SA-9 battery appeared to be practicing moving from hide positions to firing positions. The battery commander had moved his launchers back from firing positions along the road to between some buildings. While I watched, the launchers darted out and their crews quickly put the missile launchers into action. They stowed the launchers in travel configuration and drove back between the buildings, then did it again. The third time an officer in his jeep called the launcher commanders together and talked to them. After about five minutes, the officer left and the launchers went back into their hide positions. I could see only one launcher, but the soldiers on it appeared to be conducting some kind of maintenance. I nodded approvingly; here was another organization whose men looked as though they knew their business. Apparently, some Iraqi officers and units took this soldiering stuff seriously. After making a note of this, too, I called Riyadh. It took me a while to get through. I thought the phones had finally failed, but on the fourth try I connected with Rich Cassem.

He was grateful for the further locations from the map and other observations, but he had news to impart to me. Apparently the plan was for all Americans to be repatriated through Baghdad. The State Department would arrange for our flight out of there to either Jordan or Europe. Again he hit me with bad news: "*When* you're taken into Iraqi custody, Marty, be sure to identify yourself as an army officer and a diplomatic passport holder." *When* I'm taken! This is not the kind of news a person in my position wants to hear. I told Rich that his bedside manner could be improved and he laughed. The wretched absurdity of it suddenly took hold of me and I laughed as well. There was nothing else he could tell me. A sort of gallows humor about the whole thing was starting to creep into our conversation. "Just keep reporting as long as you can, Marty" was all he could say. I hung up after telling him he was a one-track kind of guy.

I went back down to dinner. The dining room was packed again. As at lunch, Iraqis sat by themselves and the hotel guests sat separately. This was not by designation but by choice. I sat for the length of the meal hours, stuffing my face and watching the officers come and go. I was counting colonels and generals. This was a big headquarters, no question about it. No doubt that many if not all of these officers were billeted in previously empty rooms. I was surprised that none were on my floor. Sooner or later someone would move us out as well. I hoped that if that happened, they would just leave us on the street and tell us to fend for ourselves. That would suit me just fine. I stopped by the door to the Iraqi headquarters and did the old look-at-the-map routine. As before, no one stopped me. It was almost eight o'clock when I got back to my room. I did the intelligence dump on Rich in the same way I had before.

Then I called Brigadier General Taylor in Riyadh, but he had no new information. The best he could offer in the way of solace was tell me not to worry about the car and the equipment in it. According to him, I was stuck. The State Department plan for getting us out through Baghdad seemed to be the agreed-upon course of action. I might actually have to apply to the Iraqis for repatriation if no one came and got me after a few more days. The thought of voluntarily walking up and turning myself in made me blanche. I told Brigadier General Taylor that I would just as soon take my chances in the desert, but he said to stick with the observation post. He told me that my parents were fine, although worried, and again admonished me to be careful.

My room seemed suddenly very small, and I decided to take another look from the stairwell before turning in. I gingerly opened the door to the stairwell and slipped inside as quietly as I could. I stood there for some minutes with my hand on the door latch ready to jump back into the hall and go to my room if I heard anyone. But the stairwell was quiet. It took me a while to climb the stairs, because I climbed very slowly and stopped on each landing to listen before I went up the next flight. After about half an hour I was at my observation post looking out over the town. Nothing much was going on. A few convoys were moving through, but for the most part the Iraqis were stationary for the evening and had only minimal security. A few patrols wandered the streets on foot or in those Toyota pickups they seemed to have so many of, but for the most part the Iraqis were clearly a "daylight only" army. Even the looting seemed to end with the passing of daylight. All the city lights were still on. That, and the lack of firing, lent the city an almost normal appearance.

I must have stayed there for two hours, jotting down the occasional note but in the main just pondering my position. It was unnerving how a simple choice of where to spend a weekend had evolved into an event that had the potential to change (or end) my life and profoundly affect my family and friends, not to mention Donna. (Christ, what must she be going through?) I thought of our plans to meet in London and the high hopes I'd had to come out of that vacation engaged to be married to her. Now I was stuck in this hotel, surrounded by an army that was a cross between the three stooges and the Visigoths.

I went back down to my hotel room and called in my last report of the night to Riyadh. Rich was sleeping, and some NCO took the call. I told him that I was going down for about six hours and would call around five or so. I looked at my watch: 10:30. I picked up my previous night's nest from the floor and made the bed. I hadn't heard a shot in hours. It looked as though the fighting was over. When I had walked into my room, I noticed that a mint had been set on my pillow. I ate it with relish, reflecting that it was the first nice thing that had happened to me all day. I set my alarm for 4:30 and turned on the TV. Mainly it was just more talking heads not saying much of anything. One thing was clear, though. The international community did not like the invasion one bit. The condemnation from the Arabic world was almost universal. This was going to get a lot uglier. As tired as I was, I couldn't get that upset about it. I turned off the TV and went to sleep. Day two down.

The plumbing still worked the next morning, so I drained the bathtub and took a long shower. I put on my last clean clothes, then switched on the TV. The official U.S. position was that Iraq must evacuate Kuwait City as soon as possible, and the Iraqis were responsible for the safety of all U.S. citizens. The Iraqis were answering back for the first time, warning the United States and the rest of the world to stay out of matters that were "not their affair." Saudi units continued heading up to the border, and U.S. naval forces were still steaming for the Gulf. In addition, the news reported for the first time that the 82d Airborne Division had been placed on alert. The most ominous news was that there was no word of any Iraqi offer to withdraw in exchange for the Rumaliah oil fields. This, you will recall, was what the analysts had suspected before the war. Now all the evidence—both before my eyes and on the news—pointed to the complete Iraqi occupation of Kuwait. Kuwait had become for all intents and purposes what Poland had become in the fall of 1939: a country that had been occupied and, in the eyes of its conqueror, ceased to exist. It would be interesting to see what the world would do.

Outside there was nothing new. The artillerymen lounged by their silent guns. It must have been pretty foul around there by now, what with two days' worth of defecating on their own perimeter. The armored company mounted its vehicles and moved off shortly after I came to the window. It turned south and disappeared from view, loose tracks flapping and one tank towing another—a real hard-hitting armored force. Other Iraqis around the hotel were either waking up or attending to housekeeping tasks. The date was 4 August 1990, and the great Kuwait City campout was entering day three.

I went up to my observation post in the stairwell for a morning look. Kuwait City was coming alive in the dawn. Soldiers were cooking their breakfasts, shaving, or rolling up their bedding. Few could be seen working on their vehicles or cleaning weapons, but by now I had grown to expect that. Some civilians, including women in their black *abayahs*, were walking about. A few shots suddenly rang out in the quiet, but I saw no one react to them. Probably just some Iraqi troop shooting at a stray cat. I listened attentively for the sounds of any door above or below me opening, but the stairwell was deserted and I was able to make my observations in peace. I systematically searched every street in my view and recorded the number and type of vehicles I saw on each one as well as any other military activity.

After about an hour I went back to my room and checked my notes on the vehicles against the symbols I had drawn on my map. Not all of what I observed fit, but a lot of it did. Good. I would at least be able to call Riyadh with my confirmation of some of the symbology.

The phones were still working and I got through to Riyadh without a problem. I gave Rich an update, which he dutifully recorded, then asked if he had heard anything new. He told me that the State Department had worked out the details of our evacuation through Iraq and Baghdad and we might be called on to assemble at the U.S. embassy within the next few days. In the meantime I was to continue doing what I was doing . . . blah . . . blah . . . blah. I don't think he believed the evacuation plan any more than I did at that point, but what else could he say? I never blamed Rich for my predicament. In fact, with his calm voice, good suggestions, and droll sense of humor, he was a tower of strength to me while I was in the hotel. He helped keep me going when the depressing reality of my situation came home to me. Like a good 911 operator, Rich helped the person at the accident scene. Unfortunately, he could not send the cops and a tow truck for me.

I went down to the hotel lobby to hang around and see whether I could get some breakfast. How quickly I had gotten used to some things. Two days before I had feared being grabbed as soon as the elevator door opened. Now I was standing outside the door of a large Iraqi headquarters looking in and watching them like Jane Goodall watching chimpanzees. Familiarity breeds if not exactly contempt, then certainly complacency. There was no breakfast, so I hung around talking to the hotel staff for a few minutes. They told me that the Iraqis were indeed occupying the previously empty hotel rooms and more officers were coming in to take rooms every hour that morning. This made me nervous, because I knew that sooner or later someone would get the bright idea of rounding us all up, if for no other reason than to make hotel rooms available. I took another peek in the Iraqi operations center but saw nothing new. Then I went back to my room and called Riyadh.

Rich told me nothing I didn't already know. The State Department was working to get Americans repatriated, et cetera. I didn't think that would go anywhere and told him so. I also told him I wanted permission to leave that night. He said he would try again, but there was little hope that the powers that be would change their minds. I almost wished that the Iraqis would just cut off the phone exchange.

I tried to get hold of Brigadier General Taylor and Colonel Noble, but both were gone, assisting the National Guard units that were streaming toward the Kuwait-Saudi Arabia border.

The news showed for the first time refugee traffic coming into Saudi Arabia: cars piled high with belongings and people; four-wheel-drive vehicles coming across the sand. Oh yes, let that be me, I thought. The Iraqis were reacting with ugly rhetoric to the announced deployment of U.S. ground forces to Saudi Arabia. President Bush fired back with "this aggression will not stand." The prospect of a shooting war seemed increasingly likely. I wondered whether we would get out before it happened. My thoughts at the time were that we should. It would take months to get the forces into place, and the diplomats would be doing their Kabuki dance the entire time. Our repatriation would be part of that dance. I hadn't for a minute begun to accept the fact that I would be captured. I would much rather try my luck at getting out of Kuwait City myself. I recognized, though, that this prospect was becoming less likely. If I could just make it until tonight, I could slip off—if I could get permission to leave. I thought seriously about developing phone trouble but then dismissed the thought. Such an action would be cowardly and unprofessional. I would be less than honest if I did not admit that the thought did cross my mind, however.

About 11 A.M. I noticed a large entourage of staff cars bring about a half dozen general officers to the hotel. I frantically recorded their car markings and ranks and reported the whole thing to Riyadh as soon as the last of the officers entered the building. It was close to lunchtime, so I thought I'd go down and see what was going on. For the first time there were guards at the door of the Iraqi operations center. I could walk by in the hall, but when I tried to stop and look in I was motioned to keep moving. The Iraqis let no one hang around in the lobby, and I didn't make it back down to lunch until after noon. The staff cars were gone by then.

After lunch I called Riyadh and told them about the tightening of security and the departure of the generals. I told Rich that in my opinion we were not going to be allowed to stay in the hotel much longer, and I again asked for permission to depart. Rich said that no one there could give me that permission. At this point I was exasperated. "Why doesn't someone grow a set of balls and make a decision?" I yelled at the phone. "This isn't going to last much longer."

I was right; it lasted another forty-five minutes.

The hotel guests were called individually and told to come down to the lobby. I could still kick myself for answering the phone; it was reflexive. I went because I figured they would be putting the word out to us but we would be allowed back into our rooms to pack. I was right. An Iraqi captain addressed the assembled hotel guests and told us that we were being taken to Baghdad and from there would be flown to our respective countries. We were to go back to our rooms and pack, then wait for further instructions.

I returned to my room as quickly as I could. I saw that another convoy was passing the hotel and got my binoculars to briefly look at the types of vehicles. They were trucks; I couldn't tell what was inside. I called Riyadh and told them what had transpired. I informed Rich Cassem that this terminated my little duty as an observation post and I would try to hide out in the hotel until dark. The stairwell seemed as good a place as any. After that I would find a vehicle and head south. I was about to start packing water bottles and food into a carry bag when the door was kicked open and an Iraqi soldier came in. Too late, damn.

Part Three

CAPTIVITY

5

DEEP DOWN I KNEW I would probably be caught ever since I was told to stay in place and keep reporting. The moment of capture was still a shock, however. The Iraqi private motioned me to put down the phone, saying, *"Halas! Halas!"*

Rich asked, "What's going on, Marty?" I could say only, "They're right here with me, Rich. I gotta go." (You might think you'd say something pithy at a time like that: *"I regret that I have but one life,"* et cetera. It just couldn't come to me.) Rich was equally tongue tied. "Ah, okay, Marty. Bye." The private, who had waited politely for me to finish, grabbed one of my bags and threw it on top of the bed (over the map), motioned for me to pack, and walked out the door.

I could only wonder at it. Here I was, a guy with binoculars around his neck, a map of the city with writing all over it on the bed, captured in the act of talking on the phone, and Private Not So Bright couldn't put it together. Although incredulous at my good fortune, I made the most of it. I tore up the map and flushed it down the toilet, then ditched the notes and other stuff. Then I decided to run for it. I didn't care what my instructions were. My contract to conduct this little observation post just expired. Exit, stage right, for this kid. I peeked out the door.

It was immediately apparent that I wasn't going anywhere. About a platoon of Iraqi troops in the hallway were helping people with their bags and escorting them out of their rooms. They were in a congenial mood, and no one was being mistreated, but just as obviously they had been sent to round us up. A couple of troops were already heading for my room again. So that was it; I would be captured. I hurriedly packed a bag and put every water bottle and piece of food I could get my hands on into it.

We were taken down into a conference room in the hotel and held there for four hours. They brought food to us and allowed us to use the rest room but otherwise kept us under tight guard. An Iraqi captain came and looked at our passports but made no comment on all the nationalities. Basically every western guest in the hotel had been rounded up. The captain informed us that we would soon be taken to Iraq, then flown to our respective countries. In the meantime we were to stay in the conference room "for our own safety." So we sat, and told jokes to keep our spirits up, and waited. I took down everyone's name and nationality, because I wanted to account for everyone in our group. I also encouraged them to save as much food and bottled water as they could. Unfortunately, I couldn't talk the Iraqis into bringing more for us.

Right before dusk, the Iraqi captain who had spoken to us before came into the room and told us to gather our belongings. We were being taken to Baghdad. It seemed plausible, especially considering what Rich Cassem had told me over the phone. So we gathered up our stuff and walked out of the hotel. The building was still surrounded by military units, and more were driving through the traffic circle as we boarded the buses. Clearly this was a major movement. I tried to remember as much as I could, but it was all a blur of trucks as I crowded onto a bus.

The first thing that struck me about our evacuation was how sloppy and haphazard it was. The captain had detailed four privates to ride the bus with us (one driver and three guards) and barked a few terse orders to the driver. The soldier stiffened and saluted and off we went. I thought this was a recipe for disaster. In the U.S. Army, the driver would have at least been given a strip map or a more thorough briefing. Here these guys were, in a new city they had just conquered and were not familiar with, and this officer just grabbed a "hey you" detail and sent them off unescorted with the general admonition to get the busloads of prisoners to Basra (and from there to Baghdad). The sun was just beginning to set as we left the hotel and headed toward the sixth ring road and the Kuwait City-Basra highway.

So of course we got lost.

The privates in charge of our bus didn't have a clue where they were going. I halfway hoped that they would take a wrong turn and head for Saudi Arabia, but sadly they turned north. On our way out of Kuwait City we saw ample evidence of the fighting of the previous days: several knocked-out tanks near a road intersection, and a bus smoldering by the roadside with charred corpses inside. All along our route were dozens of antiaircraft guns and missile launchers. Even then the Iraqis were fearful of U.S. air strikes. We could also see Iraqi soldiers breaking into stores.

I mentioned this to one of the Iraqi privates who spoke pidgin English to match my pidgin Arabic. He shrugged and said that they had received no rations since 31 July and had gone hungry for two days prior to the invasion. This certainly explained the obsession with food that I had observed the first day: the troops looting vending machines, and tanks with cases of bananas on top of their turrets. The men had been starving. By the time we got to Mutla Ridge it was already dark and we continued toward Iraq, through the Rumaliah oil fields in northern Kuwait. My companions in captivity spoke little. Maybe they were still caught up in the surrealism of the whole thing. Maybe they were like me and were soberly counting all the units streaming past and feeling overwhelmed at the scale of the invasion. That the night was warm and the buses did not have air-conditioning served to lull many of the occupants to sleep. We reached the Iraq-Kuwait border around midnight and were stopped at the border post.

We could tell that we were at the border even without the fence and the gates with adjacent buildings. The road maintenance took a decided turn for the worse: from a well-maintained, four-lane highway to pothole heaven in an instant. At the border post itself there was a short halt when the troops driving us were stopped by the Iraqi border police. Apparently no one had told the police that busloads of westerners were being taken to Iraq, and they initially didn't want to let us in. The soldiers argued with them, then the border guards left to make some phone calls. A few minutes later one came back and waved us through. While we were sitting there, convoys of vehicles and armor kept coming through the checkpoint. I was awed by the number of tanks I saw—more than a hundred—and I knew there must be a lot more. I guessed that the Iraqis had put three or four divisions into the invasion of Kuwait (I later found out there were seven). We still hadn't gotten any directions about where to go, and the troops on our guard/escort detail looked lost. The bus was hot, but the relatively lower temperatures of night air kept it from being unbearable. We drove to Basra quickly enough, but then the night turned into a series of stops and inquiries as to whether this was indeed the right place. Our suspicions were borne out that these guys didn't have a clue about where we were. We were going through our water supply fairly quickly. My companions had already drunk most of what they had brought with them, and I was worried about the next day. I had packed enough bottled water for myself for a couple of days, but a lot of the other hostages didn't have anything. Sharing my water bottles depleted them, and I was less than optimistic about my chances of filling them back up with potable water once their seal had been broken.

Shortly after dawn we stopped at a large square water tank on the side of the road, and the Iraqis let us drink from it and save water in our containers. After that it was back to the search for a place to drop us off. The Iraqis took us to a compound that looked like an army-level headquarters with all of its antennas remoted to various buildings. Several Italian-version Bell Augusta helicopters were just taking off, and some high-ranking officers were getting out of cars parked in front of a large headquarters-like building.

We stopped there for a bit while our drivers got directions. It was starting to turn hot and the buses were beginning to feel cramped. Soon the drivers came back and we were off again. The Iraqis seemed to know where they were going for a change and set off to their new destination at a good clip chatting amicably with one another.

The place they brought us to was clearly some kind of prison. It was a large compound surrounded by barbed wired and walls. We were plainly not expected, given the consternation with which the Iraqis there received us. There was some argument as to where we would be put in the compound. While this was going on, I tried to get a look around. The place was stark: one-story cinderblock barracks with wooden roofs and a seeming dearth of facilities. Garbage was piled up in places. I didn't even want to think about what the latrines looked like. There were a lot of flies. I remembered what I had read about Andersonville and Japanese prisoner-of-war (POW) camps in World War II. What killed many prisoners was disease brought on by poor sanitation. This place looked pestilent.

The compound *was* a POW camp. We saw this when we were taken to our barracks. The Iraqis had decided to keep us separate from the rest of the prisoners—Iranians from the 1980–1988 Iran-Iraq War, I was told by one of the guards—but we could still see them. Our captors put us in a single barracks, which consisted of a bare room with a cement floor. Through the windows we could see a water truck backing up to what looked like a large trough. As the water flowed into the trough, the Iranian prisoners fought for a place to get to the water. They were savage about it. All were young who, although physically debilitated by captivity, were still more than a match for the soft, older, western businessmen who made up the majority of our group. I looked at my companions and mentally evaluated their chances of surviving in this cesspit for very long.

The heat was enervating, and after being up all night some of my compatriots just wanted to lie down. Unfortunately, this wasn't immediately possible because the floor was covered with garbage and debris. We managed to scrape most of it into piles with a piece of cardboard and prevailed on the Iraqis to give us a broom, so after an hour we at least had a clean floor. However, no water was available and we were all thirsty. The Iraqis brought sodas to sell, and the one man (a Japanese citizen) who had Iraqi money bought us all a soda. The guards did not know how long we would be there, and there was no one to answer our questions. A man in his seventies went up to the guards to complain about the heat and his broken watchband. He became quite upset about it and was beginning to agitate the guards when we finally got him to sit down and be quiet. Two Kuwaiti soldiers were brought in looking the worse for wear. I took their names and tried to find out what I could about them, but neither spoke English and my Arabic wasn't good enough for us to communicate. They were soon taken out of our group. Then the Iraqis came back and took westerners from certain countries out of the group, first taking an Austrian and an Italian. I gave the Austrian a list of all the people being held in the barracks in hopes that he would get the list to his diplomats, who in turn would inform the United States. I watched the two men go with a feeling of foreboding. A prolonged stay in this place would be lethal to many of my fellow hostages. I began mentally recalling everything I had ever learned about field sanitation and survival in a POW camp.

Fortunately, we did not stay there long. After about five hours the Iraqis came and told us to get on other buses. These were like tourist coaches and were comfortable and air conditioned. Our new guards and handlers were clearly big wheels, judging by the deference the Iraqis at the POW camp showed them. I heaved a sigh of relief as we passed through the POW camp gates. I looked back to see the Iranians in the yard staring at us as we left. We weren't free, but any time you leave a place such as that POW camp vertical, it's a good deal.

We were driven through town past numerous groups of what looked like soldiers standing on the street. They were unarmed, and many were carrying bags or suitcases. I was told they were mobilizing reservists. We passed occasional convoys of armor being carried to Kuwait by heavy equipment transports. I remember several U.S.-made M577s parked by the side of the road. Because the United States had not sold any armor to Iraq, I could only assume that the M577s had been captured in the Iran-Iraq war or newly captured in Kuwait. We also drove by a surface-to-air missile battery parked on the side of the road in movement configuration. I counted sixteen missiles on the trucks and made another note.

We were brought to another compound and taken to a large room in one of the buildings. From this room we were escorted one at a time across the little courtyard into another building. From there each person was taken back to the buses, which were waiting outside. I guessed that the Iraqis were conducting some kind of sorting process, and we were taken individually for preliminary questioning. I resolved to go last so I could ensure that all the members of my group got back on the buses. I was certain that as soon as any interrogator with two brain cells to rub together questioned me and found out that I was an American army officer, I would be segregated from the group. Everyone before me followed the same pattern: across the courtyard to the other building, then back to the buses. Each person was held for about five minutes. There seemed to be no order of who should go first; the person nearest the door was taken. After a while the people in my group could see that we were getting back on the buses, so they stood near the door to be next. I hung back. Finally I was the only person left. The guards came and politely motioned for me to follow them. We walked across the courtyard and I saw my fellow captives talking among themselves on the buses, which had their engines running to power the air-conditioning.

The room I was brought into was bare and had a cement floor with drains in it. Three men sat at a table with forms in front of them. There was a chair in front of the table for the guest of honor. Four or five men who seemed large for Iraqis leaned against the wall—not threatening, but there. I was politely motioned to sit down, which I did. No one laid a hand on me. The man on the right asked in good (if accented) English, "What is your name?" I told him, and he wrote it down on the form. "What is your nationality?" I told him, and he wrote that down too. "What is your profession?" I told him, "I am an officer in the American Army."

He looked up, surprised. "What did you say?" I repeated myself. He shook his head and turned to the man on his left. *"Inta Daabit Il Jaysh Ameriki."* The man thought this over for a second, then shrugged. He asked the man on his left, who didn't know, then they put it to the other men in the room. My interrogator looked at his watch, shook his head again, and muttered. Then he wrote something down on the form.

What he asked next threw me for a loop. "What is your annual income?"

I was expecting a lot of things, but not that. It hit me with some force that I didn't have any idea how much money I made. I didn't pay much attention to it. Whatever of my paycheck I didn't spend each month I gave to my dad to invest. They were looking at me, though, and I had to say something. I blurted out, "Forty thousand dollars a year." (This turned out to be low.)

The Iraqi interrogator asked, "U.S. dollars?" I said yes. Then he asked for my home address.

I almost didn't answer. I figured that we were way past name, rank, and serial number. On the other hand, I had my driver's license in my wallet (which they could take from me at any time) and I figured we were going to get to the thumbscrews soon enough, so I cleared my throat and answered: "Nine twenty-eight Micanopy Drive, Orlando, Florida USA."

People don't believe me when I tell them what happened next, but as God is my witness it's true. The man's head jerked up from the paper and a big grin appeared on his face. He exclaimed, "Disney World!"

There are moments in life that just beg description and this was one of them. If I was open mouthed, can you blame me? The man was positively ablaze with enthusiasm for Disney World. The questions came in a rush: Was Space Mountain as fast a roller coaster as they say? Was is possible to stay at the park? How much did it cost to get in? Could they exchange Iraqi money?

His compatriots in the room picked up on his excitement and asked him what the big deal was. I couldn't make out a lot of the machine-gun Arabic, but I could make out the words *"bayti"* (Arabic for "his house") and, of course, "Disney World." I think he told them

I lived in Disney World; they seemed very impressed. A few of them asked questions, which my interrogator translated. We talked about Disney World for quite some time. All the while my antenna was way up. I kept waiting for them to segue from Disney World to "What were you doing in Kuwait, American spy?" but they never did. I couldn't see where this was going. Finally my interrogator said with a tone of regret, "We must finish. It was so nice to meet you. I do hope to visit Disney World one day. Anyway, have you declaration?"

I didn't know whether I had heard him correctly. "What?" I asked.

He repeated, "Have you declaration?"

I shrugged. "Well, I'd like to go home."

He mulled this over for a second, then smiled. "No, no. Property. Have you any property to declare?"

It hit me like a ton of bricks that this man was filling out a customs form on me. I realized that he was the English speaker in the group and the other two men at the table probably spoke other languages, perhaps French or German. This whole thing was just a procedure to clear customs. I was so surprised that I just barely managed to croak, "No." So the man stamped my passport and shook my hand, and I was taken out to the buses.

My fellow hostages seemed very worried. I had spent a lot longer in there than anyone else had. They all were asking me questions as our bus pulled out of the compound. "What happened?" "Why did you take so long?" "What did they do?" I could only smile lamely and say, "We talked about Disney World." I left them to digest this and returned to looking out the window for more bits of information.

As we drove into Basra proper, there wasn't much in the way of civilian traffic, just the yellow-and-orange taxicabs that I was later to learn were ubiquitous throughout Iraq. Traffic was mostly military, and most of it seemed to be headed south. We passed a sign in English for "UN Observer Headquarters" or words to that effect. This perked me up; maybe we would see the UN guys and I could pass our situation through them to U.S. authorities.

We reached the waterfront proper as dusk was approaching. I could see the tops of ships' superstructures over the warehouses. We turned south and drove through what looked like a warehouse and industrial area, then reached the road that traveled along the Shatt-Al-Arab. We stopped in traffic and I could see an old British river gunboat tied up at a dock as a sort of naval museum. When we entered the drive along the riverside proper, I saw the statues. Basra had one of the strangest riverfront decoration schemes I have ever seen. Every ten meters or so for more than a mile were larger-than-life statues of men in uniform: some in helmets and some in berets, a few in tanker or jet pilot helmets. Each one was dull, dark copper and looked as though it had been cast. Each statue had one arm raised and pointing toward Iran. I found out later that the statues were of posthumous heroes of the Iran-Iraq war. They made for a romantic waterside stroll for the citizens of Basra. I wondered vaguely whether some form of Iraqi national endowment for the arts had funded them.

We had no idea where we were going. Our minders had promised that we would go to "a nice hotel." I had my doubts, but by now we were all really tired and hungry. To my amazement they brought us to the Basra Sheraton. A little more than twenty-four hours had elapsed since we left Kuwait City.

The Basra Sheraton was a clean, modern hotel with a glass front and a large interior foyer. I was surprised that a building with so much glass had survived the war. (Basra had not actually been fought in during the Iran-Iraq war, but there were enough bomb-damaged buildings to give evidence of air strikes.) We were ushered in and told to go to the buffet to eat. From there we would be given rooms. I immediately ran into some British citizens who were also captives. Some of them were British soldiers from the advisory mission that the British army had with the Kuwaitis. They had been taken from their families in Kuwait and were very concerned for their welfare. A British major (whose name I have unfortunately lost) told me that the hotel was surrounded and, although we had the run of the place, there was no use trying to get out a door. Nor could we make a phone call. All the hotel phones went through a central operator. No direct dial international access here. There was nothing for us to do but go and eat.

I entered the dining area and my heart leapt as I saw two soldiers in uniform, one of them a Canadian. Clearly they were members of the UN observer mission who just happened to be in the hotel restaurant. We were told by our minders not to talk to them, but what could they do, take me hostage? I went over to the Canadian who had the flash of the Princess Patricia's Canadian Light Infantry (PPCLI) on his shoulder. I knew the Princess Pats, a good outfit that had trained at Fort Lewis when I was stationed there in the early 1980s. I stopped at their table just as they were getting up to leave and told them that I was an American army major in a group that had been kidnapped from Kuwait and would he please pass this list of our names to the UN. I will never forget this man, although I don't know his name. He was about five foot ten and on the chunky side, with thinning hair and a pencil-line mustache. Nor will I forget what he said. "I'm sorry I can't help you. Please don't talk to me." Then he headed for the door at a fast walk.

I was speechless. Here we were, kidnapped from our normal lives, and here was a representative of the world body, a member of a proud Canadian infantry regiment with a fine heritage, running away from even taking a list of names; scared that the Iraqis would say "boo" to him. I was enraged and vowed to report him when I got out of this. (I was still thinking "when"; "if" hadn't entered into my mental equations yet. As it turned out I didn't report him; it wasn't worth the energy. Even good outfits such as the Princess Pats have their losers.) The British major witnessed the scene and shook his head ruefully.

This wasn't the only missed opportunity to communicate our presence to the world. After dinner the British major and I were walking through the lobby when he overheard one of the British women say that someone had gotten through to the British embassy in the telephone exchange. Apparently there had been a shift change and no one had told the new guys that we were not allowed to communicate out. Unfortunately, the person who had gotten through simply passed a message about being late for an aunt's birthday, then hung up. Before we could get the operator to connect us, the Secret Service minders were all over us, shooing us out of the area. It was enough to make you weep.

I was drooping with exhaustion by this time, and the lobby offered nothing in the way of foreigners to pass a list of our names to. I looked out the doors and windows. Guards all over the place. Even if I could get past them, the nearest place to escape to was . . . Iran. Not very inviting. So I headed to my room, which was nice enough, and took a long shower, then I went to sleep.

The next day we assembled to leave for Baghdad around 10 A.M. The westerners must have numbered more than sixty, including people I hadn't seen the previous day and whose names I did not have.

There was no time to update my list, though, because we were already being herded on buses. At least I had managed to restock my food supplies of bread and fruit and take some water bottles. I sat down behind the British major and we were off.

We drove back up the waterfront, past the long row of statues (which were even uglier in daylight). We went through parts of northern Basra and could see ships sunk in the Shatt-Al-Arab that had obviously been there for some time. Northern Basra looked a lot more beat up than where we had been the previous day. Apparently the Iran-Iraq war had hit it pretty hard. I made a mental note about their slow postwar recovery. It was more than eighteen months since the armistice and the place was still trashed.

We entered a four-lane highway and turned north. The countryside was fairly flat and featureless except for a lot of marshes and canals. Periodically I could look over to the east and see long, built-up dirt ramparts with tank ramps built up to them. These were part of the Iraqi defense system that had finally halted the Iranian human-wave assaults (or so I had read). The ramparts looked intimidating, but against a competent army with air support such a fortification just made a handy target reference point. Still, it was interesting to see. Periodically we passed military convoys heading south. In one I counted more than sixty T-55 tanks on heavy equipment transports; the others were just military trucks. Except for military vehicles, traffic was sparse. I did see a taxicab headed north with a casket draped in the Iraqi flag strapped to its roof. Clearly it was a soldier who had died in the invasion of Kuwait. Its presence was odd because normal Arab custom is to bury the dead within twenty-four hours. The taxi passed us gradually, so I could see the casket for a long time. Immeasurable sorrow to one family, I thought, suddenly hoping that the man had not been an only son or a father. I watched the taxi slowly disappear in front of us. The first installment on Saddam's nutty ambition had been paid.

I suddenly remembered my history. We were traveling up the same route that the British had first used in 1915, then again in 1917 in their efforts to take Baghdad. Their first try had met bloody defeat at a place called Ctesiphon, then disaster when they retreated to the town of Kut-Al-Amara. More than 10,000 British and Indian soldiers had been killed, wounded, or captured by the Turkish army. I thought about an army on foot and horseback in that hellish heat, with only ox-drawn water carts for sustenance. The men were hard in those days. I looked at the ground from a fresh perspective and tried to visualize the campaign there.

Presently the buses reached Kut-Al-Amara, but it was only a way station to change drivers. I was disappointed that none of the battlefield had survived. (I don't know why; it stood to reason that they would build over it.) Kut had, of course, grown out of its World War I boundaries. All the former trench lines were now covered by houses and other buildings. I didn't get too good a look, however, because the drivers changed quickly and we kept going north almost without pause. I saw a lot of military traffic and many installations, almost too many to keep track of. It was turning dark as we got to Baghdad, and I have only a few recollections of the place. For the most part it looked like a big-city version of Al Hofuf, with all its little shops displaying their goods outside. Baghdad was also similar to Riyadh in that it didn't have a high-rise city center, just a few buildings. The most memorable impressions I got were of the weird decorations in its traffic circles. One had a strange, silvery metal ziggurat that seemed to be made out of garbage. Upon getting closer, I saw that it was constructed from the wreckage of Iranian fighter planes. I could just make out the markings on some of the twisted and rusting pieces of metal. The sculpture (if one can call it that) was at least thirty feet high. The most impressive structure was another statue that appeared to be made of chocolate marble. It was a commemorative statue of the Iran-Iraq war and takes the prize for the single ugliest piece of artwork I have ever seen. It was a life-size sculpture of a T-55 tank (yes, a tank) with what appeared to be about a hundred men riding on top of it, waving their weapons and fists and looking exultant. Beneath the treads of the tank were Iranians being crushed; expressions of unspeakable agony were on their faces. We were stuck in the traffic circle for about two minutes across from this statue, and it is burned into my memory. It exuded a strange and hypnotic fascination in its ugliness. I couldn't take my eyes off it. I could almost picture Saddam saying, "I may not know art, but I know what I like."

We got to the Monsour Melia Hotel after dark, and the British were segregated from us. Only Americans and Canadians were left on the buses. I said good-bye to the British major and settled in for another long ride. As it turned out, we were driven only a short way to another hotel, the Al-Rashid, reputed to be the nicest hotel in

Baghdad. We dismounted with our bags and were led inside. The hotel itself lived up to its reputation. Our bags were taken from us and we were given a meal in the coffee shop while our rooms were readied. Then we were brought to our rooms to find our bags already there and service as in a four-star hotel, down to the mint on the pillow. This raised my hopes that we would be repatriated soon, as I had been told over the phone in Kuwait. It appeared that the Iraqis were bending over backward to provide us with attractive accommodations. I figured they probably didn't want anyone to go home with stories of Iraqi mistreatment (little did I know). There was still no phone contact, but they could hardly hide us in this hotel. I was sure we would have contact with the Baghdad U.S. embassy in the morning. Feeling much better about the whole situation, I went to bed.

6

Al-Rashid

THE NEXT MORNING I was up early but found that we couldn't leave the floor; guards were posted at all exits and the elevators. So while I was waiting for everyone to get up, I went back to my room to look out the window. We were on the fifteenth floor, so jumping out the window to escape wasn't an option. I could see down into the swimming pool area by leaning over the small balcony. Better yet, I had an excellent view of Baghdad, which literally sprawled out before me. The city seemed much bigger than when we had driven through it the previous evening. I could see the huge war memorial and the tower with the turban-minaret top that later became famous on the first days of the war when it was lit up with antiaircraft tracers flying about it. But that was in the future; now the tower just struck me as an odd piece of architecture.

We were brought down to breakfast in one large group that included everyone on the floor. The minders and security men who watched us seemed to have only one rule: No one went anywhere alone. So we'd had to wait until the last late risers were ready to go. Breakfast itself was superb, but I couldn't eat much because I kept looking through the glass doors of the dining room for any U.S. diplomatic personnel. None showed up that day. This was disconcerting, because we were not being kept in some dungeon: Most of Baghdad had to know we were here. I was told later that people from the U.S. embassy in Baghdad had tried to see us as soon as they found out about our presence. But they had been thwarted at every turn by the Iraqis, who kept coming up with excuses as to why our diplomats could not be allowed into the hotel. After breakfast we were brought back upstairs and, although we were treated politely, not allowed down again until the next meal. We spent our time listening to the radio and hearing the English version of the Iraqi news. This was full of praise for Saddam and accounts of how grateful the Kuwaiti people were for the liberation of their country—real big brother *1984*-style propaganda. Subtlety was not their strong suit. One of the oil workers in our hostage group had a shortwave radio, and we managed to catch the Voice of America (VOA) and British Broadcasting Corporation (BBC). Every radio news program was filled with talk of a deepening crisis and ultimatums, UN resolutions, and troop deployments. Not the kind of news that would normally lend encouragement.

I took stock of my fellow captives. Most were American; a few Canadians were among us initially but were soon released. All the other captives had been in Kuwait through their employment or on business trips; ironically, I was the only tourist. All the other hostages had been captured in the first few days of the invasion, some when the Iraqis had driven up to their oil rigs and said "let's go," and some after a few days of hiding in Kuwait City. Their backgrounds were diverse. The single biggest group was the oil workers from the various oil fields in northern Kuwait. They were mostly in their late forties and early fifties and were a good group to be in captivity with. They had spent years on oil rigs in the middle of nowhere and were used to entertaining themselves. They were also physically and mentally tough people who came from a line of work into which the touchy-feely approach of modern society had made few inroads. They were hard men, brought up in a business in which results are ultimately what matter. They were not given to whining or complaining, and without exception could be depended upon in a clinch. Some of them could occasionally be cantankerous, and they sometimes looked askance at the young whippersnapper major and his suggestions. However, I never saw any one of them come even close to breaking solidarity with the group or not be instantly ready to help a fellow hostage if that help were needed. All of the oil workers had their stories of Indonesia or Iran or Saudi Arabia in the old days when Riyadh was relatively small and it was common to see tribesmen with their rifles and bandoliers come into town like something out of *Lawrence of Arabia*. There is nothing as interesting as the conversation of well-traveled companions. I realized that for all my travels in the army, compared to a lot of these guys I was a fuzz-nutted rookie. I ended up listening quite a bit. Spread through the hostage groups like leavening in bread, the oil workers were a calming influence on everyone. Laconic, skeptical, humorous, trustworthy, and helpful. America was made with such men.

The other big group was businessmen, and they were as varied as the businesses they represented. They, too, were mostly in their forties and fifties, but there were a few guys my age and a few in their sixties. Their reactions to captivity were also greatly varied. There was a prevalent, irked mind-set among them; they seemed convinced that this situation would sort itself out after a couple of days and the biggest inconvenience would be having to redo their appointments for August and September. Some men were incensed by the inability of the U.S. government to get us out; some withdrew and came out only at meals; and some tried to curry favor with the Iraqis in exchange for telephone access.

Lastly there were the families. They had been living in Kuwait or caught in transit. In age they were all over the chart, from married couples in their twenties who were on a British Air flight that had been caught in Kuwait, to a retired ex-Marine colonel and his wife who had been on a tour of the Middle East. Several of the couples had children with them, and you could see the worry on the parents' faces. I could sympathize. Being in this situation alone was bad enough; being here with your family must have been particularly stressful. The families were kept on the floor below us, and we saw them only at mealtimes.

In the early afternoon our minders came down the hall and asked whether any of us wanted to go swimming. I thought this strange, but I wasn't about to pass up an opportunity to get a better look at my surroundings. About a dozen of us were included in a large group of other guests and taken to the hotel pool. The odd thing was that no attempt was made to segregate us from the other guests. I talked to several westerners from non-NATO countries who promised to pass the word of our presence. The pool itself was large and well kept, so I killed time between swimming laps looking for new faces to say hello to. The minders left us there for a long time, but not all of us had come down to swim, so I wasn't worried about them searching our possessions. They had mealtimes to do that anyway. I was worried about missing anyone from the U.S. embassy who came by. But there was nothing I could do about it. They wouldn't have gotten to see me even if I had stayed in my room. At least at the pool I had a better chance to advertise our presence.

The rest of our first day at the Al-Rashid passed without incident. The rhetoric on the radio and TV was ugly, and I saw President Bush say several times, "This aggression will not stand." This was the right thing to do, but I sure hope that Bush will forgive me when I confess that at the time my enthusiasm for this stance was considerably cooled by circumstance. I went to bed wondering where the people from our embassy were.

They came to the hotel the next day and were allowed to meet with us in the lobby. What they told us was not good news. They were working on our repatriation from Iraq, but the Iraqis were throwing up roadblocks and delaying as best they could. In the deepening crisis it looked as though our release was a bargaining chip. No one was yet using the dreaded "H" word ("H" for hostage), but the possibility was on everyone's mind. The only good part of the visit was that we could get messages out through the diplomatic representative who came to see us (a nice young man, sweltering in the suit-and-tie uniform of a diplomat). He pulled me aside to say that the defense attaché would be out to see me the next day. I asked about the possibility of going to the U.S. embassy because I had a diplomatic passport, but he said that the consensus was not to draw attention to my status. This did not please me, but there was nothing I could do about it. It confirmed my suspicion that about the only thing a diplomatic passport is good for is getting through the line quickly at immigration. I didn't press the issue—he clearly had hassles enough as it was—and I sent two messages, one to my parents and the other to Donna.

After the U.S. diplomat left, it was the same routine of meals, a trip to the pool, and back upstairs. The young diplomat had warned us, however, about the rooms being bugged. This led to a lot of talking in whispers while the water ran in the sink. We also had notepads; we would pass notes to one another, then flush them down the toilet. I looked around my room in all the places I had seen in the movies—behind pictures, in the lamps, under the bed, in the ventilation. I didn't find anything, but I still treated my room as though it were unsecured. I also would leave my bags arranged in a certain way so I could tell whether the room was searched when I was away from it. I found that several times the bags were, in fact, moved and searched, but because I didn't have anything to speak of, it was a wasted effort on the Iraqis' part. The walking around and whispering/writing notes to one another like secret squirrels was just another surreal element in an already strange situation.

There were TVs in our rooms but not much worth watching. Endless programs on the glory, wisdom, generosity, and mercy of Saddam Hussein. Who says the most imaginative TV writers are in Hollywood? These people had Saddam looking like Mother Teresa. Interspersed with these programs were Egyptian soap operas in which the actors seemed to have learned their craft in a silent film studio. The programs were filled with eye rolling, exaggerated exclamations, and hand gestures. There was one western movie in English—a film about the U.S. Air Force with Rock Hudson as a B52 wing commander. I wondered what the Iraqis thought about it, seeing as they were putting themselves in a position to experience the U.S. Air Force up close and personal.

The situation was getting more tense. The young diplomat had said that massive U.S. forces were deploying to the Gulf, and the UN was drafting resolutions to require Iraq to withdraw from Kuwait. The Iraqis were digging in their heels and stressing that Kuwait was the "19th province of Iraq." Every radio program had more descriptions of diplomatic and military activity. Only the Canadian broadcasting service was carrying anything else: the blow-by-blow of the Ohaka standoff in Quebec. The rest of the news was all the Gulf crisis, all the time. Saddam Hussein announced the annexation of Kuwait and the dissolution of the Kuwaiti nation. President Bush was still proclaiming, "This aggression will not stand." Yep, nothing but good news. The radio vaguely mentioned huge U.S. troop deployments. Everyone else and his brother seemed to be ponying up troops for Saudi Arabia as well. Things were definitely getting interesting.

The extent of the troop deployment was confirmed to me when I was visited by the U.S. defense attaché to Baghdad (Colonel Ritchie) the next day. I didn't know it then but afterward discovered that Ritchie was the closest thing the U.S. Army had to Lawrence of Arabia. He was a senior full colonel who had come out of Vietnam to spend years as a foreign area officer in the Gulf, Beirut, and other Middle Eastern locales.

Ritchie came over to the hotel pool, where we were swimming laps under the watchful eyes of our minders. I noticed him and a young diplomat and went over to see them. The colonel introduced himself, and we went off to a table in the open that would at least make it hard for someone to listen in on our conversation. Ritchie could see that I was pretty wired, so he tried to reassure me by commending me on the job I had done in Kuwait and the lists of people I had kept. He then hit me with the totality of the situation. Although the news had said that massive U.S. forces were deploying, I knew that most newspeople wouldn't have a good grasp of military operations. What Ritchie told me put it all in perspective. He said that the entire 18th Airborne Corps, with the 82d Airborne, 101st Air Assault, and 24th Mechanized Divisions, plus the 1st Cavalry Division plus the 3d Armored Cavalry Regiment and an entire Marine Expeditionary Force were deploying to the Gulf. Fully a third of the entire U.S. Army and about half the Marine Corps. He described the massive deployment of air and naval forces and the call-up of reserves. I gave a low whistle. This scale of deployment meant that the Iraqis had backed down or there would be a war. No way could this be a bluff or a show of force. In spite of my predicament, I was impressed and very proud of President Bush. It was a ballsy decision in anyone's book.

I asked Ritchie what my chances were of being brought out of the hotel and to the embassy, me being a black passport holder and all. He shook his head. Without melodrama, he told me that I was in a precarious situation, and the less we drew attention to my uniqueness as a guest, the better. The general consensus of people who knew the Iraqis was that my best protection was to be treated like everyone else. If we made a big deal about my diplomatic status, the Iraqis might investigate me further.

I had suspected as much of course, but it was still disheartening to hear it from someone you knew had a handle on what was going on. Ritchie asked if there was anything he could do for me. I gave him updated messages for my parents, Donna, and Brigadier General Taylor. He promised to send some books and board games to pass the time. The minders came up and began to motion him away. I wished him luck, and he told me to just sit tight and keep doing what I was doing. Then he and the young diplomat with him were gone.

You may think this odd, but his visit cheered me up considerably. On a personal level, I was relieved to learn that my actions in Kuwait were approved of. I was glad that no one was calling me a bonehead for being there to begin with. Regarding the overall situation, I was happy that we were deploying such a huge force. Whatever else happened, this would not be a repeat of the 444-hostage drama in Iran.

Then we didn't have a creditable threat. Now, we definitely did. It might come to hostilities with us still being held in Iraq, but at least we wouldn't be there for a year or two.

I recounted what Ritchie had told me in general terms to my fellow captives. Their reactions varied. Some were pleased and felt that this was the best way to get us out. Some were horrified that their government would take such a step when *their* life might be in danger. I was surprised at this reaction, but then some people have an exaggerated opinion of their importance in the world. This last was a minority reaction, however. Most took it stoically.

Later that day the Iraqis began letting people of other nationalities go. Canadians were among them, and I sent messages to Donna through a Canadian diplomat who was allowed on our floor to collect the few Canadian citizens who were being kept there. There was a mixture of guilt and relief on their faces as they left. I don't think they had any reason to feel guilty; none of the Americans begrudged them their early out from what was obviously a worsening situation. They did us a favor by carrying as many letters and notes to our families and friends as they could; then they were quickly gone. With the opening of several rooms, those few people who were doubled up on the floor got their own accommodations. So it was back to playing card games, watching dull TV, or reading paperback books. It was by no means the Hanoi Hilton, but it was tedious nonetheless.

The lack of exercise was getting me down, so I ran the length of the hallway, turned around, and ran it again. It was a long hallway, more than fifty meters, and I figured about a hundred lengths was about three miles. So in the afternoon while everyone else was taking a predinner siesta, I ran. The Iraqis thought I was crazy but did not interfere with me. Run down, touch the wall, run back, touch the wall, again and again. It didn't give me much of a workout, but it passed the time. The thump-thump-thump of my footsteps was fairly loud in the hall, but no one complained. One day I had my room key in my pocket. The clatter of the key on its plastic holder was enough to cause Tony Nelson (one of the oil workers) to come out and tell me to please empty my pockets. I had been daydreaming as I ran, oblivious to noise.

A few days went by and things were starting to become routine. On 15 August we were at the pool when I suddenly heard a lot of gunfire. Alarmed, I thought for a split second that someone was attempting to rescue us and cursed the embassy people for not trying to pass a warning. Then I looked over and saw our minders smiling and slapping one another on the back. An antiaircraft gun on the roof of an adjacent building had cut loose at nothing, and I realized that what I had been witnessing was just celebratory firing into the air. I was stunned at the sheer stupidity of it. The Iraqis were firing off live ammunition and antiaircraft rounds as though bullets did not obey the law of gravity and would never come back down. I was a little nervous to be outside; who knew how many innocent bystanders were going to be hit by this "happy firing." I asked one of the minders what the racket was about. He informed me that a peace treaty had been signed between Iran and Iraq and relations between the two countries would be normal soon. I was dubious at first, but later that day the BBC and VOA confirmed the story: peace with Iran. I remember thinking that this would throw President Bush a curveball. As it turned out, he handled it just right. The reality of the situation was that the signing of the peace agreement didn't change much. There had already been an armistice in effect for two years, and even a foreign policy novice such as myself could see that the Iranians would not rush into the fray to make common cause with their recent mortal enemy against us. From where I was sitting, the Iranians would be only too happy to have us beat up on the Iraqis. You couldn't convince the Iraqis of this on that day, however. All those I talked with were convinced that this was a turning point in the crisis and Saddam had pulled one out of the hat again. "Convinced" is probably too strong a word. It was just as likely that they were aware of what they better say in public if they knew what was good for them.

The news certainly did not bear out this optimism. The United States continued to deploy troops to the Gulf, and more nations were signing up for the coalition against Iraq. Sitting in our hotel rooms listening to the shortwave radio, all we could do was quiet one another's unease as best we could. It was obvious to even the densest of us that the situation was getting worse.

The next day (about the sixth day in the Al-Rashid), we had our last visit from the Baghdad embassy personnel. No new news, just "We're trying everything . . ." They returned some messages I had sent; my mom and dad said not to worry about them and just take care of myself. Donna sent a humorous message about missing our London trip that had concern written all over it. Hearing from them was depressing, because it illustrated how far I was from them. In re-

ality I might as well have been in a dungeon for all the chance I had
of getting away.

It was a strange and gilded captivity. No thumbscrews, starvation,
interrogations, or beatings. We had a spectacular view of Baghdad
from our windows. News of the outside world was readily available
to us, and we could periodically get messages out through our diplomats. We traded paperback books and played board games. We
pooled magazines; I saw my *Economist* and *National Lampoon* making the rounds. We communicated in whispers and on notepads all
the while that our Iraqi minders reassured us that we were "guests"
of the Iraqi government and would be going home soon. So we did
our three meals a day and trips to the pool, afternoon siestas, or laps
up and down the hall. Waiting for the embassy people to arrive and
half dreading what they had to say. Listening to the military movements on the radio and in general staying in a state of suspended an-
imation.

The Iraqis found occasions to exploit the "guest" aspects of our
stay when they learned that a little girl in one of the hostage families
was having a birthday. They walked into our dinner with a huge cake
and several toys and dolls sent courtesy of Saddam. It was like something out of a hotel advertisement, with all the Iraqi staff singing
"Happy Birthday to you" along with most of the hostages. I didn't
stand up and participate because I noticed the TV cameras, but I
didn't want to freak out the kids by making a scene. Score one for
Iraqi propaganda: The birthday party made the Iraqi nightly news as
further proof of Saddam's munificence. It served as a cautionary tale
to me. Any moment we could be used for propaganda filming. It was
something we had to keep aware of.

Looking back, I think for the first few days of our stay in the Al-
Rashid, the Iraqis were actually at sea as to what to do with us. They
didn't want to repatriate us immediately because we were a bargaining chip. However, the lame series of diplomatic excuses they used to
delay our movement would gain them only a few days at best. They
had to make a decision as to whether or not we were hostages. I think
this decision was probably made a week after the crisis began, on our
second or third day in the Al-Rashid. The rest of the time we spent
in Baghdad was the amount of time it took the Iraqis to prepare facilities elsewhere. The hostage policy was probably Saddam's idea. It
fit in with what I've read since of his view of America and the West

and western weaknesses. The hostage crisis had worked for the Iranians; why shouldn't it work for him too?

With the benefit of hindsight, I realize now that we probably would have been moved anyway. However, at the time we believed that what precipitated our removal from the Al-Rashid was the arrival of American newsman Ted Koppel and his crew. (It was easy for us to make the connection, because the next day we were moved.) They came bursting into the hotel, past minders who were unaware they had come in or (more likely) unsure of instructions on how to handle them. I was standing by the pool putting on my shirt when Koppel came running up to me sputtering, "Say that you know me and we're old friends!" Surreal. I of course said that we were old buddies from Fort Irwin, California, then I told him how many of us there were, our condition, and the fact that the Iraqis were not letting us leave. I also passed to one of his cameramen a verbal message to the embassy about our status. Koppel had time to ask only a few questions about our treatment and what we knew of the situation before the Iraqis came and carted him off along with his camera crew. Then we were all hustled out of the pool and back upstairs. Dinner that night was a strictly up-and-down affair, with none of the previous lollygagging in the lobby.

Later that afternoon I began advising people to stock up on what they might need in captivity: hotel towels, silverware from the dining room, water bottles, prepared packaged food, and the like. I also cautioned people against making statements that could be harmful to the government and its cause. Dummy that I was, I didn't write down these instructions to be disseminated, which would have been possible. Instead I wasted the evening listening to the radio and looking out the window. Ah, hindsight.

We were moved the next afternoon about an hour after lunch. The Iraqi minders came up and told us to pack. The one bright spot about not having much in the way of clothes was that I was ready to go in about five minutes, with stolen towels, cutlery, water bottles, and all. Because I was known to be a military officer, one of the minders was assigned specifically to me, and we spent about an hour sipping tea and discussing the situation while the rest of the floor frantically packed all their possessions. The minder's name was Mohammed Abdullah and he was very reassuring, telling me that we were being taken somewhere in preparation for release and would see our embassy representatives soon. I didn't believe a word of it and asked him if he thought Baghdad's defenses could stand up to the U.S. Air Force. He shrugged and said that Vietnam had beaten us, why couldn't Iraq? I smiled and told him that he seemed like a nice man, so I warned him to get his family out of the city before it was too late. He said that the United States wouldn't dare bomb Iraq with us there, but I just smiled again, shook my head, and explained that we would be acceptable losses. I didn't know whether or not this was true, but never pass up the opportunity to place a kernel of doubt in your captor's mind. Unfortunately, before I could work on him further it was time to go.

We were taken out to buses under heavy plainclothes escort. A foreign diplomat whom we had seen in the hotel before saw us being taken out and came over to ask what was going on. The minders tried to shoo him away, but we shouted to him that we were being removed to an unknown location and to tell the U.S. embassy. He nodded and took off. We boarded the buses slowly, stretching out the process as much as we could. However, we could stall for only so long, and at about three in the afternoon we pulled out of the Al-Rashid parking lot and started to leave Baghdad. Signs showed that we were going toward Rutbah, a small town near the Jordanian border. The position of the sun confirmed that we were heading west. I leaned back in the seat and watched the cityscape of Baghdad gradually be replaced by desert. I rode on alone with my thoughts, thinking of my family and Donna and wondering what was to become of us next.

7

Al Quaim

THE HOPE THAT WE WERE BEING TAKEN to Jordan was short lived. More than a hundred kilometers from Rutbah we turned north off the road and started heading for the Euphrates River. It was dark and the convoy got lost several times; we stopped to ask directions. Finally we got onto a main road that paralleled the river on the south side. We were traveling due west toward Syria, and my excitement grew with each passing minute as I realized that we had to be getting close to the border. Had we been in the open desert it would have been harder to tell, but the river beside us could only be the Euphrates, and that river ran to Syria and Turkey.

The buses had been traveling along this road for several hours at about eighty kilometers an hour. Considering we had been about a hundred kilometers from Rutbah when we left the main road, we *had* to be getting close to Syria by now. Close to another country meant a possibility of escape. With every mile we traveled along the river, my spirits rose. We had gone for more than two hours when we turned off to the south and entered an industrial complex just short of a town that we could see in the distance.

We were brought to a workers' camp outside of the industrial plant. It was dark and we were shown to a community building, where dinner was waiting for us. After dinner we were brought to some of the unoccupied workers' houses and given our rooms. I took a brief walk around to get a feel for the place. I could see about forty houses. All were little two- or three-bedroom affairs, the same sort of management workers' bungalows that I had seen in Saudi Arabia. I couldn't tell much more before our minders came by and told me to go to my house. I was sleepy anyway, so I complied without comment.

The next morning before breakfast I got a good look at the place. It was slightly bigger than I had realized, with another street of twenty or so houses that I had missed in the dark. The houses were semi run down, and their interiors were nothing to write home about: cheapjack Italian appliances, a washing machine that could hold maybe two shirts, and strange-looking wall sockets that would shock you if you weren't careful. The compound itself had a lot of trees and bushes, and there were places to hide outside of the buildings. There was some shade, which was a relief because the heat was murderous—well over 115 degrees. The Gulf in August can be a physically stressful place. I went to take a look at the fence. The sight of it was particularly heartening because it was not well made. The guards in their non-air-conditioned towers drooped in the stupefying heat, and their attention was on anything but us. I walked slowly along the fence, taking in all its details, noting how in places the wire was not well connected to the poles, how in other places there were gaps sufficient for a person to shinny under. It dawned on me as bright as sunrise that as prisons go, this one was fairly porous.

The outside of the fence offered less assurance, because our compound was surrounded by other facilities. There was a radar installation to the southwest and an antiaircraft position about five hundred meters to the south. I could see a large chemical plant about two kilometers to the northwest for which this compound was obviously worker housing (at least for some of the foreign engineers and senior staff workers). Getting through the fence would be easy enough, but I would have to pay attention to find the best route past the installations and facilities that surrounded the workers' camp.

My thoughts had turned to escape because I knew about where we were. The little map of Iraq I had showed that Al Quaim was very close to the border with Syria. I had read a sign that said "Al Quaim 10KM" prior to us turning off. Al Quaim was less than twenty kilometers from the Syrian border! One good night's walk if I could avoid capture. I cautioned myself that this had to be planned well and I shouldn't go off half-cocked. I would get the pattern of things, plan the best times. Wait for the moon to go down, but not all the way down because I needed some light to find my way. Was the border with Syria mined or was there wire, or was it desert and all I had to do was walk across it? This I wouldn't know until I got there. First things first. Concentrate on getting through the facilities surrounding this workers' camp and into the open desert.

We were fed in the camp's communal building. Ground lamb and potatoes French fried in what must have been 10-30 weight oil. The Iraqis announced that we would be kept there as a guarantee against attack, but it was "only temporary" and soon we would all go home. This caused quite a bit of consternation, especially among the businessmen and the married couples. The oil workers took it with their usual laconic aplomb.

Listening to the radio that afternoon confirmed the Iraqis' "human shield" policy. We were told that we could have the full run of the housing compound but not to try to leave. We were also told not to talk to any of the Eastern European workers who still lived on the compound. The place had mostly empty houses, and the workers were probably in the process of being moved to better digs. But there were a few left, and I resolved to get them a list of our names as soon as I could. The trouble was that the Iraqis always had minders near where their workers lived. I could see that we would have to sneak them a list somehow. This was done the next day by one of our number who saw a gap in the Iraqis' coverage of the workers and gave them a list of our names. I was pleased with this, because it showed that at least some of my fellow captives had made the mental transition from disbelief to resistance.

I didn't want to be too obvious hanging around the fence, staring out all day, so I forced myself to go to the pool. It was large—about twenty-five by fifty meters—and had a strange, rubbery-surfaced bottom. The water was a wonderfully cool change from the pervasive and enervating heat, and I swam laps and generally loafed around for a few hours.

When I went back out to walk by the fence again, I checked the number of guards in the towers and tried to get a good look at their faces so I would have an idea as to how often the guards changed over. I watched the facilities outside for traffic. I figured I would get about six or seven days' worth of data before the moon was right for escaping. I was already looking for water bottles and other escape kit items.

After supper that evening, we had a meeting. It was interesting that some of the group wanted to make a statement that we were all civilians and demanded to be released. I sat there thinking what a waste of time that would be. But the thought process that some of them wanted to make a statement worried me. The last thing we needed was any of us making statements that could be used as propaganda. Fortunately, one of the oil workers, Gary Carr, defused the whole thing by reminding them that we were "not all" civilians. A few of them turned to me and said words to the effect of, er, sorry, Marty. I used that opportunity to remind everyone not to make statements damaging to the United States or its cause. I reminded them that the United States would make every effort to get us back safely, and there was nothing for us to do but sit tight. We broke up feeling not much better. Discussion doesn't improve everything.

Walking around at night I noticed several things. First, the Iraqis did not seem interested in enforcing a curfew. They let us walk almost anywhere we wanted inside the compound. Second, there were a lot of lights on the outside of the fence. Looking at my sketch map that I had made earlier in the day, I could see that the lights about lined up with the facilities I had drawn. There was nothing I had missed. Good. What I wanted was a route that would take me south clear of the lights and into the open desert. From there I would go due west. I didn't want to parallel any roads or installations for two reasons: There would be a greater chance of being inadvertently discovered; and if I followed a road, the area around the border would probably be patrolled and have obstacles or at least a fence. If I went far enough south (say ten kilometers or so) before I went west, I reasoned I had a greater chance to get to a place on the border where the fence was in poor repair or there was no fence. Also by going south initially I would be taking a route that would not be the first one my pursuers would think of. Key, though, was the ability to get into the open desert, hole up for a day, then cross the border the next night. I figured I could miss two meals (breakfast and lunch) before the alarm was sounded. I had to carry two days' worth of water and just a little food. I had no compass then. Navigation would have to be by dead reckoning. I knew about where west was. By keeping the glow of Al Quaim off my right shoulder, I would do all right. Distance would be measured in hours—so many hours south, so many hours west, and so many hours north. I would come out on the Al Quaim-Damascus highway, then hitch a ride. (Admittedly, the last part of the plan was not well thought out. I had no idea what Syria was like.)

The guards were not very attentive, and I could see that at least one of them was asleep in his tower. The other two towers weren't close enough for me to tell for sure, but I didn't see a lot of movement. I could just imagine the Sleepy Hollow guard force suddenly being mobilized to provide security for the "human shields." No, I wouldn't have any trouble getting past these shock troops. They changed out every four hours; there were no roving patrols by the fence. I made a small pile of rocks next to the place in the fence that was in the most shadow and the least observable by one of the towers.

The next day was more of the same. Breakfast of bread, jam, and cream cheese followed by walking the perimeter and casing the joint. I went swimming and felt that I was just about to regain control of affairs. I was anxious, because the escape would be a very tense and dangerous couple of days, but on the whole I thought I could handle it. God knows I had walked enough miles at night in the desert at Fort Irwin. If I was conservative in my movement (I couldn't take a chance on breaking a leg), I would do fine.

I now began to face the moral dilemma of escaping on my own and leaving my comrades to face whatever retaliation the Iraqis had to offer. The thought made me uncomfortable, especially in view of some of the senior citizens in the group. On the other hand, my sticking around wouldn't help them either, and it was my duty to escape. The other issue was that I would need some of them to cover for me the day after I went through the fence. I was sure I could miss breakfast, because half the people didn't show up for it on the two days we had been there and no one said anything. I never saw the minders actually count us in terms of an old Stalag 17 roll call. From what I could see, they counted us the way a zookeeper counts animals in a pen. If the Marty animal didn't show up for a few hours, they would assume that he was sleeping in the hollow tree. It was inefficient and slipshod and definitely to my advantage. I wrestled with whom to tell and when. I was afraid to confide in my fellows too soon, because loose talk would stand a good chance of being overheard by the Iraqis. Besides, I wouldn't actually need that much help, just lookouts and people to cover for me once I was gone.

Later that evening I talked to some of the men about what to do if a hostage rescue team came in. Some of them were for jumping the guards if this occurred. I discussed with them how to make improvised weapons from broomsticks and the pieces of trash that were lying around the compound. My main point, though, was to instruct them to just lie down, because any hostage rescue team would be trained to shoot anyone who was standing. I also discussed satellite signs and how to make something that could be seen from their air but would lie flat and be relatively unnoticeable to a person standing on the ground beside it. I left the discussion feeling newly guilty about going. Jumping the guards was dangerous stuff and should be done only in conjunction with an outside rescue attempt. The problem was, of course, that the last thing we needed was armed hostages standing up while the special operations soldiers busted in. On the other hand, if we managed to disarm our minders and hold our interior perimeter, it would make it easier for the special operations guys to rescue us. Such an action would be a desperate thing, though. I resolved to use the next few days to come up with a realistic plan that I could leave with my fellow captives, one that had three people assigned to each minder and would use the minders' familiarity and lack of security consciousness against them. We might be able to disarm some of the guards, but getting all of them would be a true stroke of luck.

I watched the guards again that night; their shifts changed about the same time as before. The guard in the tower closest to me was not asleep but was listening to a transistor radio and facing away from me. The other two seemed equally inattentive. I went to sleep feeling pretty confident. There was a lot to do: Finalize the escape plan, and spend the next few days exploring the best way for our group to disarm the minders and hold an inner perimeter in the event of a hostage rescue attempt (or make an honest appraisal of the hostages' capabilities and try to talk them out of it). I also had to find more water bottles and get my kit ready for escape.

I made a mistake in doing all of this, and it was a bad one. It was about the biggest mistake I made during my entire captivity and one that had far-reaching consequences into my immediate future. I made the mistake of thinking that the Iraqis would adhere to my time schedule. My mistake illustrated that although I had been captive for some weeks, I had yet to internalize the fact that I was not fully in control of the situation. As a result, I was making assumptions about the time available to me that I had no right to be making.

The next morning after breakfast, we were told that some of us (about two-thirds of the sixty or so people there) were going to be moved. This threw me into a quandary. Here I was working to escape, and now I could be moved again. I realized what a fool I had been for thinking that I could take a leisurely approach and get everything just right before I struck out through the wire. Idiot. Now I could lose everything. But there was nothing for me to do but wait and see who got selected to go. There was no point in trying to escape through the wire in broad daylight. Even as sleepy and inattentive as they were, the guards in the towers would have spotted me like a roach on a billiard table. Even if I did by some miracle avoid their detection, I would surely be missed before an hour was out, and there would be all kinds of daylight left. No, the only thing to do was wait to see whether I was among the lucky one-third of us or so who would remain at this housing project.

I was not.

What happened next is embarrassing to relate because it does not reflect well on me, but I resolved when I started writing this to tell the truth and sometimes the truth is embarrassing and unflattering. And the truth is I panicked. For the only time in my captivity, I lost my cool and became noticeably agitated. The disappointment of having my escape plans dashed by this random act was absolutely crushing, and I did not react to it well.

We were told to get our bags and return to the community center to have lunch and wait for transportation. I packed my bags hurriedly without thought as to what went where. I was not behaving normally. I took a half scissors that I had found and secreted it in the bag. I had a vague idea of jumping our guards and commandeering the bus. I thought that if I could get a few more guys to buy into this little plan, we could make a dash for the border before the Iraqis could stop us. I kept thinking, fifteen-minute drive, twenty minutes tops. I was not rational.

There were more holes in this little flight of fancy than a Swiss cheese: jumping the guards with a half scissors on a moving bus; then, assuming that worked, traveling toward Syria on roads we had never been on and breezing through border posts who would just smile and wave us on. No police pursuit either. I'm embarrassed now when I think about it, even ten years later. Dumb, dumb, dumb.

Worse, it made my fellow hostages nervous. When I asked a couple of the guys if they would help me jump the guards, they looked at me (correctly, I might add) as if I had lost my mind. Finally, Gary Carr pulled me to the side and told me to calm down. I mentioned to him all that I had planned, and he shook his head ruefully. His words were kind but at the same time served like a cold slap in the face. He told me in effect that I had lost this one and there was nothing I could do right now. The important thing was not to frighten everyone else (especially the women) and to start planning again as soon as I got to where they were taking us. I realized what a spectacle I was making of myself and made an effort to pull myself together.

Shortly after lunch, twelve of us were told to load ourselves into cars to be taken to a new location. So much for my plan for grabbing the bus driver. I said my good-byes to Gary Carr and the others and went toward one of the cars. Paul Eliopoulos was put in the front seat of the car and I was put in the back between two security men. We pulled out of the housing complex shortly after noon and drove toward the main road. There we turned left, away from Al Quaim and Syria. I looked back to see the town receding in the distance and felt inconsolably miserable. What a wasted opportunity. I resolved to never lose my cool again and never let another opportunity like this slip by me. Gary Carr's advice to start planning again resonated with me. I would do better the next time.

There was an unfortunate upshot to this part of the story. The married couples with us were released early along with all the other families. Once they were released, they called the families of everyone who had given them their phone number. I had passed them mine along with others, because we had hoped the women would be released. They told my parents that when they had last seen me I was in good health but "looked upset." I learned several important lessons from this failure to retain my composure. The first was that the biggest reason for keeping your cool isn't so you look like some movie hero but so you are not a burden to your comrades in adversity or to your family at home. Fortunately I found out about this after it was all over. Had I known then, I would have been even more ashamed.

I also learned that I had psychologically let myself in for a big fall. I had made assumptions about available time and had paid because of it. I learned that hope is necessary, but ignorant and uninformed hope is cruel. I finally internalized the fact that I was a prisoner and much of my life was no longer under my control. I also came to the conclusion that the Iraqis were not going to inform me of their schedule and could be entirely innocent of my plans, yet still screw them up with random changes such as this one. My hope evolved from a buoyant hope to a hard and introverted hope that expected to meet with setbacks but would still keep working toward escape and helping my fellows.

We drove into a little town on the river with trucks and donkeys sharing the same crowded street. People ignored the big official cars for the most part, although I noticed that they were quick to get out of the way whenever there was a traffic jam. We came to a floating bridge and crossed it with the wind whipping spray onto the windshield and the car shimmying with the sway of the bridge. We climbed the bluffs on the other side of the Euphrates and headed deeper into the desert. I did a lot of thinking as we drove back into Iraq. I knew I had failed and I was ashamed, but I also knew that it would be dangerous to dwell on this. I was still a prisoner. I would just have to hang on and do better the next time.

BAIJI

After driving through a long stretch of desert, we arrived at Baiji, another nondescript Arab town with what looked like a military airfield outside of it. Unfortunately I didn't get as good a look at the airfield as I wanted to, due to being wedged between my minders. I probably wouldn't have gotten one anyway, because we passed it quickly. We were soon through Baiji and on a main north-south highway. In the distance I could see a huge oil refinery off to the left. Also on the left was a large ridgeline that stretched as far as the eye could see. There wasn't much vegetation, although the ground was broken up with wadis and natural folds. Difficult country to hide in, but not impossible.

As we reached the refinery we turned left (east) again. I thought for a moment that we were going to the refinery, but we drove past it. I got a good look at it, though. It was an enormous facility, at least four kilometers long and almost as wide. It seemed to go on forever in one huge, sprawling mass of pipes, tanks, and burn towers. I couldn't help but think what a target it was. Evidently it had already been attacked in the Iran-Iraq war, because it was ringed with anti-aircraft batteries of various calibers. I was sure that the surface-to-air missile (SAM) sites were not too far away either. I made as many mental notes as I could about the refinery and its defenses as we drove past, hoping to get a private moment at a rest stop soon and sneak some observations into my notebook. (I needn't have bothered. I was to see a lot more of the refinery in days to come.) Soon we were past the refinery, and I figured we had to be getting near the Tigris River soon. Sure enough, just as I was thinking this, the car crested a little rise and we saw the river, sluggish and wide, making its way toward Baghdad. Hooray for land navigation, I thought. My relief in seeing a new landmark and getting a better idea of my location was tempered by the knowledge that I was now about as far inside Iraq as possible and not be in Baghdad itself. Depressing. This had certainly been one of those days.

Instead of crossing the river, the car turned left (south) into a large power plant next to the river. Clearly one of the main power sources for Baghdad, it was an immense complex of about a dozen huge buildings and transformers with power lines all over the place. There was a guardhouse by the main gate that looked as though it could accommodate about a platoon of people. There were three guards at the gate itself, and towers on the surrounding fence. The fence itself didn't look like anything special—just chain link with a strand of barbed wire on top. It didn't look well anchored at the bottom. I got to drink in this detail because ours was not the first car of the convoy, and the lead car had stopped at the gate. I could see the head Iraqi Secret Service guy conferring with the lieutenant from the guard force. The officer didn't look pleased and kept making furtive glances toward us. We could see that we spelled trouble in this guy's little world. He had been suddenly cast from his sleepy guard mount on a power plant to guarding the "guests" of Saddam. There was no upside to this for him. If one of us nutty, unpredictable foreigners made trouble or escaped from here, it would be on him. I could read the expression on his face. In spite of my depression at the moment, I had to chuckle. I feel for you, dude, I thought, but from my position I can't quite reach you. After a few minutes of discussion, however, the lieutenant let us go through. Clearly we had been expected. The officer had made no phone calls, and no other officials from the power plant had come to the gate. The few minutes of interlude at the gate had given me a precious opportunity to get a look at some of the security forces and appraise the fence—about all I could do at the moment.

We were brought to an office building and shown to a conference room with a large table full of food spread out in traditional Arab style. Although there were only a dozen of us, there was enough food for easily a hundred people. This was typical of an Arab host who wants to make a generous show of the bounty he puts before his guests. There were no armed guards in the room with us; they waited outside. We were hungry and commenced eating immediately without being invited to do so. The Iraqis left us alone. Presently a man in his mid-thirties came in and introduced himself. His name was Ra'ad (pronounced "rod"), and he was a plant supervisor charged with our care during our "stay" with them. He said our quarters were being finished and we would be shown to them within the hour. He expressed hope that this "difficult situation" would be behind us soon and we would be allowed to go home shortly. He also requested our cooperation to ensure that our stay was a smooth one. I thought this was his lead-in to, "If you try to escape you will be punished," but oddly enough it wasn't. Ra'ad's concerns were that he didn't want us wandering around the power plant getting hurt. He launched into a ten-minute lecture on safety and promised that he would show us around later. For now, he insisted that we stay in the vicinity of our quarters.

Our quarters was a dilapidated barracks trailer that could house about twenty people. If the intent was that we be used as human shields, the barracks didn't fit the bill. It was in a corner of the complex well away from the power plant itself. The trailer wasn't exactly the Ritz, but it was air conditioned, which was critical in that blast furnace of a summer. The trailer had a single long hall of rooms. There was a large living room with a TV, and a kitchen and latrines at the other end. You could tell that it hadn't been used recently because of the dust and its overall dilapidated condition, but at least some attempt had been made to get it ready for us. Ra'ad's efforts no doubt. I felt sort of sorry for him. Imagine being a plant manager suddenly told that you're keeping prisoners that you have to treat well. It was probably as disorienting an experience for him as it was for us. At least that was the impression I got. On the other hand, it could be just another day on the job in Iraq. I imagined that after a decade of Saddam, the people had gotten used to weird requests.

We were billeted two to a room, with thin foam mattresses covered with cloth and white sheets. Blankets were available, but no one wanted one. Even with the air-conditioning, it was warm. My roommate was Paul Eliopoulos, the computer salesman who had been caught in Kuwait. The other guys were either oil workers or businessmen: Tony Nelson, the ex-Marine; Chuck Tinch; another crusty, old oil worker nicknamed "Peanuts"; Rodenbush, another oil worker who was a good guy; a businessman named Frank; and nine others whose names I can't recall. Mostly older guys in their forties. Paul and I were the two youngsters.

The days at the Baiji power plant settled quickly into a normal pattern of activity. Three times a day, for meals, we would travel from the trailer to the meeting room in the big office building. Ra'ad continued to put out a good spread for us, and we also had water and soda at our billets. The Iraqis let us have the run of a specific area of the compound that encompassed the large, shaded overhang next to the barracks trailer and the road that led to the buildings in the compound itself. They also let us walk around in the yard wherever we wanted. They would not allow us into the power plant area proper. So our little world was about two hundred by three hundred meters.

Television reception was spotty because of the proximity of the transformer to our barracks. Not that there was much to watch: shows on the greatness of Saddam and old TV shows dubbed in Arabic. We had a shortwave radio that one of the guys had managed to hold onto, so we could pick up the VOA and BBC in the mornings. We did not draw attention to our use of the radio, but I'm sure that the Iraqis knew about it. Oddly, they didn't seem to care. The news that came out of the radio was not good. Well, not for an Iraqi. The United States was sending more and more forces to the Gulf, and the coalition against Iraq was forming. The Iraqis were continually defiant in their responses, and the fate of the hostages didn't appear to be even a small priority. Things did not look good for a peaceful resolution to the conflict, and I kicked myself for not running in Al Quaim the second I had realized where we were. Discussions of what was going to happen occupied a lot of our time. I reassured everyone that the United States would slaughter these guys. Only Tony was skeptical. A Vietnam vet, he had heard that before. I described to my fellows the waves of aircraft and the targeting of installations. I told them in no uncertain terms that we were a target and pointed out to them the safest place to go if we were bombed. The whole thing still seemed dreamlike.

We did a lot of exercising in those days, walking back and forth from one end of the enclosure to the other. It was here that we first hit upon wearing shorts and going bare chested as a sign that western hostages were being kept at this location. (Arab men never walk around bare chested.) We also got the idea of making satellite signs—flat arrangements of rocks and boards that if looked at from overhead spelled "hostages here." Unfortunately our first efforts were clumsy and not very big. The one I put together was an arrangement of rocks to make letters, but they were only about three feet long. That, and the contrast with the ground they were on (light tan rocks on brown ground), made them not very readable. Unfortunately at the Baiji power plant there were not a lot of materials available, but we did the best we could. We also got a good impression of the size and composition of the guard force and their times and habits. They were definitely not supertroops. Most were older men who had clearly seen better days of soldiering. Only the officers were even halfway energetic. The heat sapped them the way it did everyone else. This was brought home to me when on one of my walks I noticed a guard tower unmanned for the first time. Curious, I walked to it and looked up. I could just make out the top of the guard's head as he slept with his body wedged against the side of the little guard box on top of the tower. Amused, I did another lap and stopped. He was still asleep. I walked for about half an hour before I saw him wake up and stretch. He saw me looking at him and waved lazily. Yessir, really tight security here.

The perimeter fence could be breached easily by a determined man. The fence was chain link but not dug or cemented into the ground; nor was it well lighted in all places. There were several gaps and shadows that left places for unobserved movement. Getting under the fence would be relatively easy. The problem was where to go on the outside.

I knew we were by the Tigris River because I could see it sluggishly passing the power plant to the east. It was warm enough for a swim I was certain, but the problem was that it was going in the wrong direction. North of Baghdad (as I was sure we were) the river would merely take me deeper into enemy territory. Not having Baiji on my map opened up all sorts of questions. Although we were probably north of Baghdad, were we north of Tikrit? I would have to walk north to Turkey, but how far was that? Considering I would be hiding by day and walking slowly and carefully by night, I figured that I was more than a two-week walk from Turkey. I didn't yet have any gear and resolved to unobtrusively start accumulating things that I would need to escape.

In the meantime the routine went on. Ra'ad actually surprised us by making good on his promise to take us on a tour of the power plant. He walked us all over the plant like a kid's class on a school tour. He was obviously proud of the place. It was an impressive facility, with large turbine generators made in Germany and a clean, modern control room. As he walked us through the facility, I made as many mental notes as I could: where interior guard posts were and where open gates were, ways through the buildings that offered cover and concealment, places to hide. He took us down to the river to see the hydroelectric sort of half dam that had been built to power the turbines. We got to walk out onto this facility, then walk back to the plant. This gave me a priceless look at the riverside within the plant. It was as I had hoped: There was no fence. If I could get through the plant at night and reach the river south of the dam, I could swim beyond the fence, then skirt the plant on my movement north. I felt bad because Ra'ad was obviously trying to do the best he could for us, and here I was repaying his kindness by planning an escape with information that his tour had given me. But Ra'ad was the enemy—pleasant and well meaning or not—and it was my duty to escape.

I was not the only one who played a dirty trick on the Iraqis from this little tour. When we were brought to an automation room, the man in charge briefed us on the type of computers they had, then confessed that he was having trouble with one of the systems. Paul Eliopoulos piped up that he knew about the systems and could probably fix them. He worked on the computers for a while, then told the Iraqis that he was sorry but he didn't have the right software. They took it philosophically, and Paul was returned to our group. He later confided to me that he had programmed a virus into the system while he was working on it.

Paul was a good companion to have in adversity in that he had a wonderfully droll sense of humor and was endlessly cracking jokes to relieve the tension. He told me of his wife, Angelica, and his two daughters. I told him about Donna and our planned trip to London. We talked about places we had been and things we had seen in our lives. His descriptions of the Greek islands were so wonderful that I could almost see them. It was certainly a distraction from the skillet-hot desert we found ourselves in.

Entertainment in general centered around a few paperback books that we'd had or the Iraqis had procured for us, card games of all sorts (cribbage was very big with the oil workers), and listening to TV and radio. The news was never good: threats flying from both sides and more and more forces heading to the Gulf. The radio kept fading in and out. One morning we got a Canadian radio broadcast describing the departure of Canadian warships from Halifax with the announcer making repeated comments about how the ship's guns had been taken from monuments in parks, refurbished, and installed on the ships. I remember shaking my head and thinking, what next? The only news of hostages was how the United States would hold the Iraqis responsible for any harm that came to us. This was about what I expected, but it upset some of the other guys. News of what's going on in the world is important if you're a prisoner; it's just not always encouraging. I did my best to keep my comrades' spirits up.

The Iraqis even took us swimming at a pool once. This was a major event, not only in terms of a break in the boredom but because I would get an additional look at our surroundings. The trip through the power plant gate revealed that nothing had changed since we had first seen it. But while we were driving to the pool, I managed to get a good look at some of the surrounding installations and had a much better idea of what was immediately around the power plant—valuable information if I ever got through the fence. The Iraqis took us to a place a few miles from the power plant; we could still see the plant in the distance. The pool was at a recreation club for plant workers; it had a playground and a small auditorium building with changing rooms. The pool water was murky but cool. The only thing that marred the event was that the Iraqis took photographs of us and wanted us to pose for pictures with them. I refused to pose, but they got some of me anyway. I made a point not to smile. The other men also did their best not to appear photogenic, but the Iraqis were soon satisfied with their pictures and left. (A few days later I was astonished to be handed a little packet of pictures, with me in them, that had been taken by the pool. Crazy.) We spent a long time at the pool and came back just in time for dinner. They promised to take us again but never did while I was there.

Paul Eliopoulos helped pass the time by telling my fortune with a deck of cards. He would lay out the cards, then arrange them in a kind of solitaire pattern. He would then say that various face cards reflected fortunes or humors and numbers represented good or bad fortunes. He predicted that we would be incarcerated for a time but would be all right. He also told me that I would marry Donna and we would be home by Christmas. I asked him what his methodology was. He tried to explain it, but I could see he was making it up as he went along so I dropped it. The funny thing was, I think we both saw through each other. He could see that I was pissed off and worried and tried to reassure me, and I could see that doing this helped him cope with his own fears. In truth, he had much more on his plate than I did; he was married with two little girls, and the thought of what was going to happen to them wore on him. He told fortunes; I spoke of rescue, going over all the ways the satellites could track us (I wish) and what to do when the helicopters came in to get us. Not that I really believed it, but it helped keep my spirits up. We were all whistling past the graveyard.

Three days after the visit to the pool, Ra'ad came in with our minders and told us that our group would be broken up. Four of us would stay there and the rest would be taken to other places. He said he hoped our predicament would not continue for too long, then paused for a moment. He suddenly blurted out, "Please don't think badly of us." Then he was gone to hide his own embarrassment. I genuinely felt sorry for him.

Our minders divided us up. I was put in a group of three along with Paul Eliopoulos and Chuck Tinch, an oil worker in his fifties who was a quiet and pleasant man whom I hadn't gotten to know yet. Chuck was always a little sickly looking (at this point I didn't know how desperately sick he really was), and I hoped that his illness wouldn't be exacerbated by captivity. We waited with our bags packed for a few hours. Finally a car with Iraqi Secret Service minders showed up to take us away. We waved good-bye to our friends and left. I kept a list of everyone who was still there and those who had left before us.

I was expecting a long trip similar to the one from Al Quaim to the Baiji power plant, but in fact we traveled just five minutes down the road to the large refinery we had passed earlier just before entering the power plant. As we entered the refinery gates, I craned my neck to take in the details of the place. It was huge and surrounded by antiaircraft gun positions. The refinery complex itself was at least two by two kilometers with an exterior fence more than a kilometer beyond that. We drove to the center of the complex. On the north side of the road was a series of small workers' houses. We pulled into one of the compounds and we were told to get out of the car. I received the disconcerting news that only two of us were to stay here— Chuck and I. Paul would be taken to a camp farther north. I offered to trade places with Paul so he would have another American companion (and so I would be closer to the Turkish border; I will not deny that selfish motivation), but it was nothing doing. I wished Paul Eliopoulos luck, then he was gone with his minders. Some Caucasian men came out of one of the houses on the compound and looked at us. Chuck and I picked up our baggage and walked to meet them.

THE BAIJI REFINERY GROUP

The three men by the house stood their ground and didn't approach us. We could see that they were sizing us up warily. I introduced myself and Chuck and they relaxed visibly. They helped us to our own little workers' house as they introduced themselves: Dave Freeman, Mick Finan, and John McCollah. They were British army sergeants from the British army advisory group in Kuwait.

They explained that there were two other British sergeants here from the Royal Air Force (RAF): Reg and Mike. All of them had been captured on the second day of the invasion. In addition, there were four Frenchmen, three Germans, and three Japanese. Chuck and I were the only two Yanks in the group. The British soldiers had just that morning said good-bye to their family members who were being released. Upon hearing this I inwardly cursed our luck at missing them, because I had lost an opportunity to slip a hostage location update to one of the women. But it couldn't be helped, and I didn't mention this to my new British friends because they were upset about their families being taken to begin with. The fact that this had happened surprised me, and I asked how it had come about. What I got was a torrent of bitterness that was shocking but, as the story came out, certainly understandable. To use their way of saying things, it was a complete "balls up" from the start.

On the first day of the invasion the British advisors had been told to remain in their housing complex south of Kuwait and pack up their vehicles in preparation for the less than one-hour drive to Saudi Arabia. They were quickly ready to do this but could not get permission from their commander to drive for the Saudi border. Their ambassador had told everyone to stay in place. So they sat, all night, with an open road to Saudi Arabia and safety less than an hour away, waiting for the word to go. The order was never given. The Iraqis came the next morning and rounded up all the soldiers, put them on a bus, and drove them to Baghdad. Their families remained in place for almost a week, unprotected and helpless, as Iraqi troops ransacked their houses and looted them of most of their possessions. The wives and children were not evacuated to Baghdad and linked up with their husbands and fathers until a week later. Soon after that, they had been put out onto hostage sites at the same time we had been taken to Al Quaim. Listening to their story, I could only shake my head in disbelief. The sheer spinelessness of it was shocking. It had left some very bitter people in the British army.[1]

Having put our stuff away, I left Chuck and our new British friends and had a walk around the compound. It was larger than the place we had been kept at the Baiji power plant. It was also much greener and had large bushes and a lot of shade, with trees interspersed among the houses. The compound had two rows of two houses on either side and a fifth row of houses in the middle on the eastern side. On the western side in the center was a community building that had outdoor basketball and volleyball courts. There was only one road entrance into the compound, and the first house next to it on the eastern side was where the guards and minders set up shop. There appeared to be six minders and about a dozen uniformed armed guards, with two and four on duty at any one time, respectively. There were also the guards that roved the perimeter of the entire complex and provided security on adjacent installations within the complex. The northern side of our little complex was open all the way to the outer perimeter fence, about a kilometer away. The only thing between us and the fence were several 57mm antiaircraft positions, which were part of the defenses that ringed the refinery. These seemed to consist of positions of two guns apiece with twenty to thirty soldiers manning them. They were interspersed about five hundred meters apart around the perimeter. There were always a few troops sitting on the guns, but they came up to full strength only when there was an alert. Still, they would be another thing to get by if we ever tried to escape.

I met the rest of the crowd at dinner. The Germans were Ingo Fruedenberg, Herbert Hoffman, and Manfred Locher. Ingo and Manfred spoke excellent English. Herbert spoke only a little. Their

---

[1] There was a sad footnote to this. The 18-year-old son of the Colonel in charge of the British advisory group was later killed in an ordinary traffic accident in Baghdad while waiting to be released. I am sure not a day of the poor man's life goes by where he does not think about whether or not he should have ignored his diplomat's instructions and gotten his people out. The burden of command is hard enough, whatever I say about the unwillingness of the British embassy to make a decision, I can only express my sorrow and sympathy to the Colonel for this cruel loss.

backgrounds were varied. Ingo, a tall, thin, ruddy man in his mid-fifties, was a merchant marine captain who had been hired by a firm to evaluate wrecks in the Shatt-Al-Arab for possible salvage. He had a sailor's sardonic humor and a gift for gab. Herbert was a business-man who had been trapped in Kuwait along with many other West German citizens. He was shorter than Ingo but weighed more—a real large hoffbrau German. His English (or lack thereof) was a barrier, but he was always ready to pitch in and help. Manfred Locher was a businessman in his early fifties who had spent a lot of time in Iraq and had many contacts within the Iraqi government. When I asked him whether any of his friends could be prevailed upon to effect his re-lease, he snorted and said something to the effect that people in Iraq couldn't even save their own family members much less foreign friends. Manfred was an interesting character, and his insights into working with the Iraqi government confirmed my overall impression that we were in deep shit. He portrayed the Iraqis as dishonest, spite-ful, and vicious people who were ruthless when it came to getting things their way. When asked if doing business in Iraq wasn't a little too stressful, he shrugged and said, "Sure, but the money's good." I was surprised to learn that Manfred was an ex-Luftwaffe (the post-war, not World War II) flight officer who had flown F4 Phantoms and served under the command of the great German World War II ace Erich Hartmann. Manfred looked like a college professor, with his thick glasses and graying hair. He had a soldier's outlook on captivity, though, and was determined to escape when the time came. He never talked about the possibility of release. His previous business re-lationships with the Iraqis had convinced him that we would still be in captivity when hostilities started.

The French were from the crew of an Air France airliner that had been trapped in Iraq. There were four of them, all men in their late twenties to mid-thirties and all in good physical condition. The senior one was the aircraft's senior steward, Jean Pierre, with Etienne Boussineau, the purser, and Phillipe and Jean Francois, who were flight attendants. Jean Pierre was the leader, and the crew members kept their discipline in an informal but effective way. All had been with Air France for some time and were indignant over what had happened to them. Their attitude was something of a revelation to me. If you had asked me before captivity, I would have said that the French were the most likely to collaborate with the Iraqis. Nothing could have been further from the truth with this bunch. They looked upon the Iraqis with thinly concealed Gaulic contempt and on occasion baited them openly. Jean Francois and Etienne spoke good English, but the others spoke almost none. This language barrier did not stop them from fully participating in our efforts of resistance, and the French could always be counted upon to lend a hand for lookout or stealing something. *"Vive le Resistance!"* was their battle cry. The only thing that occasionally concerned me was that someday they might actually go too far.

All the Japanese were petrochemical engineers: Schochi Hasegawa (Sho), Kiyoshi Odagane (Doug), and Toshio (Tosh). In his mid-forties, Sho was by far the senior. Doug and Tosh were both in their late twenties or early thirties. None of them was especially small (they were all about five feet six), but they were different in their build, which gave an impression of variations in height. Doug and Tosh were stocky guys with a low center of gravity and muscles from physical activity. Sho was slight and brainy. All were pleasant, quiet, and polite men from a nation of pleasant and well-mannered people. They had some interesting hobbies. Sho played the flute and was an accomplished sketch artist. Doug was a movie buff. Tosh, who couldn't speak English well, was an excellent badminton player. Sho was especially invaluable to the group because he could look at what was going on in the refinery and tell what was happening. Refineries were his line of work. The Japanese kept to themselves at first but gradually became part of the group. They maintained their outer serenity better than any of us did. Although I knew they were concerned about what was happening, I never once heard them complain about it. They met the experience of captivity with an interested but detached serenity. Their behavior had a calming influence on the rest of us. Anytime we felt pissed off, we had but to look at Sho Hasegawa calmly drawing in his sketch pad or Doug walking the perimeter and we would feel ashamed at letting our emotions get the better of us. The Iraqis never once disturbed the Japanese *Wa* (their concept of serenity).

Among the other nationalities in our little group were the Brits. They were in a class by themselves. There were the two RAF sergeants, Reg and Mike, and the three army sergeants, Dave Freeman, Mick Finan, and John McCollah, who were to be my closest companions during captivity.

Dave Freeman was a company sergeant major (the British equivalent of a first sergeant in the U.S. Army) from the Queens Dragoon

Guards (an armored outfit). He was an imposing figure. He pronounced phrases such as "isn't it?" as "innit" or "all right" as "ar-rite,"
and he tended to substitute an "s" in words that ended in the letter
"t." So I had to pay attention to get all that he was saying; otherwise,
the meaning of "thas ar-rite then innit?" might escape me. People who
annoyed him were "gits." My rank did not spare me from being la-
beled an "idle American git" on the odd occasions that I angered him.
He did recognize the need for solidarity among the hostages and for
us to follow our respective military codes of conduct. He was at all
times helpful, gregarious, and very funny. You could tell when he was
serious because he didn't say much and his voice took on a low, calm,
level tone. Occasionally, captivity would depress him and during
those times he would walk by himself.

Mick Finan was a bomb disposal NCO who had won the George's
Medal (a high award for valor) in Northern Ireland and had been sent
to the Kuwait advisory group as a "break" from his duties in South
Armagh. The irony of this was not lost on him. Like the others, his
family had been reunited with him after several nights of terror in
Kuwait and was initially in the Monsour Melia Hotel with the rest of
the captured Brits. When the hostages were sent out to strategic facilities, they had come to the Baiji refinery as human shields as well.

Mick was small and wiry with thick glasses and an unwavering
gaze. While he was in the Monsour Melia, he had become a small leg-
end by crawling through air ducts from room to room, looking for
routes of escape and passing messages. He was usually a person of few
words, but on the odd occasion he opened up he told amazing stories
of bomb disposal and operations in Northern Ireland.

John McCollah was an "artificer sergeant" (in the U.S. Army he
would be called a mechanic) who worked on heavy armored vehicles.
He was about my age but looked ten years younger with a boyish
Dennis the Menace face and a natural grin. He was a perpetually
good-humored person who could put anyone at ease and always be
depended upon to say the right thing. He was also the practical joker
among the Brits, and I learned to tread carefully for booby traps if I
saw him leaving my room. He played only practical jokes on those of
us who looked as though we could take it in good fun, and I counted
it an honor that he included me in that category. He never played
jokes on Chuck, because Chuck was sick. Being a mechanic, John had
a natural ability to work with his hands and was generally acknowledged to be the Mr. Fixit in the group. He missed his wife, Heidi, and

daughter, Danielle, very much but did not let it shake him. He was kind, reliable, and unselfish.

The last of our group was Chuck Tinch. Although I had been with him since the beginning in the Al-Rashid, I didn't know him well. I was to get to know him better during our subsequent captivity. Like all the oil workers, he was an interesting character. In his late fifties, he stood about five foot ten and was rail thin and weather beaten. He had spent most of his adult life on one oil rig or another all over the Middle East and Asia. He had been in the air force in the early 1950s and was stationed in England, where he had met his wife, Eileen. They lived in a little town called Saint Olaves on the coast of Britain, or in Malaga, Spain. Chuck was typical of all the American oil workers I came in contact with. He was physically tough, given to few words, and very well mannered. He played cribbage and backgammon exceptionally well and was much better adjusted to confined surroundings than the rest of us. At first this struck me as curious, but it made sense the more I thought about it. After all, he had spent his life working in areas much more confined than the places we were being held. He had worked on rigs long before satellite TV or VCRs and was used to entertaining himself. The captivity I'm sure he found disconcerting; but being a man who had spent his whole life among other hard men, he kept his misgivings to himself. When he voiced an opinion, you knew he had thought about it first.

Chuck was sick and in bad shape, though. He had a stomach condition exacerbated by ulcers. He had trouble keeping down much of the food the Iraqis gave us, and after a while this made him physically weak. Worse, he did not have sufficient medicine and had not been able to get more prior to our being moved from the Al-Rashid in Baghdad. As a result he periodically had painful attacks, and his condition gradually deteriorated. None of us realized how sick he was at first because he kept from us the extent of his illness and the effect it was having on him.

I did not know it at the time, but this was the group that I would stay with throughout the remainder of my captivity. I was to come to know and depend heavily on all of these men during the next few months. They never let me down.

After introductions we sat down to dinner. Although the area we were being kept in was more agreeable than that at the power plant, the chow in the Baiji refinery was a comedown: U.S. grade D ground lamb, potatoes, and tomato and spinach salad. We wouldn't starve, but compared to the relatively opulent plates that Ra'ad at the Baiji power plant had set for us, I could see that dinner would not be the pleasant distraction it had been in other places. There was a TV and a ping-pong table in our community center, and we watched the Iraqi news after dinner. Unflattering pictures of Bush and Thatcher flashed across the screen as well as pictures of stalwart-looking Iraqi troops. Yawn—same old, same old. After a while I went to take a nap. I was going to be up tonight.

That evening after supper, Chuck and I went over to the Brits' cabin and listened to the BBC on one of their short wave radios. The stories were about talks to get the hostages released and Iraqi demands that the United States remove its forces from the Gulf. Nothing new or encouraging there. The Brits wondered where their families were and whether they had gotten out yet or (an unspoken horror) the women and children had been moved to an even higher priority hostage site to protect something such as chemical weapons or nuclear production. The separation from their families preyed on the Brits more than the rest of us because they had first been taken from them at gunpoint in Kuwait and now a few weeks later were forcibly separated again with only the Iraqis' word that the women and children would be released. The Brits wouldn't put their worry into words, though, and I admired them for their forbearance. Stiff upper lip or whatever else you want to call it, they weren't the over-sensitive, whiny adult males that we often saw on TV in Britain and America; they were men. Conversation led to our previous experiences, and we continued to fill in one another. The Brits had been brought straight here from Baghdad with their wives and families and spent all of their captivity here. It was odd to them that we had been moved so much, but the policy clearly was that each hostage group would consist of somebody from each country. The theory I supposed was that no one country could dare bomb anyplace without being fearful of hitting its citizens (as if that made any difference, I thought). The U.S. Air Force would pound this place to rubble with us in it. Sixteen guys were acceptable collateral damage for an oil refinery.

I was impressed with the way the Brits appraised the situation and remembered thinking how fortunate I was to have been placed here. It looked like a good group. I wondered how Paul Eliopoulos was doing. Because I couldn't help him, I concentrated on the job at hand. I was killing time until we all went to bed. Then I could make a good reconnaissance of the place and see how alert the guards were.

Chuck and I went back to our house around ten that night. About two hours later I slipped out the door and moved cautiously into a shadow near the house. The first order of business was to sit for about fifteen minutes and watch for movements. I could see the minder's house, but there was no movement near it. I thought about waiting all night to watch the minder's house, but I figured I would do a once-around of the whole place and work on details after that. I knew I was repeating my pattern that had lost me my chance of escape in Al Quaim, but Baiji was different. I was too far away for any overnight dash to the border. Escape would more than likely be unsuccessful unless I prepared meticulously for it. So it was back into deliberate planning mode for me.

I left the shadow and walked quietly from house to house, heading back toward the end of the compound along the interior road. The trees and houses threw shadows, which were easy to hide in. I wasn't making much of an attempt to stay hidden, however; if challenged, I would say I was out for a walk. If I could get around the entire compound without being seen, so much the better, but it wasn't necessary to my reconnaissance. I stopped again by the trees and waited for a few minutes. I could see the whole fence on the south side of the compound in the glow of the streetlights of the main interior road. The fence was not patrolled. There was only a guard at the little guardhouse at the entrance gate to our compound. This was probably because the fence was on the interior perimeter of the refinery, and there was no apparent need to patrol it. This struck me as odd, because it showed that no additional security measure had been put on it even though hostages had been here for some time. I made a note to myself to check on this again. Maybe the guard was eating dinner or talking somewhere with his buddies. If not, this part of the fence would be easy to get through. Trouble was, it led to the interior of the compound instead of away from it. I crossed the open yard onto the other side of the compound by the fence at a fast walk. I expected to be challenged but wasn't. I gradually went up the other side of the compound, stopping every few meters to watch and listen. There was more activity: The antiaircraft guns each had three or four soldiers on them and lights showing on each position. Watching the men, I could see that they had the bored attitude of soldiers who had sat on the same guard post for too long. There was also a roving guard on this side of the compound, probably because it was an exterior fence. I watched him from the shadows, a man in his early twenties, AK-47 slung on his shoulder, hands in pockets, ambling along the fence in his own little world. He walked close to me but did not see me; in fact, I never once saw him look into the compound. I sat and waited for him to come back, which he did, then he turned and came back again. About ten minutes a revolution—five out and five back.

After watching the guard I continued my eastern movement up the compound to the end of the row of houses. From the shadows I could see a line of fences (in better repair) that divided our compound from another one. Many of the buildings in this compound still had lights on, and I wondered who lived there. I waited but no one came out, so for now it was a mystery. The young guard came up and went past the place that the two fences intersected. This told me that the guy was guarding the entire fence line, not just our compound. I looked for a guard patrolling the fence line between the two housing compounds, but none appeared.

I went back toward my house, walking along the interior line of houses that the French and the Brits lived in. No one challenged me and I became bolder. I decided to walk down the row where the guards and minders lived. I would try to see how many there were and how many lived in each house. The Germans lived in this row, too, so I could always use the excuse that I couldn't sleep and was going to see them. I got about halfway down the row when two uniformed men came out and talked outside the minders' building. They lit cigarettes and laughed, then slowly began walking toward the community center. I watched them as they did a lazy stroll through the interior of the compound and chatted amicably. So there was in fact an interior roving patrol. This was an unwelcome surprise, but if they all talked that much they would at least advertise their presence.

I waited until they were out of sight, then walked to the minders' house. Three fairly beat-up cars parked outside the house provided extra cover. I had to cross the road to get back to my house, and that meant being exposed to observation from the guardhouse at the gate. I watched him until I was sure he wasn't looking my way, then I darted across the road into a shadow, trying to make as little noise as possible. I turned around and looked at him from the shadow I was hiding in. He was reading a magazine and facing away from me.

Good. I went back to just outside my house and watched the roving patrol return to the minders' house about ten minutes later. That was a long walk around a small compound. I wondered how many times they did that a night. I looked at my watch, almost 2:30. I had been out for a little less than three hours. It appeared that someone was up in the minders' house twenty-four hours a day. I wondered whether the guard on the exterior fence was based out of there. Lots to learn yet, but I'd had a good first look at the inside of the Baiji refinery hostage camp. It was time to call it a night.

The next morning I got up for breakfast, then just loafed around for the rest of the day. It was easy to see how many guards and minders were on shift in the daytime, and I spent some time by the north fence looking at the antiaircraft crews at drill. Each position of two guns had between fifteen and twenty people, so they had to be billeted close by—within running distance. I couldn't see their barracks, but I surmised that they were behind some trees in another compound past the one immediately next to us. I shot some baskets at the basketball court in the afternoon and generally wasted time until evening, when I could get another look at the night shift of the minders and the guards.

After dinner, however, an incident occurred that gave me insight into the mentality of our captors and my fellow captives. We were watching the Iraqi news when the picture of Saddam Hussein meeting with the hostages and patting the little British boy, Stuart Lockwood, on the head came over the television. I thought the Brits were going to come unglued. They started swearing at the television set and cursing Saddam Hussein. The minders were surprised and acted nervous. Several of the Iraqis in the room with us started edging toward the door. I was a little surprised myself. The picture of Saddam with the obviously frightened child was disgusting, but we had seen a lot of propaganda on the Iraqi TV channel so I didn't understand what made this different. John McCollah explained to me that the boy was the son of one of their fellow sergeants in the British advisory group and the playmate of their own children. The Iraqi minders who spoke English tried to explain that this was meant to show that Saddam loved children. The minders could not understand the Brits' anger. Mike and Reg went back to their house in disgust. John McCollah in civilized and dignified tones tried to tell the Iraqis why this display had made them so angry. Mick and Dave, however, shouted abuse at the minders, and their faces had "kill" written all over them. Violence seemed a distinct possibility. I positioned myself between them and the Iraqis in case one of them lost it and went for our captors. (Not that I would have been effective. I would have had about as much chance of stopping Dave Freeman as stopping a charging cape buffalo.) It wasn't that I liked our captors, but if we assaulted them they might jail us and restrict our movements. The "white collar" sort of captivity we were in right now had its advantages.

Fortunately, physical restraint (or attempts at it) was not necessary. Both men were soldiers and masters of themselves. They regained their composure and left for their house. No one followed them. It was obvious that they were better left alone. The group broke up that night early and somewhat chastened. I know that our minders were more alert and on guard against us after this incident. Before, we had been sullenly cooperative. Now they'd had a glimpse of the rage that simmered in many of us just beneath the surface. It was not reassuring to them.

8

I LEARNED A LOT about the camp over the next few days. There were always three minders on site. They traded out every twelve hours or so. Normally they hung around and talked for about half an hour at trade-off. The roving patrol inside the compound was not made up of minders from the special police but uniformed guards from the Baiji refinery on detail. They based out of the house next to that of the minders, and there were always six on site. The rotation at the guardhouse came from this six as well. They seemed to trade out every twenty-four hours, so it was a sleepover post. That meant six rifles in the one house. The minders also had AK-47s; I had occasion to see in the door once in the daytime and two were in a corner near a table. The exterior fence patrol did not base out of our site but started somewhere else, probably from a larger guardhouse along the fence that we couldn't see from where we were. Our food was not prepared for us on site but was brought in a small panel truck; there were always two men on the food detail. There was no place to hide on the truck, so sneaking out on it would have been difficult. Garbage was taken out of the Dumpsters about once a week in the daytime with a guard watching the Dumpster truck.

Our minders were from the Iraqi special (read "secret") police and for the most part didn't try to engage us in conversation, especially after the hostility involving the TV program with Saddam and the boy. They were gray men who lacked personality. Mostly they kept to themselves and only occasionally came out to check on us. They counted us at mealtimes in a surreptitious and informal way that I guess we weren't supposed to notice but we all did. Only three of them stood out: Mohammed, Abdul Rahman, and Khalid.

Mohammed and Abdul Rahman, in their late thirties to early forties, were, if not actually friendly, less stiff than the others. Both were married and showed us photos of their children, and occasionally played backgammon or chess with one of us in the recreation room. They seemed resigned to the situation and appeared willing to live and let live as long as we were also willing. Khalid, however, who was in his late twenties, was very full of himself. He was given to waving weapons around and had threatened the Brits with his rifle before we got there. He pulled his pistol on me once and gave me a ration of shit about America, but I just smiled at him. I didn't tell him that if he was going to threaten me with a pistol, it would help to put the magazine in it. For the most part he was just an irksome, bad-ass wanna-be who was a little ticked that his prisoners didn't take him seriously. He was full of stories about the Iran-Iraq war, but from his descriptions I doubt he had ever seen action. He didn't appear to have many friends among the other minders, all of whom were ten to fifteen years older than he was. As I watched him go from our little encounter I thought, great, just what we need, a nutcase. I made a mental note that Khalid bore watching.

In the meantime I continued my efforts to advertise our presence to the outside world. During my walks around our compound, I discovered numerous orange roof slats about two and a half feet long. They were lying as discarded debris all over the compound. I got the idea to lay them out on the ground and spell words with them. The grass behind the community center building was about two feet high in places, and I figured I could lay them down in letters without it looking too obvious. It took me most of a day to do it, making the letters a bit at a time to avoid suspicion, but eventually I had made a sign that read, "16 Hostages Here" in letters that were three slats long. My only concern was that the orange would not show up well against its background, but there was nothing I could do about that.

The change in diet did not sit well with Chuck. The greasy fried food worked havoc on his stomach, and he couldn't eat much. He had run out of his medication, and we could see that he was suffering. We had prevailed upon the Iraqis to take him to the hospital, but they only took him to the refinery clinic and a doctor there gave him nothing more than the equivalent of Pepto-Bismol. Chuck took it but it didn't help. He said he could stand the discomfort and tried to eat only fruits and vegetables. He didn't want us to make a fuss over him, but I was worried. I tried again to get the minders to take him to the hospital, but they refused, saying that he had been given medicine. They probably thought he was playing sick in hopes of winning an early release. For now there was nothing to be done but keep an eye on him. Hopefully we could get Chuck treated by prevailing upon one of the Iraqi officers who showed up from time to time.

Food became an issue for all of us when, the next day, Saddam Hussein exclaimed that because the Iraqi people were starving due to sanctions, the hostages would be starved too. I saved some bread from our meals in case we went on short rations. Manfred Locher and I discussed hunting some of the numerous feral cats on the compound to supplement our soon-to-be-starvation diet. I found an old broomstick and tied my half scissors to it, making a kind of a spear. Manfred said that after the war it was common for people in Germany to eat cats. "Roof rabbits," he called them. Fortunately for us, it didn't come to that. The minder Abdul Rahman told us that we would not be subjected to any reduction in rations. The Iraqi minders were true to their word, and the quantity of food did not change. On the other hand, neither did the quality improve, so we still had the problem with Chuck.

As the days dragged on, we played volleyball often. I was in my element at the net. Being tall has occasional advantages. We usually stopped before lunch due to the heat. We also played basketball, but the heat was such that we could play for only a few minutes. As at the Baiji power plant, some of us walked outside without our shirts on, advertising that we were Caucasian and therefore out of place. We called it "being Caucasian." We would take turns, so at least one of us walked around in daylight with his shirt off.

After we had been at the refinery for about a week, the Iraqis told all of us to get our towels and shorts and said they were taking us to a pool. I was hesitant at first. The "you're-going-for-a-shower" routine was on my mind. Not that I thought we were going to be killed, but I was worried that we might be taken to another location without notice. However, not all of our group wanted to go, which the Iraqis didn't mind, so my fears were allayed. Chuck and I boarded the bus along with the Brits and the French. The bus went back down the same entrance road we had used coming in, only now that I was sitting higher I could see more. The first thing I noticed was a deep drainage ditch that paralleled the road and ran toward the outside of the compound. I could not see the bottom of the ditch even from my height in the bus, so a person standing or driving in a car could see even less. When we got to the gate I could see four people in the guardhouse, one of whom came out to lift the barrier. The ditch went under the fence to a culvert that passed under the main highway. I couldn't see whether the culvert had grates or anything else that would prevent a person from crawling through it. I was excited, though, because I had seen what looked like a covered and concealed route out of the camp. All I would have to do is cross the road inside the camp and drop into the ditch. The big question was, could I get under the fence and through the culvert to the other side of the main road. As we turned onto the highway heading south, I resolved to look into those two things as we returned.

I thought we would be taken to the same pool we had been to before, in the Baiji refinery. I hoped that we would meet up with other hostages there and I could pass on more information about our group. No such luck. We soon turned off the main road away from the Baiji power plant and went to another pool. Apparently each major industrial site in Iraq had its own recreation complex. This one had a twenty-five-meter pool, tennis courts, and volleyball courts. The pool was somewhat run down, but the water was clean and cool and there was plenty of shade. I swam laps until I was exhausted, then watched with small envy as the young Frenchman Jean Francois, who had started about the same time I did, swam twenty more laps than I did. Oh well, we can't all be in killer shape. The Iraqis further surprised us by bringing out a couple of cases of the local beer in big, unmarked brown bottles. The beer was ice cold, and the first one was gone in a blink. I looked around for cameras or other propaganda recording items but couldn't see any. It was a hot day at the beginning of September, and home seemed pretty far away. My companions were already into their second and third bottles when all of a sudden a "what the hell" mood came over me and I reached for my second bottle. It was certainly not the most professional thing I had ever done. By the time we were finished at the pool that day, we were all pretty drunk. After three beers I started to feel a little drowsy, so I decided to stop drinking. No one needed help getting on the bus, but we were all weaving slightly. On the way back through the refinery gate, I could see that there was room to crawl under the fence, but I couldn't see whether or not there were grates on the culvert. We made it back to our place just in time for dinner. I did no reconnaissance that night.

The next day I observed the Iraqi antiaircraft batteries at practice.

There was an alarm and the soldiers all ran for their weapons. The batteries within my field of vision were fully manned within five minutes. Afterward the Iraqis did manipulation drills with the weapons, traversing them back and forth in unison and alternately elevating and depressing the barrels. This drill lasted for about thirty minutes. I thought this would be it, but as a finale to the exercise they conducted a live shoot, with all weapons concentrating their shells at a prearranged firebox at about 10,000 feet. All the shells exploded in proximity to one another and made a dense little cloud of explosions. The two guns in front of me fired a total of about twenty rounds. It was obvious that the guns were optically rather than radar directed, and just as obvious that the gunners were practiced. I hoped our planes came at night.

I remember that day because it was the night of our big bonfire. The British have a holiday called the Last Night of the Proms. I never did get the entire history or the why of it, but the bottom line was that the Brits would set a big bonfire, then sit around it and sing. I'm sure there was more to it, but that was the gist of what I got from my fellows. The Brits worked industriously all day preparing for the bonfire, finding pieces of scrap wood and other burnable materials and putting them in a big pile in the middle of the little soccer pitch by the basketball and volleyball courts. They were enthused about the celebration and invited the rest of us to join in. After dinner we went out and sat on logs that we had placed in a "V" around the fire. The BBC carried the entire celebration from London, and John McCollah brought his shortwave radio from their house, using some of its precious battery power for the occasion. Night fell and the stars were beautiful. It was warm and pleasant with only a few mosquitoes. The bonfire was lit and soon it was roaring impressively. The radio played the London Symphony Orchestra along with other artists in an impressive performance. We sat in the light of the fire and listened to the music. Some of the minders came up and told us to put out the bonfire, but we told them to "piss off." That night we were all British, and the phrase summed up our contempt and anger wonderfully. The minders went away, but their lieutenant came back a few minutes later stressing that we had to put out the fire and go back to our houses or there would be trouble. Again we told him in fairly sulfurous terms to go away. The program was nearing its end and the London Philharmonic and choir broke into its finale—a rendition of "Land of Hope and Glory." Each one of the Brits was singing as loudly as he could along with the radio, and the rest of us joined in as we could pick up on the words. We belted it out into the night; not one of us could carry a tune in a bucket, but we sang with wrenching gusto. We sang it like a battle hymn, roaring our defiance to the heavens with the flames of our bonfire lighting our faces. The Iraqis stayed back, watching us from a distance. The song ended and we sat there in the firelight feeling giddy, happy, and strange.

After a few minutes the gate to the compound opened and a fire truck from the refinery fire station came through. It was like one of those air crash trucks where the nozzle can be manipulated from inside the cabin. The truck pulled up to our fire but we didn't move. The Iraqi firemen motioned us away, but we all sat where we were. It was an act of useless, truculent defiance, but that's how we were feeling at that point in time. Finally the firemen shrugged and went to talk to our minders. They came back to the cab and started spraying the fire, being as careful as they could not to get any of us. We all got splashed with water and wet ashes, but none of us moved. After the flames were extinguished, the firemen could see us sitting exactly as before in the moonlight with the smoke from the embers wafting around us. They took their truck and left without saying another word to the minders. None of us moved from our little "V" around the soggy remains of the bonfire. After a few minutes the minders went back into their house and left us alone. We didn't say much to one another. It was just before midnight when there came a sense that the night was over. We said good night to one another and went to bed. I lay down but did not go to sleep immediately. I knew that something special had occurred and I wanted to think about its meaning.

The entire episode had been an effort of the collective unconscious. It was unplanned and unrehearsed, but all of us reacted in exactly the same way. The effect was almost palpable. The Last Night of the Proms in 1990, whatever significance it held for people back in Britain, had served to make the Baiji refinery hostages a tighter-knit group. We took from that night a sense of community—unspoken and inarticulate but very real.

Chuck continued to deteriorate slowly. He couldn't eat much because the greasy food irritated his stomach. He tried to keep himself hydrated, but more than once I caught him being sick when I walked into our house. The heaves, with their attendant dehydration and the fact that he couldn't eat much, meant that Chuck was getting weaker by the day. He didn't engage in any unnecessary activity, although he would sit and talk and be congenial. There was an unspoken agreement among the rest of us that Chuck would never be required to do any of the common details until he got better. Still, he did his part whenever he could. He must have found our solicitous help in emptying garbage or cleaning the house annoying. He always maintained that he was fine. He was one of those people who would say, It's only a compound fracture, Marty. No need to trouble you. I'll be fine. We were all worried about him.

Our minders in the Baiji refinery were completely unhelpful in this matter. To them we were an annoyance, and Chuck was obviously faking it. They took him to the refinery clinic where some quack (who had probably graduated from the University of Basra medical school and janitorial hire) had given him the local equivalent of Maalox and pronounced him cured. To the minders this ended the matter and they refused our subsequent attempts to get Chuck medical treatment or to speak to a higher authority.

It came to a head one day when I walked into the house and found Chuck passed out on the floor. I checked his airway to make sure he was breathing, then tried to wake him. He awoke saying he was dizzy and couldn't stand up. I sat him against the wall and told him I was going to get help. I went to the Brits' house, and soon everyone was milling around asking about Chuck. I knew we had to get him to a hospital. Leaving one of the Frenchmen with Chuck, we all went to the minders' house. They wouldn't answer the door at first, and the armed guards at the gate eyed us nervously as we banged on the minders' door. Finally Khalid opened it, acting irritated that his sleep had been disturbed. I described Chuck's condition and demanded that he be taken to a hospital. My request was angrily denied by the minders, all of whom were standing at the door now, shouting at me and telling us to go back to our houses.

I was mad and so was everyone else. What we did then wasn't rational, but I was way beyond that point. All of us returned to the minders' house and began beating on the door, breaking one of the windows. The uniformed guards—about five in all—were out of their house by then with their weapons. The minders came out with their weapons, and Dave Freeman hollered at them that they had better get Chuck to the hospital *right now*. They were scared by the sight of us and fingered their weapons nervously. The air was electric with violence, and I belatedly realized that we could all get killed over this, but I was too mad to care. It was a standoff of the worst sort, with neither side wanting to back down and no one willing to talk or negotiate. We were all hollering at one another and waiting for the other side to make the first move. My whole world had come down to going for Khalid before he could bring up his weapon. After that I had no plan other than to continue to do violence to whatever Iraqi was handy. The tension in the air was unbearable, and something had to break it. Deus ex machina, something did.

The officer of the guard for the refinery, a lieutenant, came around the corner, saw the confrontation, and started screaming at us. He demanded to know what was going on. We told him. He started yelling at the minders, who looked surly and answered in monosyllables. They went back to their billets and slammed the door. The whole thing lasted about a minute, but what a minute it was.

The officer of the guard said in passable English that the ambulance would come soon and for us to get Chuck's things ready to go to the hospital. I realized that we probably owed the officer's intervention to a phone call from the guardhouse at the front gate. God bless that Iraqi soldier, whoever he was. We all stood there uncertainly, but the officer was insistent that we get Chuck ready. I went back to the house to help Chuck get his things together. Sure enough, in another five minutes an ambulance showed up and we put Chuck into it. The Iraqis refused to let one of us go with Chuck, but considering his condition we didn't have any options but to trust the men. Chuck thanked us, not realizing what had just happened and how close we had come to violence. I told him not to worry and just get out of Iraq if he could. The ambulance pulled away and all of us drifted back to our houses. I let out a long breath when I reached mine and looked at Chuck's empty room. I said a prayer for Chuck and hoped he would get out of the country. The Iraqis had been shown releasing sick hostages on TV, so it was possible. If anyone needed to be released, it was Chuck.

I thought about our minders' reaction and their uncertainty with their weapons. They weren't pointing them at us and had allowed us to get close to them. We would have been able to rush them if we'd had a plan. This of course was silly. Overpower the minders and take their weapons, and then what? The only reason we had been confrontational was because of Chuck. What it had showed, though, was that the minders must have had orders to treat us with kid gloves, maybe even to the point of being threatened with consequences if anything happened to us. We could see it in their faces—the animosity but also the confusion, as though they were thinking, Uh-oh, don't wanna hurt Uncle Saddam's hostages. He'd be pissed. This seemed an exploitable weakness.

The other interesting thing about this incident was how the uniformed guards from the refinery guard mount hadn't stepped in to help. This was not the first time I noticed that the two groups mixed only perfunctorily and that the minders had an arrogant air about them that the refinery guards did not appreciate. We could tell that the uniformed guards were conflicted about the whole incident too. On the one hand, they would probably have been delighted if we had beaten up the minders; on the other hand, if they had just stood by and done nothing, it would have gone bad for them later on. It was certainly one of them who reported the confrontation to a higher authority. So, we had a rift in our security force. Good. It occurred to me that we must do as little as possible to anger "Sergeant Shultz" and his little group of lackluster refinery guards. They could be possible allies against minder mistreatment.

The incident also brought home to me how anger can be deadly. We had no plan other than to demand that Chuck be taken to a hospital. We could have done all sorts of other things. We could have set a building on fire and claimed that Chuck was a smoke inhalation victim, or we could have thrown things at passing vehicles within the perimeter to attract attention. Instead we just pounded on the door and forced the confrontation: risky and too dependent on chance. We hadn't even known whether the officer of the guard was available, much less whether he would intervene decisively on our side. Chuck was in bad shape, but he wasn't dying. We could have taken an hour and come up with a plan (or, better yet, thought of one beforehand). Instead, my anger made us confrontational. Effective in this case, but only by chance.

It was good to know, though, that we all stood shoulder to shoulder (almost literally in this case). The power of America had seemed far away to me, and the helpless rage of not being able to do anything for Chuck was consuming me. I was never prouder to stand with any men than with those Britons, Frenchmen, Germans, and Japanese who looked armed men in the face and demanded succor for their friend and would not back down.

After two days Chuck was brought back to us. I was disappointed because I thought for sure he was sick enough to be released in a "humanitarian gesture." He said that the doctors had looked at him and decided to treat his condition with new medicine. They had rehydrated him and given him some proper food, and he looked a lot better. The medicine helped some, but we could see that it was only keeping the condition on hold as opposed to curing it. Chuck still looked pretty wan, but he held on and actually walked around more.

One of the upshots of the incident was a general improvement in the way we were treated by the Baiji refinery staff. The food improved, with more items that Chuck could eat. And the minders, although present, kept more of a distance. They even brought us a small pile of books that they were able to acquire from various locations. The books were mostly in English, but there were a few in French and German as well. They were nothing special—mainly romance novels that were about thirty years old. There was one book, however, that I picked up and kept. Sitting there in the pile of romance novels and cookbooks was *The New York City Guide and Almanac 1957–1958*. Its cover boasted 544 pages of information, 750 illustrations, 135 maps, and 1,001 subjects. Everything you ever wanted to know about New York. It had a little stamp in purple ink on the front cover that read, "Cornet Bookstore, Merjan building, Baghdad" in English and in Arabic. How the book had made its way here had to be a story in itself.

It was a fascinating book, not only for the details of life in the 1950s that I could immerse myself in but because at the time my father had been stationed at Fort Monmouth, in New Jersey, right across from New York City. I imagine that my parents went to New York City on several occasions when they could get someone to watch my sister and my two-year-old self. Maybe they went to see the 1956 Broadway premiere of *My Fair Lady* with Rex Harrison and Julie Andrews. No, probably not, not on a first sergeant's pay with a couple of kids. Maybe they took in the Hayden Planetarium or the Long Island Automotive Museum. Dad would have liked that, or going to Rockefeller Plaza or Radio City Music Hall. I tried to imagine them as young adults, but it was difficult. Your parents are always your parents to you, and it's a stretch to ever think of them as young. But this travel guide was their world. My dad was a couple of years older than I was when this book was printed; my mom was a few years younger.

As I read the book, the innocence and optimism of the times came home to me. I'm not one of those who longs for a return to a golden age that I was too young at the time to remember, but it seemed that the people in this book were particularly blessed. The nation was not at war and was bustling along. The book showed a city of people seemingly at peace in Zion. Even allowing for the rose-colored glasses of a travel almanac, New York in 1957–58 looked like an interesting place to be. I wondered how much of the stuff I read about was still there. I kept the book; periodically when I got bored or just wanted to daydream I immersed myself in the world of 1958 and pictured myself in blue jeans and a white T-shirt walking around on Coney Island checking out the babes. Escapism comes in many forms. I always had a tremendous ability to daydream (if such a thing can be called an ability; I was a lousy student because of it) and could easily lie down and pretend I was somewhere else. I never would have bothered with such a book had I been at liberty. The picayune detail of it would have been too much for me. At best I would have used it for reference material. A footnote for some paper I was writing for school. Now as a literal captive audience with little else to read, I took great pleasure in the intimate details of New York during an era in our country that is as remote to me as the Civil War. As I write this I still have the book. It sits on my bookshelf with its broken spine and faded cover. It looks shabby and out of place among my many volumes of military history and other books, some of which I've even read. I wouldn't part with it for the world, though. It is an old comrade in adversity. Every now and then I take it down and remember details about the Merchant Marine Academy or former mayor La Guardia.

In addition to all of this, the Iraqis let us go to church, which turned out to be quite an undertaking. One day the bus pulled up and it was announced that anyone who wanted to go to church could ride to it on the bus. Most of us did, and in a few minutes the bus was heading down the refinery's internal road toward the gate. Instead of turning north, however, as it did when we went to the pool, the bus turned south toward Baiji proper. I was able to get a good look at the culvert going under the road and could see that there was no grating on the culvert and I could fit through it easily. I also saw that it emptied into a wadi. So this route out of the camp was viable after all. The trip to church was already worthwhile and it wasn't even five minutes old. I grinned happily as the bus kept on heading south.

I thought we were going to Baiji. But when the bus reached the intersection on the road leading to the river and the Baiji power plant, it suddenly turned left and headed toward the plant. I was instantly alert and thought for a second that we might be taken to a central location from which several hostage groups might be given a church service or otherwise collected. I checked the lists of names I had copied earlier and put in my pocket. But we did not stop at the power plant, and I didn't see whether any of the hostages were still at our old trailer.

We crossed the wide, sluggish, muddy brown Tigris River and continued into Iraq. Right across the river was an antiaircraft position with three dual 14.5mm antiaircraft guns and a few soldiers lounging about them. I looked around for other positions but couldn't see any. There were probably more on the Baiji side and I told myself to look for them when (if) we returned. I wrote down all of this information in my notebook. Not that I had a way to pass it out, but I could never tell when the opportunity might present itself.

I asked one of our minders, Mohammed (who had not been there the night of the near riot), where we were going. He said Kirkuk, about an hour away. There were three minders on the bus. Mohammed didn't look as though he fancied the company of the other two and sat down in the seat in front of me, right behind the driver. We ended up talking for most of the trip. He had been in the special police for about six years. Before that he was in the army as a tanker. He told me stories about the Iran-Iraq war and how the Iraqi tanks were much better than the Iranian tanks. He knew I was in the American military and sought to impress me with his stories of the war. I asked him all sorts of questions about Iraqi tanks and how they trained. He was proud of his service and answered willingly. He said they went on exercises two or three times a year and each tank crew fired a dozen main-gun rounds and several hundred machine-gun rounds per year. They also practiced with something his English failed him on. After a while I figured out what he meant—a subcaliber device for the main gun that allows you to shoot rifle bullets out of the tank cannon, a money-saving training system. He also said that he liked the old Russian T-55 a lot better than the newer T-72 because the older tank was simpler and more reliable. He couldn't resist getting in a dig by telling me that the Americans had lost Vietnam and the Iraqi army had very skilled tankers.

What had been meant to impress me and fill me with awe at the power of the Iraqi army actually had the opposite effect. I hadn't been that impressed watching them in Kuwait City, and now that I talked to someone who could tell me something of their training standards, I knew why. These guys didn't have a clue how to train. They fired less than a tenth the ammunition per year that a U.S. tank crew did, and what firing they did do was under canned and artificial range conditions, as opposed to the realistic tank battle runs on U.S. training ranges. I thought about the big M1s going down the Drinkwater Valley in Fort Irwin getting first-round hits at more than 2,000 meters while moving. I thought about the T-72s I had seen come into Kuwait City with their tracks loose and flapping, and the lack of maintenance I saw while I watched them for two days. I looked at Mohammed and felt sorry for him and others in their army. They didn't even know what "good" looked like in terms of being well trained. They had no concept of what Saddam was getting them into.

The conversation helped fill the void of the drive, because the country between Baiji and Kirkuk was flat and dreary. Few vehicles passed us; the only thing I noticed was trucks full of produce. It would take a long time for sanctions to starve these people out, I thought. Even with inefficient farming techniques, the Tigris and Euphrates valleys could produce a lot of food. The cradle of civilization still managed to support large populations thousands of years later. Only the traffic and occasional mud-hut and cinder-block villages broke the monotony of the drive. I enjoyed it, though. After being cooped up at the Baiji refinery, any outing was a refreshing break.

Kirkuk was a surprisingly big town, a city really. We started going through its outskirts about an hour after we crossed the river. There were numerous refineries and natural gas projects to the north of the road and even more near the town proper. The town itself was made up of white and tan buildings and stretched up against the side of a ridgeline, beyond which were even larger ridgelines and mountains as far as the eye could see. These mountains led to the border with Iran and extended north toward Turkey. We passed a refinery that appeared to have suffered a major fire some time before. I pointed it out to Mohammed the minder, and he shrugged, mentioning that the refinery had been destroyed in an Iranian air raid some years ago. I remember thinking, Don't you guys fix things in this country? But I didn't say it. No point in picking a fight. The burned-out refinery and the presence of the others still operational certainly helped explain the numerous antiaircraft installations we passed: 57mm and 37mm guns as well as radar and surface-to-air missile sites. Even on a quick drive-by, it was obvious that Kirkuk was a heavily defended town.

It was also a bustling one. Our bus drove by many souks whose stores were crammed with all kinds of consumer goods. They were doing a brisk trade. A small sea of people moved in and out of the little shops and along the streets carrying all manner of items. We passed produce souks brimming with vegetables and meat souks full of lamb and goat carcasses hung up for sale. The bus moved through the town at a fairly slow pace, and I got a good, long look at everything around me. There were school kids in blue-and-white uniforms walking home from school chattering with one another and playing, and old guys in mechanic and blacksmith shops working metal with sparks flying. There were a lot of little mechanic shops all in a row with cars being worked on in front of them. The cars on the road in Kirkuk were unusual: Japanese subcompacts that I later found out were made in Brazil. Almost all of them were taxis, painted white and orange. Mohammed told me that all the taxis were in fact family cars and that people received a government subsidy to buy them if they would also perform the function of a taxi. It seemed strange, but then this was Iraq. The people didn't seem terribly concerned about the crisis, and there were a lot of smiling faces in the crowd. A few who saw us looked at us curiously, but for the most part the world was oblivious to our presence. We were just another bus on a crowded street.

We inched our way for what seemed like almost an hour. Some of the turns the bus took were very tight. It was clear that we were going into an older section of town. Suddenly we were at the church; it was worth the trip just to behold. It was an orthodox Christian church that must have gone back centuries. It was tan and ornate with latticework and stained glass windows. I know nothing of art, but I knew that I was in the presence of something old and special. The inside of the church looked Eastern Orthodox or Coptic, with old statues and paintings of saints and only a few light fixtures. Most of the light came from candles, and the place had the musty but fragrant smell of old incense. Pillars led down the aisle to the altar, and there were knaves on either side of the church near the back. (Mr. Sussel in high-school humanities would have been proud of me for remembering the term *knave*.) The altar itself was slightly raised. Directly above it was the small dome of the church, giving an impression of greater space than there actually was. The pews were dark wood, as were most of the other fixtures, such as the confessional booths and the railings. The combination of poor lighting and dark wood made it a place of shadows. I think this was intentional. What lights there were seemed to center on the altar, but people in the pews could sit in the shadows almost alone with their thoughts even if other people sat beside them. We spent some minutes wandering around this strange and wonderful church before the priest came. Our minders, uncertain at this Christian place, contented themselves with remaining outside in the shade of the trees.

The priest came out after about fifteen minutes. He was in his late thirties or early forties—younger than I expected. He spoke very good English and welcomed us to his church. You could see that he was a little confused and distraught at our status. He was familiar enough with our minders to know that the special police were serious bad news and that we were people whose very lives were in the power of an evil regime. We could see his sympathy for us but also fear. Nothing good could come of our visit to his church. At best he would give us the comforts of our religion and we would leave. At the worst, the secret police would suspect him of trying to help us and come down on him. It was probably difficult to be a Christian here anyway. This visit did not make his life any easier. I had thought to pass him a list of names and locations in hopes that he could get it to U.S. authorities through the church, but after talking with him I decided against it. It was obvious that he wouldn't do anything like that, and he might even turn my note into the minders. Priest or no, he was still an Iraqi.

He did say Mass for us, I'll give him that, and for it I was grateful. I had always been a haphazard Catholic. I was never one for the ritual of the church. My career as an altar boy had foundered on the fact that I could remember no Latin except for *"dominus vobiscum et cum spirit tu tuo."* I had always believed in God and on occasion prayed for friends and family, but I had never been a religious person. Still, I found myself praying a lot more in captivity. I thought it helped. My prayers were not of the "Oh-God-if-you-get-me-out-of-this-I'll-go-to-church-every-Sunday-and-never-get-into-trouble-again" variety. I couldn't be that dishonest. One of my few firmly held religious beliefs was that I could not bullshit God. My prayers were mainly for my family and for Donna. I knew that all of them would be very worried. I don't think I ever prayed for myself. Not that I was unselfish—far from it. It's just that so far I could handle what was happening to me. My main worries were for my fellows (particularly Chuck) and my family and friends back home, my parents especially. I knew that the uncertainty and anxiety of it all must have been killing them.

The service went on, and sitting in the shadows I began to day-dream, as I almost always do in church. It was a reflexive action that even my unusual present circumstances could not change. I remembered going to church with my parents when I was a small boy and how my father and I had played silent little games such as thumb wrestling or paper-scissors-stone. Periodically he would make me laugh, and my mother would give us a black look. My sister, sitting between her and Dad, normally didn't get to have as much fun, but she was better at sitting quietly than I was. Later on, when I was a teenager, my dad and I would sit and whisper to each other, evaluating the young women present at the Mass. I would whisper, "What about her?" and nod toward a young girl walking by to Communion. He would appraise her with a critical eye, then say something like, "Naw. She's all right now, but look at her mom. By the time she's thirty five, she'll have an ass as wide as the back porch." Dad always had a way of making me laugh at Mass.

My father the retired sergeant major occupied a special place in our little parish. He had run the bingo and had straightened out the church's hopelessly kept books. He was not one for piety and never read from the lectern or otherwise participated in the Mass. One Saturday morning while my dad and I were setting up the bingo, Father Brown (our new priest) walked in on us. I was busy putting the red poker chips in the plastic Tupperware dishes and the markers by each place, wondering why I couldn't be at the beach like a normal teenager. (The trouble with being an only son in a military household is always being on the duty roster.) My dad was setting up the bingo machine. We both had a rhythm to our work and riffed off each other quite well. Father Brown, a nice man in his early forties, walked up to my father and introduced himself as the new parish priest. Charles R. Stanton, without missing a beat at what he was doing, said, "Well, Father, the last two priests before you got married and the one before them was queer. I wonder how long you'll last." Father Brown was abashed and managed to stammer some reply or other that I didn't catch. He thanked my dad for his work for the church and left quickly.

Over time they became fast friends, although Father Brown did on occasion run off at the mouth during the sermon. When he did this, my dad would hold up his hand like a kid asking a question in class, then make the flapping-your-mouth gesture by opening and closing the fingers of his hand with his thumb. My mother would dig him in the ribs, and the people around us would giggle or look horrified. Once Father Brown saw him do it and said, "Oh, stop that, Charlie. I'm almost done." My mother and sister were mortified, and I almost split a gut holding in my laughter.

I thought about our old church, which was a big wood frame building with a tin roof and a big tree that everyone used to try to park under because of the shade it provided against the Florida sun. I thought about the new church, which was shaped like an upside-down bowl. It was roomy and cool but didn't have any of the character of the old building. My dad didn't like the painted statues of Christ imported from Spain. He had pronounced them "guinea" in taste, but had contributed to them all the same. I looked at the Iraqi church with its ornate orthodox or Coptic icons and wondered what he would say. Not much probably. He had a respect for old things if not an appreciation of them. He was a fairly traditional person, and the folk mass, hosanna, let-us-offer-each-other-the-sign-of-peace modifications that he had seen creep into the traditional Catholic Mass did not sit well with him. He absolutely would not hold hands with anyone during the saying of the "Our Father." Although he helped manage the church's finances and secular affairs, he steadfastly refused to read the gospel or take an active part in the Mass. He had a low tolerance for the aggressively devout and told more than one holy person in our community that he was glad they were related in Christ because there was no way he would *choose* them for a friend.

So I sat in the dark with my companions in an old, ornate, and beautiful chapel, listened to an enemy priest say Mass for us, and thought of my father. I had Donna, whom I hoped to marry, as well as a mother and sister who must have been in an agony of not knowing. But try as I might, I couldn't conjure them up. I rose to my feet or kneeled as did everyone else when the ritual of the Mass required it, but in reality I was an automaton. My mind was a world away. The church brought my dad to me and I could see him back in our house, concerned but stoic, consoling my mother and keeping the family calm. The thought of him steadied me. Sons spend part of their lives living up to their father's expectations. I was no exception. I knew that wherever I was, my dad would expect me to do my best and keep faith with my comrades. Sitting invisible in the dark seats of the chapel, I prayed to God that I be given the strength not to fail my friends or my father. I also prayed for God to give strength to the rest of my family and Donna. I sat back content and reconciled. The mass ended soon afterward.

The priest came out and gave absolution to all who wanted it. I was one (cover all the bases you can; you never know). Afterward he shook our hands and disappeared into his church. The minders put us back on the bus and we drove into Kirkuk. We left town on a different route past even more souks brimming with produce. It almost made me suspect that this was a propaganda ploy to show us as much as possible of normal Iraqi life going on in spite of the sanctions. This suspicion was further compounded when our bus and its escorting cars stopped at a store and our minders bought us Popsicles. I didn't enter the store and stayed as close to the bus door as possible. I was looking for a photographer but couldn't see one anywhere. The people in the store and on the street looked at us curiously, and there was a great buzz of conversation at our appearance. It occurred to me that this show of kind treatment might be for the population's benefit to back up the claim of the Iraqi government that we were "guests." You can bet that no Iraqi taken into Saddam's custody ever got a Popsicle. After a few minutes we loaded back onto the bus and continued to Baiji. The one other thing I noticed was large numbers of uniformed men with suitcases and duffel bags at several major bus stations. All the men appeared to be in their thirties and forties and looked like reservists being called up to active duty. Officers with clipboards were calling out orders, and the troops responded in a lackluster and hopeless fashion. *There's a real morale challenge,* I remember thinking. On the way out of town we passed a military airfield with a lot of activity, but it was too far away to see what types of aircraft were kept there. Then we were in the desert for the long, empty trip back to Baiji.

I was taking my turn walking around the fence to our compound "being Caucasian" when I noticed three men at the fence in the compound next to ours. Unquestionably European, they froze when they saw me. What they did next was interesting to watch. Without saying a word, the one in the middle motioned to his two friends to stand lookout. Immediately they both peeled off, one to look back down the road they had just traversed and the other to look up the road toward the gate to their compound. Both men gave little "all clear" nods to the man in the middle, who then motioned me forward. After looking around quickly to see if the roving guard was in the area, I came up to the fence.

The man was almost as tall as I was, with jet black hair but very fair skin. His eyes were blue and he said in accented English, "Who are you?" I explained that I was a hostage and that there were sixteen of us hostages here. He said that his name was Josef and he would help us. He looked at his watch and said, "Come back tonight, nine o'clock." I would like to have learned more about Josef, but the man watching the gate whistled and they all took off.

I went back to the Brits' house feeling somewhat confused. On the one hand, the presence of Europeans next door who wanted to help could be a very good thing. On the other hand, could I trust them? Were they people being used by the Iraqis to set us up for something, such as being caught trying to escape? I talked it over with John McCollah and the rest of the Brits, and they all agreed that it wouldn't do any harm to meet the man and hear what he had to say.

The only awkward thing was that the meeting time was early at night, right before the guards went to bed, so someone usually began his rounds then. We would have to develop a system of warning. Fortunately we had some clever and inventive people in our group. The house closest to the place I was supposed to meet with Josef was the French house. To warn me of a coming guard, the French would sing "La Marseillaise" or some other French song. The Brits would keep lookout and signal to the French that someone was coming my way. The spot by the fence could not be seen from the minders' house or any of the guardhouses. There was a direct line of sight to the antiaircraft batteries, but this spot was too far away to be seen by them at night. My big fear was being surprised by a guard.

That night I left the group in the community building as though I were going for one of my normal walks. There was nothing suspicious or unusual about this, and none of the minders or uniformed guards in the community center with us gave me so much as a glance as I left. I quickly stole along the exterior fence, then hid in a bush next to one of the last houses in the row where I could observe the meeting spot. I waited for about half an hour, but it seemed a lot longer.

Sure enough, Josef and his pals showed up. The three of them came out as though they were taking a walk. They went past me and down to the end of their compound and out of sight. It was obvious that they were doing a recon of their side to see if the coast was clear. On the return trip one man dropped off and took his security post; the other kept going past the meeting site to take his post. Josef stood by the fence and looked around anxiously. It was now or never. I left the shadows and walked out to join him at the fence. He gave a start when he saw me but quickly recovered. I was about to say who I was, but he beat me to the punch. He said, "I Pole, me help." I told him there were sixteen of us and that Chuck was in rough shape. I passed him a copy of the list of names of everyone and where I had last seen those men from the Baiji refinery. He took the papers and promised to get them to the U.S. embassy. He also asked if we were being starved. Apparently he had heard of Saddam's threat to starve us in retaliation for sanctions and was worried that the Iraqis might actually start doing so. I told him that this had not yet occurred. I asked him for a large-scale map of Iraq and a compass and he agreed to bring me what I wanted. I also asked who was in the compound with him and where they lived. He told me of the Rumanian group of petrochemical engineers who worked in the Baiji refinery. There were a dozen of them and their families, although most of the wives and children had gone home for the summer. They were trying to go home themselves, but the Iraqis were stalling. They did, however, have freedom of movement inside the country. This meant that they could travel to Baghdad, where the U.S. embassy was. I found out that someone in their group went to Baghdad each week to shop and get mail.

Josef and I then discussed the security situation around the refinery. He was able to fill me in on what posts there were on the sides of the refinery that I couldn't see. He also confirmed what I already knew of the guards on our side and at the main gate. From this I estimated the guard force at the Baiji refinery to be about two hundred people, not including the antiaircraft troops. With what Josef told me of the numbers of air defense positions on the other parts of the perimeter, I figured that the site was defended by about a battalion of 57mm antiaircraft guns, which would add another 250 to 300 troops in the immediate vicinity. There would also be surface-to-air missile batteries farther out that I couldn't see. Josef also told me that within a ten-kilometer circle of Baiji, there were four large military camps with lots of soldiers or airmen in each one.

We talked for a little more than five minutes. Our discussion was hurried, furtive, and somewhat hampered by Josef's limited English and my nonexistent Polish. We both kept glancing to the sides and behind us, still speaking while we were looking away. Josef took a faded blue denim bag with a rip in it from his pants pocket and showed it to me. He told me he would have the map and compass in the bag tomorrow and would place the bag in a small rubbish pile by the fence, so that it looked like just another piece of trash. We chose a spot and made sure that I could reach through the fence to get the bag. He said that if I had a message for him, I should leave it in the bag at the same spot. He then looked up at me and said, "Have courage. We will help all we can." He shook my hand through the fence and disappeared. I left the fence as quickly as I could and returned to my normal walking route. I went back by the Germans' house and past where the guards and minders slept. I saw nothing out of the ordinary. Good. We had not been observed. I returned to my house and thought about the meeting.

Josef and his friends were taking a huge chance in talking to us, let alone offering to help. The Iraqi regime had shown itself to be both savage and perfunctory in dealing with people it suspected to be guilty of espionage. Shortly before the war the Iraqis had actually hanged a British journalist they had accused of spying. I had no doubt that Josef and his friends would suffer the same fate if their contacts with us were discovered.

At the same time, I was excited at the potential of contact with the U.S. embassy in Baghdad. There, Americans were confined but not under actual Iraqi control. The embassy could communicate to the States. For the first time since Al Qaim, I was able to send out a message on the composition and status of our group and where I had last seen other hostages. Admittedly it was an act of faith; Josef and his friends were like a radio with a broken speaker. I could transmit messages through them, but I could not receive.

I must confess that I had some doubts as well. Was this whole thing set up as an elaborate hoax by the Iraqi security services? I remembered Robert Graves as the German spy in *Stalag 17*. Maybe the Iraqis had something like this going on at each hostage camp. Maybe my preparations to escape had been too obvious, or maybe the Iraqis had seen or figured out one of the satellite signs. There was also the possibility that Josef and his pals were playing it straight but their embassy officials would turn in my messages to the Iraqis. The old Soviet bloc states in general were close to Iraq economically and politically. Captivity had made me suspicious, and I did not trust any-one outside my small circle of comrades.

After debating with myself, however, I decided to continue the contact. It felt genuine, and my feelings were about all I had to go by. Besides, what choice did I have? I could ignore Josef and his friends and stay out of contact, or I could send messages through them and maybe some would get to the U.S. embassy. I rationalized that if the Iraqis were going to trump up espionage charges against me, they would not have to rely on legal niceties or the truth; they could just make up something. After all, they had already kidnapped us; they could do whatever they pleased. I lost nothing through continuing the contact. Still, I wondered how much help the men at the fence would be. My request for a map and compass would be a good litmus test of their ability and intentions.

I spent most of the next day on pins and needles waiting for dark to see whether the bag had anything in it. Around 9:30 I left the community center and the people who were watching TV and took my usual nightly walk. Some of the Brits and the French had gone back to their houses earlier and taken their positions as lookouts. I walked by their houses to make sure that they saw me and knew to sound the alarm. I did a thorough look-around to make sure that we hadn't missed a guard or minder who was now wandering about. There wasn't anyone. So far so good. I waited in the shadows by the house as I had the previous night and identified the place where Josef said he would leave the bag. Screwing up my courage, I left the shad-ows and went to the fence. Immediately I saw the bag and in a sec-ond more it was in my hands and I was walking quickly back to the shadows. I felt a surge of excitement because there was clearly some-thing in the bag. I walked as nonchalantly as I could to the Brits' house. Running would have been criminal folly because it would have called attention to me, as would have sneaking around. No, the thing was to act normal. Just the same nutty American on one of his nocturnal prowls that the Iraqis were used to seeing.

Inside the Brits' house I emptied the bag onto the table, and John McCollah, Dave Freeman, Mick Finan, and I looked at the contents. There were three items: a very good compass, a large tourist map of Iraq, and a letter written in green ink. The compass was first rate and immediately went into my pocket, because I felt nervous about leav-ing it out for even a second. The map was intriguing. It was black and white and of poor quality, but it gave me the scales of distances and the major towns. From this I could figure out exactly where we were and approximately how close we were to the nearest borders. This last information was not especially encouraging. We were north of Tikrit but 120 miles as the crow flies from the Syrian border and 140 miles from the nearest Syrian town. Turkey was 150 miles away, but even with the bad map I could see that we had considerable mountain ranges to contend with on that route. We were as close to smack dab in the middle of Iraq as we could get. Damn. I also saw just how close Al Qaim was to the Syrian border and felt that momentary pang of loss, but I quickly mastered myself. No time for recriminations now. All of this I learned from a minute's glance at the map. Dave Freeman was reading the letter written in green ink. He showed it to me with a blank expression on his face. The English was poor, but the block capital letters were formed with a schoolboy's almost deliberate precision. The writer had clearly meant to be very careful that we understood the words he was putting on paper. The message said:

My Friend

Don't be worry! Letters will be sent to your country. We think you receive reply 4–5 weeks. We give you map of Iraq, but please believe us that escape has no chance. Now it is impossible!! Don't ask why. We make everything for your freedome. If you like give us more letters of your friends, we can send its off. Write! What you need. Please to contact every Thursday in this same time as you did last propose.

Yours, W.2xY.

I didn't know what to make of this. The W.2xY was obviously some form of abbreviation for himself or a code sign so I would know that the letter was from him. No, what puzzled me was the content of the letter in contrast to the man's actions. This guy was risking his life to give me the tools to conduct an escape and virtually in the same act was warning me that I had no chance and not to do it. That it would be hard to escape all the way to safety I already knew. In virtually all of the places we had been held so far, getting away from the actual confinement facility would not have been difficult. The problem was what to do once we were outside the wire. At best we could get only a two-meal head start before someone got suspicious and our absence was discovered. From there it would be a simple matter of cordoning off a perimeter and conducting a search. From what I had seen of the police state that was Iraq, assembling manpower for this would not be a problem.

9

MY MENTAL APPROACH to escape was evolving. I realized the futility of just getting out of jail, so to speak. All of Iraq was a jail. Unless the Iraqis moved us again and put me in a position where it would be a walk of seventy-two hours or less from an international border, escape prior to hostilities was not practical. So Josef's warning was not necessary, but he didn't know that. I could understand his concern, even from a selfish point of view. If I got caught, he and his friends were in mortal danger for helping us. What I found interesting was that in spite of this fear, he still provided me with the map and compass I had asked for. If he had wanted to control the situation, he could have simply passed our messages and said he couldn't obtain a compass or a good map. This would have kept his assistance to us at a level he felt comfortable with. If he ever got scared, he could just pull in the blue bag and that would be that. Trusting me with the map and compass just because I was an American was a huge leap of faith and added an element of utter unpredictability for him. Yet he still did it. I think this single act, more than anything else, convinced me that Josef was genuine. He had nothing to gain by it and his life to lose if I was foolish.

The arrangement with Josef also worried me a great deal, because it confirmed to me the tenuous situation we were in. Had Josef not felt that we were in real danger, it wouldn't have made sense for him to do this. What he was giving me was the ability, in extremis, to make a run for it. The unspoken message behind the gift was chilling. Josef, a man who had worked with the Iraqis for some time, must have believed that the situation we faced could become so bad that a desperate escape attempt would be preferable. Bluntly, bad meant dead. I had been thinking over our status as hostages. The rationale for our use as human shields was to prevent attacks on key Iraqi targets. This would present the coalition forces that were forming in Saudi Arabia with the unpalatable prospect of killing or wounding captive civilians from coalition nations to strike key Iraqi targets. The Iraqis would be quick to publicize the "unfortunate" deaths of human shields in the wake of any strike. If no hostages were actually killed in a strike, I had no doubt that the Iraqis would execute a group of hostages and bring their suitably burned and blasted bodies to a bombing site as "evidence" of coalition-caused hostage deaths. What was even more disturbing was the realization that they would have to do it to an entire group. They couldn't take just a few men from each group of hostages because someone would be left to tell the tale. If this happened, a little group somewhere (maybe mine, maybe Paul Eliopoulos's, maybe the people left at Al Qaim or the Baiji power plant) would simply disappear and there would be no survivors. From where we were positioned in the refinery, I was reasonably sure we could survive an air strike (assuming of course that the bombs hit the actual refinery as they were supposed to, instead of the administrative and housing areas). The awesome risk that Josef and his friends took in giving me the map and compass conveyed to me with a silent eloquence that merely surviving any air strike might not be enough.

What made the situation even worse was that I would have little or no warning of when bombing was going to commence. The radio would not be a help in terms of tipping us off beforehand, although it would help us find out as soon as the war started. The disturbing thought was that we would probably be taken into closer custody as soon as the war started, at which point our "guest" status would change to that of actual enemy prisoners. What it all boiled down to was that I would have at best only a few minutes' warning in which to run unless I took the bull by the horns and escaped prior to hostilities.

The timing on this would be critical. I had no illusions as to my long-term prospects of escaping from Baiji in the police state that was Iraq. Six-foot-three white guys who don't speak the language tend to stick out in the Middle East. The best possible outcome would be to escape within twenty-four hours of the commencement of hostilities. Once war had broken out, at least there would be a major distraction to any search effort. The Iraqis would not be able to use the troops from the antiaircraft batteries or the nearby airfields or military bases to look for me. They would have bigger fish to fry. The problem was, of course, judging the correct moment from listening to the BBC and VOA, but these would be imprecise indicators to say the least.

The prospect of retaliation against my fellow prisoners did not escape my thoughts. This was one of the harder possibilities I had to come to terms with. Although it was clearly my duty to escape, the thought of leaving my friends, particularly Chuck, made me feel as though I were planning to desert. I hadn't at this time entertained the possibility of taking any of the others with me; this would come later. So preparing to escape brought a sense of guilt and shame that I had to master. Rationally, there was no reason for it. My presence added nothing; I was just one more guy to be shot if the whole situation went bad. It actually would be advantageous to the group if one of us did make it out. A missing individual meant that the Iraqis could not execute the group without running the risk that the escaped prisoner might gain his freedom and expose the fact that the dead prisoners had actually been alive at a different location on a certain date.

My preparations for escape at first centered on finding suitable water containers and rations. The key to staying at liberty was to be self-sustaining for as long as possible. The more food and water I could carry, the longer I could avoid habitation to steal my sustenance. I was under no illusions about my ability to live off the land. Euell Gibbons couldn't have lived off the Iraqi desert. Using the map, I plotted two general courses of action. One took me west toward Syria and the other north to Turkey. Both had their strong and weak points. I had already seen the route to Syria; it offered smooth, flat going that would allow me to cover twenty to thirty kilometers a night. The main problem with the Syrian route was the distance between certain water sources. The large tourist map showed the tip of a lake near Habbiniyah and other locations that looked as though they would have water, but I had no idea whether they were dry lakebeds or held water year-round. I didn't know whether I could carry enough water to see me through from source to source. The walk to Turkey paralleled the Tigris River, so water wouldn't be an issue, but the area was extremely mountainous and I'd be lucky to make five kilometers a day in places.

Once more I scoured the little workers' compound for anything useful. Unfortunately it had been well cleared of empty plastic containers, which are the number-one item of choice for budding young escape artists like myself. The only thing I found a lot of was janitorial equipment such as mops, buckets, and brooms. I did find one foul container, though: a gallon jug that had been used for ghee, an Indian version of clarified butter. Screwing off the top released a nauseating smell, and peering into it I could see about a quarter inch of muck on the bottom with some bugs in it. Charming. I could ill afford to toss away such a sturdy plastic jug, though, and I painstakingly went about cleaning the interior with hot water and soap. It took me some days of work before the water tasted barely potable, and I was worried about getting the runs from the jug, so I kept cleaning it out every day. Working on the evil-smelling jug for the first time that night, I resolved to ask Josef for clean water jugs and a haversack to carry my escape stash of food and other necessities.

The appearance of Josef and his compatriots had certainly added a new aspect to my existence in captivity. They had caused me to fully and completely appreciate the gravity of the situation. If my suspension of disbelief had been eroding before I met Josef, it was now gone for good. I realized that my life and the lives of my companions could well rest on my ability to escape and remain at liberty. I also realized that there would be no second chances. A misjudgment in timing, be it too early or too late, would have equally unfortunate results. So, when to go?

Decisions, decisions.

We were taken to church at Kirkuk once more, a week after the first meeting with Josef. The trip was about the same. Still more reservists being called up and more military convoys on the road. The priest at Baiji wasn't quite as nervous to see us the second time, and the Mass was less stilted and awkward than the first one. I again spent a cool hour in the dark daydreaming about my childhood (a habit that continues to this day). After the Mass, the priest stayed to talk with us for a few minutes and even patiently listened to the confessions of those who wanted to do so. I didn't confess because I couldn't bring myself to confess to an Iraqi, even an Iraqi priest. Besides, God knows what's in your heart.

Kirkuk seemed to be as bustling and prosperous as ever. Sanctions didn't appear to be having much effect. The airfield had a lot of activity; aircraft seemed to be taking off and landing on a regular basis. Even in the church I had heard their distant roar periodically throughout the Mass. The Kirkuk airfield was clearly an active fighter base. I wished I could get a close look at it. In a touch of incongruity, jet fighters took off as men walked beside rubber-tired donkey carts. Our bus passed people in the fields still at work with draft animals attached to plows or other bits of animal-powered farm machinery. Iraq was a study in contrasts. The cradle of civilization, where the fertile valleys produced enough food for cities to begin. Their agriculture looked as though it hadn't changed appreciably since the days of Ur, but they had jet fighters. We drove west into the setting sun and left the donkey carts and their drivers to make their timeless, phlegmatic way into town.

I never failed to be fascinated by glimpses of normal Iraqi life made during my captivity. In Saudi Arabia, one occasionally encounters traditional medieval attitudes and mind-sets. In Iraq one encounters the Middle Ages on a daily basis. Mud bricks and microwave towers, blacksmith shops and Sony televisions; it was as though the fourteenth century had met the twentieth century in a huge train wreck, and the pieces of both were strewn intermingled with one another.

As fascinating as it was, I had to discipline myself to pay attention to militarily useful details. On each bus trip I surreptitiously jotted down a few more notes of everything I saw and transcribed them that night in order to pass them to Josef. I didn't know whether any of the messages I put in the blue bag were getting through, but they kept disappearing and I had to keep trying. I wanted very badly to talk to Josef again to update him on Chuck's sickness, give him my family's phone number to call, and just talk to a free man. He was way too cautious and clever for that, though, and the little bag was our only contact.

I had given more thought to my escape and believed that my best bet would be to head toward Syria. It would allow me to stay away from populated areas on ground that offered good going. This open, level ground would also facilitate rescue. I had come up with a scheme to signal anyone who might be looking for me. I would walk parallel to the power lines leading from Baiji to Habbiniyah, just in sight of them at night. I would stop an hour before light each morning and shine the flashlight in half-minute intervals at the sky through a cardboard tube. I would then hunker down and stay in place all day and shine my flashlight in a similar manner after it got dark, moving about two hours after darkness fell each night. I communicated this in a note I sent through Josef. I had no idea whether there would be any rescue attempt, but I wanted to make it as easy as I could to find me. Having darkness as the only safe time for movement would eliminate three hours each night, but I had to leave enough time to find a hiding place to hunker down and allow my eyes to get used to the darkness for the oncoming evening. I only hoped that some satellite, sensor, or imagery analyst would notice the flashlight in the desert. If not, I would just keep walking. It wasn't much of a plan, but it was the best I could come up with at the time.

I had sent out several messages through Josef and hadn't seen him or gotten anything in reply after the first message that warned me not to escape. The requested containers did not show up, which led me to wonder whether Josef and his pals had second thoughts about providing me with escape equipment or whether they just couldn't find any suitable vessels. Every time I checked the blue bag, my messages would be gone, so I knew at least that someone was picking them up. It tried to keep the messages to a page of notebook paper apiece so they could be easily hidden or destroyed. Each report had the status of our group, an update on Chuck's illness, and observations of the Iraqis to include number of guards and minders and all that I knew about the security of the site itself. On the later messages I also added estimates of production based on observations by Chuck and Sho Hasegawa, the Japanese petrochemical engineer. I related items of military intelligence such as my observations of activity in Kirkuk on our visits, any convoys of military equipment we happened to see on the road near Baiji, and the status of the antiaircraft batteries surrounding the site, to include manning and frequency of training.

This was a lot of stuff and it went way beyond what Good Samaritan Josef had originally intended by offering to help. I was honor bound to tell him. From a more practical standpoint, if he spoke English, chances were that he had read it too. After all, he had gotten somebody to write that note to me. I put in a note that I needed to see him. The next day he showed up after dark.

I could tell that he was skittish in the way he approached the meeting. Looking over one's shoulder must have become a genetic trait in the former Eastern bloc, because he did it as naturally and unconsciously as breathing. I asked him whether he had gotten any water containers and he shook his head. I told him to be careful because my notes contained other than just personal information. He looked at me with exasperation. "I know this," he said. "Do you have any other messages?" All of a sudden I felt very foolish. Of course he knew it. He had read everything I put in the bag and would no doubt destroy it if he felt it were dangerous. I hastily updated him on Chuck's illness, then departed. There was no point in exposing him any longer. He knew the score and was not intimidated by it. He also clearly saw face-to-face meetings as dangerous. I would not jeopardize his life again in such a manner.

The news at this point came mostly from the BBC and had a definite British slant to it. The foreign minister, Douglas Hurd, had said in an interview while touring the Gulf that he "doubted the crisis could be solved peacefully." Meanwhile, British and American forces continued flowing into the Gulf. All women and children (including Stuart Lockwood) made it out of the country in the first week of September. This news buoyed the spirits of my British compatriots considerably. Iraq, meanwhile, consolidated its hold on Kuwait and restricted all foreign airline flights into Baghdad, which was convenient because the airlines had all stopped flying anyway. The Iraqis also announced that they would target both Israel and Saudi Arabia if war broke out. Iraqi television had a lot of coverage of the visit of Foreign Minister Terek Aziz to Tehran, the first one since the war. To watch it on Iraqi TV, you'd think it meant something. There were also a lot of anti-American protests in Baghdad that looked about as spontaneous as the Miss America pageant. Things just kept getting uglier.

In the second week of September we were informed that we would be taken to a new camp and told to collect our things. After almost a month at the Baiji refinery, I looked upon this change as ominous. Once again I was being taken from a place that escape was possible from and into the unknown. In addition, I would lose touch with Josef and the other Poles who were helping us. The minders, of course, did not say where they were taking us.

I was even more concerned about the reason for us moving. The other moves could be explained as either staging for further dispersal, as at Al Qaim, or moving individuals to mix up the nationalities in groups, as when Chuck and I were moved to the Baiji refinery. All this had been done and the Iraqis were still moving us around. I was concerned that they did not want us getting too buddy-buddy with any of the people at the facilities in which we were being held. The Stockholm syndrome is a two-way street. It would be harder for Iraqi soldiers and guards to shoot prisoners that they knew. This indicated at least to me that the Iraqis had weighed the possibility of violence against us. I am personally convinced that all this switching around was to facilitate the eventuality that hostages would have to be killed and placed on the sites of coalition bombing attacks.

The worst thing about being moved was that I wouldn't be able to meet with Josef again. I couldn't even leave word as to where we were going because we weren't told. Leaving anything at all in the blue bag was a risk. What if the Iraqis found it? On the other hand, I didn't want Josef getting curious and coming too close or, worse, sneaking into our compound to try to find out what happened to us. I agonized over the situation and finally left a one-word message in the bag: MOVING. Once again this was a lesson learned too late. I should have come up with a set of prearranged signals, such as hanging a towel out a window of one of the last houses in the row so he could see it and know we were gone. Now I had to leave a message. A cryptic message to be sure, but a message nonetheless. I hoped he would get it, but I had no way of knowing. I also went back behind the community center and destroyed my satellite sign by breaking up the letters and spreading the slats over the ground. I didn't know for sure whether we were going to be replaced, and I didn't want to leave a misleading sign. In addition I went into my house and wrote all of our names and the dates that we were here on the wall by the bed. I did this in some of the other buildings too. If another hostage group were brought in, hopefully they would see the writing and record our names. I also put a couple of lists on paper under the mattress of my bed and Chuck's bed in case the names were erased from the walls. Hopefully, the Iraqis wouldn't look under the mattress (and just as hopefully any new hostages would get to change their sheets eventually). "Hope" is not a method, as some wise man said, but when you're a prisoner, you have little else.

After that there was nothing left to do but wait. We piled our baggage on the volleyball court and waited in the shade for the bus to come. It showed up a little after ten. All our worldly goods were loaded in a pathetically short time, and we said good-bye to the Baiji refinery. As we left I took a last look at the escape route down the ditch that I had planned. I was sure it would have worked, at least to get me outside the refinery. After that, who knew? But I wasn't emotional, not this time. I had become hardened in my captivity. My house of cards had once more been kicked over. Time to pick up the cards and start again.

KIRKUK

We traveled east across the bridge over the Tigris and down the road toward Kirkuk. I craned my neck for a look at the Baiji power plant, to see if I could spot any westerners at the barracks trailer we had lived in, but I couldn't see anything. I knew we probably weren't going to go north because the main north-south highway from Baghdad to Mosul was right in front of the refinery we had just left. I was curious to see whether the Iraqis would take us past Kirkuk itself. On the way, I looked for the landmarks I had become familiar with on our two visits to the church in Kirkuk. The antiaircraft defenses were still in place around the bridge, complete with bored troops sleeping by the weapons. The bus trip was uneventful, and there wasn't much traffic on the roads. Although I tried to stay focused and keep an eye out for detail, the dullness of the country made it difficult.

Just short of Kirkuk proper (which we could see in the distance), we turned north toward a fenced-off housing complex in the middle of a large, open field about five kilometers from a large refinery. At the complex we could see another bus similar to ours and a cluster of cars and military trucks. My heart leapt when I realized that this meant there was another hostage group there. I instantly reached into my bag and got one of the lists of names I had written and kept it ready to hand over.

I had a moment of panic when it looked as though the other group would be put on their bus before they had a chance to talk to us, but then the Iraqis relented and let us all talk. I recognized Tony Nelson and spoke to him about his experiences since we were separated at the Baiji power plant. He couldn't tell me much; he had come straight here from the power plant, where they had been mixed with hostages from other nations. I did get a list of everyone in his hostage group and passed him my list. He looked well and said they received reasonable care. The food was plentiful and the civilian head of the refinery, a man named Abdul Karim, seemed a decent person. We traded our opinions about what was happening. No one was optimistic about release, and the unspoken consensus was that we would be stuck in Iraq when the war started.

Meeting the other hostage group was awkward, like meeting relatives we hadn't seen in a while. But it was good to see other faces after being in the same group for so long. They gave us advice about the guards and the lowdown on the general living conditions. All too soon, the Iraqis broke up the meeting and Tony's group left, waving out their bus windows, with their escort trailing. Their minders went with them, though, and ours stayed with us. Too bad. I would like to have seen the last of Khalid. He was too unstable for my taste.

Our accommodations were large and airy: a step up from the rundown workers' camp we had been kept in at the Baiji refinery. We were put into two dormitory houses with long hallways and individual rooms, common bathrooms, and a TV room up front. Our minders lived in another building. We were given lunch, then left alone to get settled.

As soon as I could, I took a walk around the compound. There were about a dozen or so houses or barracks along with other communal buildings. All were one story and painted dull white. The fence was chain link topped by barbed wire. There were no guard towers, but guards patrolled the perimeter. There was a small guardhouse at the gate. The compound didn't look difficult to break out of. It would definitely be easier than the Baiji refinery. The best thing about the place was that it presented an easy target for a rescue operation. It was away from other built-up areas and had a limited guard force. The ground around it would be perfect for a helicopter landing zone. By this point in our captivity I no longer believed that rescue was imminent. All the same, it was pleasant to be in a place that would facilitate any rescue effort.

The next step was to make more satellite signs. Fortunately, no one was watching me and I found a can of paint while I was walking around the houses. It was sticky and did not spread easily, but it was the only thing at hand. In my walk around I had discovered that all the empty buildings were unlocked and had doors that accessed their flat roof. I chose an unoccupied building away from the billets where we were being kept and went onto the roof. Fortunately there was a low wall on top of the building, which helped conceal me. I managed to paint the words "16 Hostages Here" on the roof in letters that I hoped a satellite imagery analyst could see. I didn't have enough paint, and I had to use a piece of cardboard to spread it, but I did the best I could. Then I went back downstairs, rubbed the paint off my hands with sand, and washed up. The whole process took about an hour. I thought for sure I would have been missed, but when I returned to our quarters no one said a thing.

Right after I got back, Abdul Karim came by. He explained that he was the plant manager and we would be his "guests" for a while. He was a slightly rotund man of middle height, about fifty years old, with graying hair and a mustache. His English was perfect and only a trifle slow. His manner was friendly and gave the impression that he was trying to make the best of a bad situation. He pledged that he would do everything possible to make our "stay" more comfortable. We asked him a few questions about release but didn't press it. It was clear that he didn't know anything, and there wasn't any point in picking a fight.

That night while watching TV, I saw the first clip of "Guest News." These were filmed interviews that the Iraqis did with hostages that showed hostages making pro-Iraqi or anti-U.S./UN intervention statements. At the time, I thought these remarks had been coerced; I couldn't believe that anyone in our position would make statements supportive of our captors. Later I found out that the statements had been made voluntarily. The British sergeants were especially outraged to later see one of their number make statements on "Guest News." They all knew the man and were surprised that he would do such a thing. John McCollah intimated to me that the man was in deep trouble and would probably be court-martialed if he had actually volunteered the statement.

The other piece of news on TV that evening was a heart-rending segment showing Iraqi prisoners of war being repatriated from Iran. The condition of the men was shocking, but what was most painful to watch was how the special policemen, in green uniforms, were manipulating these men for the cameras. We could see them getting these men to do the Saddam chant and kiss pictures of Saddam Hussein for the cameras. The announcer said proudly that after a short home leave these soldiers had announced their "eagerness" to rejoin the army and go to Kuwait to face the American aggressors. Oh yeah, they looked really eager. Some of them had been in POW camps for almost ten years. Not one of them looked less than fifty, although most of them must have been in their early to mid-thirties. Here they were, finally being released and getting shoved right back into it. Most of the time Iraq had a sort of comic opera atmosphere. In spite of the seriousness of our situation, I could laugh at the silly propaganda. This, however, was not funny. I looked at the wan, wasted men getting off the bus and listened to their frail, pathetic chant. How could anyone send these men back to the army? More than anything the Iraqis had done to me, this mistreatment of their own former POWs solidified my contempt for Saddam Hussein and the Iraqi regime. The Iraqi leadership plainly needed killing. You could see that the sight of them had affected others in the same way. "Poor bastards," John McCollah muttered; others grunted their assent. Our little TV session broke up after that, each of keeping our thoughts to ourselves. My main thought was that I was glad I hadn't been born an Iraqi. I went to sleep feeling slightly depressed.

The next day right after breakfast I began to study in detail where we were being kept. The compound was bigger than our place at the Baiji refinery, but it still took only about ten minutes to walk around. I discovered that virtually all of the housing units were unlocked as well as most of the other buildings. I resolved to go through each house to see what useful items I could pick up. I also noted the absence of roving patrols in the interior of the compound. The guards didn't seem interested in us, and our minders tended to stay with the larger group near the TV room or at their own place across from ours. The old pattern from Baiji held true here. As long as we didn't make a fuss, the minders could care less what we did inside the wire. They counted us at meals and at bed check, but that was about it.

The land outside the compound was bleak and barren. There were no plants to speak of, and the only features were the refineries and some large communications antennas between our compound and the refinery. Aircraft flew low over our compound continually throughout the day, and it was soon evident that we were in the traffic pattern of a military airfield. I identified Shukoi Seven fighter-bombers and MiG-23s. I kept track in my notebook of what planes I saw when.

I occupied my time with writing our names on the inside walls of some of the buildings so if we were traded out again, another hostage group would find them. That done, I started looking for useful things to steal. It was amusing to me how naturally I fell into this mind-set of automatic theft, although I didn't take things that looked as though they would be missed immediately or were too big to hide. Tools were of primary importance to me, and in searching the buildings in this new compound I hit the jackpot: a dirty but serviceable electrician's screwdriver and a cross-tip screwdriver that had been left on a table. Both were covered with dust, and it was apparent that no one had been in the building for some time. I immediately pocketed my finds and continued to search other structures. There was a long, low building that appeared to be a storage shed. All of its doors were padlocked but the hasps had been put on wrong, so the screws that held them to the doorjamb were exposed. I looked into the rooms through the windows; all but two of the rooms were empty. The building was visible from the fence, and I had to wait for the guards to walk by. They took no notice of me as they trudged slowly along the fence like beasts of burden. I waited until they passed, then quickly attacked the doors with my new screwdriver. I had the hasps off in a jiffy, then went inside to see what was worth taking. The first room was no joy: just plumbing fixtures and the like. The second room had thin orange blankets in plastic bags and, of all things, padlocks. I took three of the blankets (they would be useful to cut up and use as panel markers when the time came) and a couple of the padlocks. I didn't know what I would use these for, but they were small and easily concealed. You never can tell. I screwed the hasp back into place and moved as unobtrusively as possible back to our billets, then I stored my new finds near my bed. There were enough blankets for everyone, but I figured I'd keep my theft a secret for a few days to make sure that none of the Iraqis missed what I had taken.

That night I went over to the French guys' house to see whether they had heard any useful information on the radio. Etienne showed me his book of French history, and I had an enjoyable few hours looking at the pictures and trying to figure out from the words what was going on. After this, a walk around the dimly lit compound at night excited no attention. Good. Our minders were used to the fact that I always walked around the compound, and the guards obviously didn't care. By the time I got back to our house, everyone was in bed. One of our minders was sitting watching TV. He barely gave me a glance as I came in. I checked on Chuck; he seemed to be sleeping OK, so maybe the medicine he had been given was doing some good after all. Down the hall Dave Freeman was already snoring like an organ. Familiar, comforting sounds. I went to bed in high spirits. This place had possibilities.

The camp was a definite improvement over Baiji. The digs were pleasant, the guards were inattentive, and the food was a step up from what we'd been given at the Baiji refinery. This new place impressed us all as much more organized in terms of accommodations. I liked it because it would be a lot easier to escape from than the Baiji refinery. There wasn't much perimeter lighting, and I felt that when the time came there would be little trouble in getting through the fence. All in all, not a bad place to be held hostage.

So of course we were moved again.

I found out later that some of the hostage sites had been taking the word "guests" a little too literally. They were putting up their hostages in housing compounds and actual guesthouses that were a good distance away from the facilities they were supposed to be human shielding. This was the case at Kirkuk. Abdul Karim had initially put the hostages allocated to his liquid natural gas plant in the housing complex that we now occupied. I can see his point as plant manager. The housing complex accommodated his "guests" and kept them out of the way of plant operations. Unfortunately, some Baathist Party bigwig had come through on an inspection tour and complained that the hostages were not being used correctly. Orders came down that we should be sent to the refinery proper. Office workers had been turned out of a single-story office block on the compound, and it was converted into a barracks for hostages. Abdul Karim regretfully told us that we would have to move into the plant.

The word that we were moving came as a blow to me, because this was in so many ways the perfect camp and we had been here only a short while. But I was much better prepared psychologically for this move from having endured my previous three moves. After digesting the initial news of it, I realized that I needed to destroy the satellite sign I had made. Getting to the building would be easy enough; I would simply tell the minders that I was going for another one of my walks. Destroying the sign would be the hard part. It was fairly large, and I had no paint. Fortunately there was a shed with lubricants and waste oil in cans in one of the corners of the compound. I took a small can of the latter and went up to the roof. In a few minutes I managed to smear the sign into a series of big black blobs. Below the blobs I wrote the word MOVING in oil and drew an arrow toward the refinery.

I didn't know whether this was the right thing to do. Maybe the Iraqis would bring people into this compound after us. I didn't think so, though. Our minders had said we were simply moving over to the refinery itself. On the balance I thought it better to erase the sign, because that's what I had done in Baiji. It pays to be consistent. Having done this, I went back and packed my stuff along with everyone else. Then we waited.

Presently a bus came to get us. Our minders traveled with us or in their cars. I watched with misgivings as the compound receded. The refinery would be better guarded and difficult to break out of. In addition, we would be close to a real target again. On the credit side, I had picked up some useful tools, particularly the screwdrivers and orange blankets. I still wondered how I was going to contact the embassy now that we were no longer near any European camp, but all I could do was keep an eye out for opportunities. There was nothing to do but look out the bus window for useful bits of information and wait to see what this new place would bring.

THE JAMBUR AND AL HASSAN PROJECT (PETROLEUM STABILIZATION PLANT #2)

The bus ride lasted only a few minutes. We were brought to the large refinery-like compound that we had seen off to the east. Immediately inside the gate the bus stopped in front of a large, single-story office building. Mohammed and Khalid the dick came out of the building and stood watching us dismount, then they led us into what would be our new digs. The building was T shaped; the minders were billeted on one side of the top of the T and we were billeted on the other. There were more bedrooms in the base of the T, along with a room with a large table and a makeshift barbell made from a piece of pipe and some large coffee cans with cement in them. Near the intersection of the T was a recreation room with couches, game boards, and a TV. The minders let us find our own billets and work out who stayed with whom. Chuck and I stayed together at the end of the hall. Right across the hall were Dave Freeman and John McCollah. Everyone else staked out rooms mainly by nationality. The Japanese next to me on the same side of the hall, the French and Germans closer to the recreation room. Because the rooms could not comfortably hold three beds (although the Japanese managed), Mick Finan later decided to take up residence in a large closet next to the recreation room. The Iraqis expressed surprise at this but let him have his way.

After putting down our stuff, we were escorted outside the gate to a large, prefabricated building that served as a mess hall. There we were served a passable lunch of goat meat and vegetables. At least the portions were adequate. The small but congenial kitchen staff was made up of a gawky giant named Yusef and a wizened man about five feet tall who looked like the late Jimmy Durante. They smiled as they served us our meals and said "hello" in broken English as though they meant it. I found out later that both were Kurds, which served to explain their friendliness toward us and their standoffishness toward our Iraqi guards. After lunch Abdul Karim briefed us. He told us that we were his "guests"—that damn word again—and had the run of the refinery as long as we behaved ourselves. His only caution was that we were not to go outside the fence or touch any of the refinery machinery.

I was perplexed by this. Just from an industrial safety point of view, this was not very smart. What plant in the States would allow a bunch of people off the street to rubberneck around their facility? From having observed the Iraqis at Baiji, it was fairly clear that they had no occupational safety rules, but the casual "y'all walk where you want to" attitude of Abdul Karim was still shocking. I have never been a person to look a gift horse in the mouth, however, and as soon as Abdul Karim finished his little talk I went out and explored the compound. What I found was revealing in more ways than one.

My first discovery came almost as soon as I exited the front door and looked to my right. Next to the building, about fifty meters away, was a long line of huge waste gas and secondary chemical storage spheres, with pipes running to the processing plant. Although the spheres had been plainly visible, I hadn't noticed them before. Now I took them in fully and realized at once their import. In the compound we had just left, we were out of danger unless the compound was specifically attacked. But here? Here we were in deep trouble. If these spheres were bombed, no one in our building would have a chance. There wouldn't even be rubble left, much less any grease spot remains of us. The bomb shelter outside the door might protect us from near misses if the bombs just exploded on the ground, but if the tanks went up, forget about it. I remember thinking, this is not good, as I walked toward the tanks following the road that traced the fence.

The perimeter fence was a good mile long, if not more. It took about twenty minutes to walk it at a fast pace. In places it took me under suspended pipelines that were connected to pipes outside the perimeter fence. The pipelines formed ready-made paths over the wire—useful in an escape. The perimeter road also passed by several sheds and a dump for discarded equipment and spools of industrial cable. For the most part, though, it skirted the large complex that it encompassed, and I could look in at the tall towers, which were used for petroleum separation and stabilization. A maze of pipes and cylindrical containers rose several stories high. The actual industrial plant was about six hundred by five hundred meters and was criss-crossed by roads that led from the perimeter to the interior of the plant. A smaller tank farm near the western side of the perimeter faced the housing complex that we had just been moved from. It had three conventional oil tanks. All of the conventional oil tanks on the compound had ladders leading up their side, and the Iraqis didn't seem to mind if we climbed them. Later the tanks would serve as a good vantage point from which to gain information about the surrounding countryside and plant defenses. Past the oil tanks on the western side was another office building and a fire department. The fire department had three modern-looking fire-suppression vehicles, and firemen were always on duty. (I was later able to count a shift of about fifteen.) Next to the fire department was another small storage building, then the main entrance and our own building: the office block cum hostage hotel. Our mess hall was a large, prefabricated building right outside the gate.

Interspersed throughout the facility were bomb shelters dug into the ground with an entrance at both ends and a cement roof. The shelters looked professionally done, but I knew that they were just a placebo for some of the workers. If those liquified natural gas (LNG) tanks went up, the overpressure of the explosion would kill us all before we even had a chance to burn. We would simply vaporize. Still, we could see that the Iraqis had done what they could to minimize the risk. Earthen blast walls about fifteen feet high and five feet thick surrounded the tanks and other critical facilities, and there were alert system speakers all over the complex. With Kirkuk being fairly close to Iran, I felt sure that this facility had seen a few air raids during the Iran-Iraq war. (Later this was confirmed when I found several light poles and other pieces of industrial equipment in the disposal yard that had obviously been punctured by 20mm cannon fire and shrapnel.)

After my initial look inside the fence, I started looking outside it. What I saw was not encouraging. Unlike our previous compound, there were other facilities beyond the fence in two directions: a communications installation of some sort and an annex to the separation plant. They were both within two hundred meters of the fence, so even if I got through on those two sides, I would almost immediately have to get by another group of Iraqis without attracting attention. That wasn't all. The separation plant we were in had a much larger number of guard posts around it than did the refinery at Baiji. Towers or guardhouses were spaced every three hundred meters or so around the perimeter. From what I could see (and later confirmed), they were all manned. The ground around the plant was flat and, worse, light tan in color. Unless I escaped during a low moon phase, someone my size would be easy to see in the moonlight. Not good. Worse was the presence of several antiaircraft positions right outside the perimeter, on the northern and southern sides of the compound. Determining their relief timings and activities was an essential addition to my observations.

We could pretty much write off a rescue as well (assuming that anyone would even try such a thing). The fact that the communications facility had about five large antennas (more than three hundred feet tall) in immediate proximity to the refinery limited helicopter approaches. The presence of numerous automatic antiaircraft cannon on the perimeter wouldn't make it easier either. Also, the number of light posts and buildings on the compound itself made for a tricky landing site for a single ship. I had no doubt that any of the helicopter pilots I knew could do it—in the daytime with no one shooting at them. I was also sure that if hostilities commenced, and a hostage group looked retrievable, some effort would be made to get them out. But here, in this place? Forget about it. It was too far into Iraq and too complex a tactical problem, given everything else that would be going on. The hostages who would be rescued (if any were) would be low-hanging fruit that happened to be close to the border in places such as Al Qaim or Basra.

Given this, I almost decided not to put up my satellite sign. I certainly didn't want anyone risking a mission to come and get us out of here this deep into Iraq. But, as I said before, it pays to be consistent. I ultimately decided to put up the signs when I got the chance. The only question in this huge place was, where? I walked several laps before it got dark, then went back into the building full of thoughts. This location presented many new difficulties. We had definitely hit a chute on the hostage game of Chutes and Ladders, but I wasn't about to let myself go into a slough of despond. There was far too much to do.

We spent the next week exploring the place in detail. Abdul Karim was as good as his word, and we were pretty much left alone. I found several places in the fence that were in poor repair that a person could shinny through. I made another break in the fence when no one was looking. Two of the exits I banded back in place with bits of chicken wire I had found. No point in leaving the fence open for someone to see and fix. When the time came, one good kick and we'd be through. We also helped some of the Iraqi workers move a large spool of industrial wire to the scrap yard and place it next to the fence. They thanked us for our efforts, and we had a ready-made hop, skip, and jump over the fence. The workers treated us as though we were slightly addled relatives. The sight of us walking bare chested around the compound caused the workers great amusement at first. Soon they got used to us and we weren't even a novelty anymore.

Abdul Karim set up some sports equipment for us—a volleyball net and badminton net—but for the most part we just walked and worked out with the barbell. We got good TV reception, and we always crowded in whenever the news program's music (performed by the Iraqi men's moaning chorus) came on. For doses of reality we continued to listen to our shortwave radio. Oddly enough the Iraqis knew of its presence but no one appeared to mind. After a while we didn't even hide it.

The news at this stage was full of further UN resolutions and tightening embargoes. Saddam Hussein and Terek Aziz were attempting to link the resolution of the Gulf crisis with the settlement of the Arab-Israeli dispute, but no one was buying it. It made for great propaganda in the Iraqi news, though, and the TV carried footage showing Palestinians clashing with Israelis as part of general strikes in support of Iraq. King Hussein of Jordan was trying to distance himself from Saddam Hussein but was in a deep hole because of his previous support. Foreigners continued to leave Iraq and Kuwait. One of them (a British subject of Indian extraction) complained bitterly to the BBC about having to wait at the Rutbah border crossing for two days. The British NCOs' comments upon hearing this were scathing: "Goddamn chapatti wallah, curry-gobbling bastard! They ought to send his arse here! Oi, he's British arright. Bleed'in Indians." I couldn't help but laugh. We heard the name Yevgeny Primakov for the first time. And the American forces continued to flow in.

The Iraqis drove us to a pool about a week after we took up residence in the refinery. The pool was located in a recreation complex near another refinery in the vicinity. The clubhouse in the complex had seating for more than a thousand, and big murals of the Roc and other tales from the *Arabian Nights* were painted on the walls. After the dusty refinery, the pool was welcome, and I swam laps while the others dove off the high platforms like happy kids. There were no cameras around, and it seemed at first that this was yet another of Abdul Karim's attempts to be nice. One of the French guys lost his wedding ring in the deep end of the pool and we spent some time looking for it. I finally found it for him and we all prepared to leave refreshed and well pleased with ourselves.

Unfortunately, it wasn't that simple. Our minders told us that a party was being thrown in our honor and we would be obliged to stay. This had my antenna go up immediately. I could see it now, us all over guest news. I told everyone not to make any statements and to avoid having his picture taken if possible. If cameras could not be avoided, I suggested doing something crude such as making obscene hand gestures or picking your nose.

It turned out to be a very weird party. All the oil workers and their families had been told to show up for this. They were happy for the free food but were clearly ill at ease with us and the Secret Service minders. For our part, the presence of the women and small children kept us from being too crude or confrontational. It didn't seem appropriate to be openly argumentative. The families didn't have any choice about being there either. The cameramen hovered around us, but I don't think they got any good photos. Every time I caught one of them looking at me, I picked my nose or scratched my privates. To my knowledge, at least, we never showed up on "Guest News."

The food was good and the beer wasn't bad either. A few of the Iraqis came to talk to me, and I told them that they all seemed like very nice people and they needed to evacuate the city before it was bombed. They paled at this but spouted the party line about how they would face us down. I shook my head sadly, feigning drunken sincerity. "You guys need to get your families away before it's too late." I gestured toward the city and the refinery with a sweep of my hands. "All of this will be in flames once we start bombing you, such a waste. You really must tell Saddam to release us and return Kuwait. It's the only way you can avoid destruction." Never pass up a chance to create doubts in your captors' minds. I'm sure we were quite a downer.

Shortly after the pool party I managed to find and steal enough paint to put up a good satellite sign. I noticed some buckets of it put out to do a painting job on one of the main pipes in the refinery, and as quick as you please I had filled both of my large shampoo bottles with new black paint. Actually, painting the sign on our roof would not be as easy as in the previous compound. Workers always seemed to be around, and the guardhouse was right down the road less than a hundred meters from our building. In addition, the roving guards on the perimeter could see me. The project was always well lit up. So we would have to keep watch in order to choose the right time. Then we would need lookouts to keep watch while I was on the roof. I had my brush and my two shampoo squeeze containers of paint, so I was all set. I would throw them onto the roof before I climbed up. I could only hope that the surface would, in fact, take and contrast paint. I had not been able to find a vantage point upon which to climb and look down on the roof, so I could only guess its color and surface material. I was betting that it would be a light cement color and porous but I wasn't sure. I remember thinking that it would be just my luck if the roof were black. Then I would have to find some chalk, because light-colored paint did not seem readily available. But there was no point in delaying any longer. If the roof were black, I would have to try again later. You can "what if?" these things to death.

Dave Freeman said he would help me get onto the roof. He could bench-press a small cow, so supporting me as I scrambled for purchase would not be a problem. We would be the only culprits caught if we were apprehended in the ascent onto the roof, a fact that Dave accepted with one of the usual monosyllabic grunts that were his manner when he was serious about something. After he got me up, he would slip back inside the building and ensure that the door was left open. I could get down by myself (gravity is a wonderful thing), and landing in the dirt next to the building shouldn't make much noise. The rest of the guys would take lookout positions in the foyer outside the minders' rooms and in various windows, ready to pass the word of dangerous movement on the part of our unwitting captors. We were ready. All that remained now was to wait for the right time.

Most of us had to make it look like another normal night, so after we turned in, the last of the minders went to bed. A little after midnight the guards had just walked by on the outside fence, and no one was outside the guardhouse. A quick perusal of the plant showed no one in evidence outside the back door. Now was the time. Dave and I slipped out the back door. I threw the shampoo bottles and the brush onto the roof. The brush landed softly, but the shampoo bottles landed with a pair of thuds that made us wince. Dave cupped his hands for me to step in, and I was up and grasping for the top of the building. Dave was straining to lift me and cursing under his breath. "Ooof! Bloody American orificers weigh a fuggin' ton. It's fat you are, mate," or words to that effect. I almost started laughing as I got my hands over the sill of the roof and began to pull myself up. I remembered to stay low as I came over the sill. I got one leg up, then slid over the sill onto the roof like an octopus. Below me I could hear Dave scurry into the building. I lay there for about five minutes listening for any sounds of alarm or unusual movements, but there were none. So far so good.

The roof could not have been better for our purposes. The actual sill that ran along the edge of the buildings was about eighteen inches above the roof itself. As long as I didn't stick my big butt up while crawling, no one would see me unless they were looking at the roof from above. The other good news was that the roof was light gray concrete. It would take paint very nicely. There was a lot of dust on the roof but no signs that anyone had been on it anytime recently. No doubt about it, we were in business.

I retrieved my paintbrush and bottles from where they had landed. The next quandary I faced was how big to make the letters. Nothing would be more embarrassing than running out of paint halfway through the message. I had originally thought to make the letters two body lengths long. But seeing how the concrete let the paint spread only so far, I realized that I would have to make my letters smaller. I settled on one body length plus an outstretched arm. This would make a letter six and a half to seven feet long. I lay on my side and started to paint as straight a line as possible on the first character.

Try to paint a big sign lying down. It's not as easy as you might think. I shifted and reached around a lot to get the letters properly spaced. I had to crawl between letters as the words were formed. In doing so I had to be careful not to smear any of the letters I had already painted. I crawled down the roof and began my second row. The paint started to run out, so I made smaller letters (about six feet, or one body length).

It was a hot night and the sweat was streaming off me as I worked. The dust from the roof covered my clothes, and after about ten minutes I was pig dirty. Occasionally I stopped to listen to people walking by or the guards on the fence. I would have to keep an eye out when I was done. But my biggest focus now was to finish the sign.

Lying on the roof in the moonlight, squeezing paint out of a shampoo bottle, then spreading it as thin as I dared to make it last, I was acutely aware of my surroundings, but I was not agitated. For all the danger of being caught, I didn't feel an adrenaline rush. The whole thing took on a workmanlike aspect. Finally I was done, and I crawled along the edge of the building to where I had ascended. I looked back along the letters I had painted and could clearly make them out in the moonlight:

16 HOSTAGES HERE
STANTON

Not a bad night's work. Now for the tricky part—getting down. I was not in communication with the lookouts, and they had no way of warning me even if they saw someone coming. I would have to judge my own timing for descent. Peering over the ledge was nerve racking, but I had to do it to see whether anyone was around. I also had to wait for the roving guards to go past on the fence, but they weren't looking at the building. I probably could have jumped off the top of it onto a piano unnoticed for all that they were paying attention. But I waited for a few minutes anyway, then looked again to make sure no one could see me. I dropped the brush and the shampoo bottles onto the ground beside the building, then did my full body octopus slide over again. There was no one there to support me as I fell heavily into the dirt with a muffled, teeth-rattling thud. I was a little dazed, but I hid the painting materials behind a loose cinder block on the side of the building, then quickly made my way through the door that Dave Freeman held open.

I returned to my room and stripped, then showered, washed my dirty clothes at the same time, and hung them on the window to dry. Everyone who was up smiled and made little thumbs-up gestures to me, then we all went to bed. Chuck Tinch grinned and told me "good job" as I lay down on my bed. Suddenly I was too excited to sleep and worried that some Iraqi would see the sign. I drove away those thoughts as best I could. For better or worse, the sign was done. What good it would do I didn't know, but at least I had done something. I went to sleep feeling content.

Listening to the BBC one day in late September, I was surprised to hear that the station was beginning a program of allowing hostages' families to send voice messages over the radio to people being held in Iraq. This quickly got all of our interest because we'd had no contact from our families. We were all excited and upbeat about this development and wondered whether our families would get in on this action. As it turned out, we didn't have long to wait. Soon the Brits started hearing from their families. The messages were all the same at first. Basically "we love you. We're all okay here. Take care of yourself." Later in our captivity the messages became more detailed and personal, talking about kid's schools and things that had happened to family members. The looks on my friends' faces as they heard their families were bittersweet—relief that everyone was okay, and sorrow because they were still captive. Listening for the radio messages became a staple of our daily activities.

I didn't expect to hear from my folks over the BBC, so I was surprised one afternoon when John McCollah said he had heard a message for me from my father. We waited until the repeat of the Gulf link program four hours later. Sure enough, my father's deep, raspy voice was assuring me that my mom, sister, and Donna were okay and cautioning me to take care of myself. At the end he said, "Your advancement is effective 1 September." This meant I had actually been promoted to major and was now getting paid as an O4 as opposed to just wearing the rank. About three hundred extra dollars a month. Fat lot of good it would do me here. Dad sounded his normal, irascible self, and I knew that he would take care of my mom and sister, who must both have been worried sick.

Emotionally, hearing from my family was a double-edged sword. It was great to hear Dad, but in truth I had put them in the back of my mind. Now the thought of all they must be going through came home to me and I was really depressed. I wished I could tell them not to worry, but there was no way of getting messages out now that we had left Baiji. It was just another thing to deal with, and I forced myself to return to the matters at hand.

About a week or so after the BBC started Gulf link, the VOA began its own message service and I got messages over that as well. As in other places, the news played a large role in each day. We watched Iraqi news for its propaganda and listened to the BBC or VOA for a more objective view. While waiting for the news to come on, we played backgammon with one another or the minders (one of whom was always in the TV room). Backgammon is a popular game on the Arabian peninsula and in many ways is the perfect metaphor for being a hostage. It has a certain amount of strategy but ultimately is dependent upon a dice roll; therefore, the elements of chance and uncertainty reign supreme. I had never played it before, but it helped while away the time. Chess was another pastime for the group, but I had been a chess player in high school and I beat everyone so quickly that no one would play with me after a few days. It was fun to thrash the Iraqi minders, though. One of life's little victories.

Soon after we got to the Jambur and Al Hassan project, Jean Pierre started holding French lessons for anyone who wanted them. He did this to give himself something to do and to help the rest of us. Reg and Mike, the two Royal Air Force sergeants, participated, as did Schochi Hasegawa and Toshio. They usually spent two hours, between about 10 A.M. and lunch, going over their lessons, with Jean Pierre patiently explaining, *"Nous avons, vous avez, tous avec"* to his charges. I tried it for a couple of days but found that I couldn't concentrate on such matters and begged out as politely as I could. The Brits, however, got pretty good at French, especially Reg, who could *parlez vous très bien* by the time December rolled around. Although it wasn't in me to participate, I heartily approved of Jean Pierre's efforts. Anything that passed time constructively and made the days go by more easily was helpful.

If Jean Pierre was the professorial type, Etienne Boussineau was the practical joker. Etienne had clearly been a mischievous kid in high school. He was a senior steward, one step below Jean Pierre in rank (they let us know this. Very hierarchical those Air France guys) and clearly a troublemaker in the best sense of the word. He was pleasantly defiant of the Iraqis, and his battle cry was *"Vive le Resistance."* His favorite trick was taking down the large picture of Saddam Hussein from the foyer of the office building and hiding it. This drove the Iraqis crazy, and they threatened to keep us inside until we returned the picture. We would tell them it was in one of the stalls of the latrine and they would get mad and hang it back up, threatening all kinds of retribution for this display of apostasy toward their saint. A few days later the picture would be gone again, only to be found in the bushes outside the building.

Etienne's other great coup was in casting aspersions on the minders' personal hygiene. He would sit down next to Abdullah or Khalid, then make a subtle show of having smelled something unpleasant. He would then look at the minder and say, "My friend, you smell bad. Have you showered this week at all? You really do stink." The expression he carried this off with was so absolutely Gaulic and snobbish that it was all that we could do to keep from laughing and giving away the joke. The expression on the Iraqi's face when he realized what Etienne was saying was priceless. Here was this member of the Gestapo, a group that everyone in the country lived in fear of, and this French guy was informing him that he was "ripe." What was worse, the minder couldn't do anything about it.

By this time in our captivity it was clear to us that the minders had strict orders to treat us with kid gloves. The fact that we had suffered no repercussions whatsoever for the Chuck Tinch incident in Baiji was our first clue. That they generally let us walk around inside the compounds and did their best to feed us also reinforced that we were in a sort of special protected status even though we were prisoners. We could tell that the minders were uncomfortable with this. They were clearly used to more hands-on and up-close-and-personal attention with their captives. Now they had instructions to treat us as though we were made of porcelain, and they didn't know how to handle it. Especially when one of them would practice his "intimidating" looks on us and we would make fun of him. A show of guns didn't help either. The Brits would tell them that their weapons needed cleaning. I would mention that I could buy the same pistol in the United States for less than a hundred dollars. The French would make snide comments about penis envy.

Ultimately, the minders seemed to give up. They couldn't just leave us alone entirely, because it was their job to keep an eye on us. But if they tried to intimidate us, we just laughed at them. Seeing that this was no use, they ended up just watching TV or playing backgammon or chess with us. Mohammed, the older one, was the best backgammon player; I beat him only once. Khalid was too impetuous, and I could usually beat him by playing a conservative game. I would work on beating them at anything that required brains. Not that it changed the situation, but it gave me a lift and established a certain intellectual ascendancy. (Or sumthin.)

10

If the minders had given up trying to intimidate us, the Iraqi government hadn't. A few days after the pool party, a news crew with some Ministry of the Interior people (Gestapo) came by and called us together. They wanted us to do spots on "Guest News" giving our views on the situation. In other words, they were asking us to do the same thing we had seen the British sergeant do a few weeks back. There had been others on the news since the Brit, and I had half wondered when it would be our turn to be "interviewed." I already had my responses ready. I told them that no one in the group would give an interview to them and we had no desire to go on Iraqi television.

They looked away from me to the others in the group who were there, but all of them shook their heads and said "no." The Iraqis made the mistake of asking Dave Freeman directly. His reply was frosty in its full English sergeant major's dignity. When they pressed him, his face clouded and he said, "Piss off, you, we're not talking." The Iraqis were taken aback and looked confusedly at our minders, who shrugged. In truth, I think the minders were enjoying the discomfiture of these big wheels from Baghdad.

The news crew and the Ministry of the Interior people didn't know what to make of this. Apparently this was the first case of outright, blatant refusal they had run into. They asked Abdul Karim to convince us to cooperate, but we were adamant in our refusal. We were much more polite to Abdul Karim because we respected him and could see that he was trying to do his best in circumstances he couldn't control. But it was no-go. No interviews.

The powerlessness of their position caused the news crew to suggest a compromise. We wouldn't have to do interviews at all. They would just take pictures of us walking around and living our comfortable hostage life. They said it would show our families that we were being well treated.

I wasn't having any of this. There was no way I would allow them to use us for propaganda purposes. Having been ambushed at the pool party was bad enough. I turned to my fellow captives and told them to go to their rooms, close the door, and remain there until the camera people left. My fellows looked at me for a second, then started shuffling toward the door. Then Dave Freeman spoke up, "No, no, Marty. Wait! Let's take off all our clothes!"

The sheer brilliance of this idea hit me in a millisecond. Arabs cannot handle public nudity. You will never see Arab women at a swimming pool with anyone of a different gender. Arab men, as has been pointed out, never walk around bare chested, even in the worst heat. The presence of sixteen pasty, pale streakers on the refinery site would be, to say the least, disruptive. And the Iraqis could never put it on TV. I immediately picked up on the idea. "Right, you guys," I said. "Get those cameras out of here or we're all going to walk around naked." My fellows started unbuckling their belts and unbuttoning their shirts. The Iraqis stared wide eyed. Abdul Karim stammered, "You must not do this! You must not do this! Stop!" The camera crew looked aghast. I repeated, "Get the camera out of here!" Abdul Karim said something in Arabic to the Ministry of the Interior people and the camera crew, and they picked up their gear and moved to the door. The Ministry of the Interior people were clearly furious. One of them turned and said to us, "You are bad men. You are very bad men!" and then left, pursued by our jeers. The TV crew left, never to return. We all grinned at one another and at Abdul Karim, who slowly smiled and shook his head. It was a small but satisfying victory. I hoped the Gestapo would always be this powerless.

Soon after our near bare-assed triumph over the forces of evil, a new member was added to our group, a German named Rolf Wachter. Rolf had been an elevator salesman who had managed to avoid capture in Kuwait for some weeks, in spite of the fact that he didn't speak any Arabic or English. The other Germans were particularly glad to see him, although the stories he told made them furious at their ambassador in Kuwait. Apparently, the man had refused to take in German nationals on the German embassy grounds (that was the story anyway), and this set off the Germans on a new round of cursing their diplomatic corps. I remember thinking that there would be a lot of unhappy diplomats in Germany and England if any of us were actually released. Rolf's evasion was the product of his staying in the basement of a large apartment building and manipulating the elevator so that it would not go to the basement except on his command. He had a mechanic's turn of mind and, as such, was a valuable addition to our group.

One of the benefits of us fellows living in the same building for the first time was that I discovered things about some of them that I hadn't known before. Sho Hasegawa was an accomplished flute player and occasionally treated us to little concerts. He would sometimes go outside and find a shady spot on the refinery site and play Mozart or Chopin. We would be walking around the fence and suddenly hear flute music. Sho was also an accomplished sketch artist and made drawings for many of the people in the group.

Sho was also something of a saboteur. I found this out one day when we were walking the fence and he looked at me and grinned. He stepped into a maze of pipes and valves and turned one all the way open. He came back to me and said, "In about ten minutes we should hear an alarm." Sure enough, about ten minutes later a foghornlike alarm went off and Iraqi workers started running everywhere. Sho looked at me and giggled.

Sho wasn't the only saboteur. I saw one of the Frenchmen breaking suspended light bulbs with rocks. Others of us stole tools and threw them into oil sumps. I was of two minds about this. Granted it was satisfying and gave a feeling of resistance, but in the larger context of our captivity it was somewhat stupid. If the Iraqis caught on to the fact that we were doing it, they might restrict our movements. This would have a negative effect on our escape preparations and our ability to collect intelligence information on the outside world. I passed the word to knock off sabotage and concentrate on just observing our surroundings. It was difficult not to strike back, but I couldn't take a chance that our movements would be restricted.

Around the second week of October we experienced a large wind- and dust storm that lasted several days. We felt as though we were being sandblasted when we tried to walk the perimeter fence. So I spent a couple of boring days staying mainly indoors and was grateful when the winds abated. Everywhere on the compound the Iraqis were cleaning filters and generally recovering from the dust inundation. This led to one of the worst scares of my captivity, because they had to repair the roof of our building. As we came out of the mess hall, Ingo Fruedenberg poked me in the ribs and pointed up. My stomach turned over as I saw a work crew of Iraqis replacing ventilation fixtures on the front part of the office-building roof. Although they were not actually standing on the sign, it was difficult to believe that they couldn't see it. Hypnotized, I watched the workmen as they moved around on the roof. I waited for one of them to exclaim and call his fellows over. After about a minute I realized that standing and staring at the workmen would do more harm than good, so I forced myself to go inside our office building. I could hear them walking around on the front part of the roof. I mentally composed myself and prepared to be taken away. I would tell the Iraqis that the act was mine alone and I had no help. That was the least I owed to Dave Freeman and the rest of them. I thought of all the heroes of fiction I had read about—men who met situations such as this with aplomb. I felt like a trapped rat.

No word from the roof yet, just working sounds and normal voices. I strained to hear but couldn't understand most of the Arabic anyway. Maybe they had seen the sign first thing and had already told our minders before we even came out of the mess hall. Maybe our minders were calling and asking for orders. (They wouldn't do anything on their own initiative, of that I was certain.) I walked by their rooms and peeked in. There were only two of them; one was sleeping and the other was reading a magazine and didn't see me. Perplexed, I went back to my room.

After about an hour I couldn't take the inactivity anymore and went out for my usual afternoon walk. The last thing I wanted was to do something that seemed out of the ordinary. I walked around the compound about a dozen times. Each time that I came to where I could observe our office building, I expected to see workers gathered around my sign exclaiming and calling the guards, but nothing like that happened. Finally on about lap eight, as I rounded the corner, I saw the workers coming off the roof carrying their toolboxes and the ventilator parts they had replaced. They waved at me as I walked by—just another crazy American walking the fence. I grimly finished my walk and came back just before supper, as I always did. Most of the guys were in the TV room playing games or watching television. John McCollah was playing backgammon with Khalid the dick. I looked at John enquiringly, but he just smiled and said hello. I asked Chuck whether there had been any commotion about the roof; he said no. Unbelievably, the whole day had passed without anyone saying anything. As far as any of us knew, no one on the roof had told the guards or the minders about my satellite sign.

This cheered me up considerably but then got me to thinking. Something must have happened to the sign. I couldn't conceive of anything so big and contrasted as that being missed by even a casual observer. I realized I would have to go up again and have a look. Later that night, with the assistance of the usual suspects, I did. I took only a brief glance over the lip of the sill. I could barely make out the letters; they were covered with dust and sand from the big storm. The same thing that had caused the mechanics to change the filters in the ventilators had covered my sign! It's always some goddamn thing or other. I dropped back down and told my friends that the sign would have to be repainted, but first we would need more paint.

Finding paint was harder than I imagined, because the open storage place where I had found the first paint was now locked. Apparently Abdul Karim was a more efficient plant manager than those where we had been kept previously. I finally got a mixture of tar and sump oil that had paintlike qualities and didn't fade after a few days. Squeezing it into the shampoo bottles was messy, and I had to be careful not to be seen before I could scrub away the spills. I also had to get the stiff paint out of the bristles of the brush; I used a wire comb and my fingernails. The results of my efforts weren't perfect but they would serve. After waiting a couple of nights to make sure that no more work would be done on the roof, I went up and started painting again. The dust on the original letters was thick, and I had to carefully trace over them. The oil and tar mixed well with the dried paint, and after half an hour of crawling around on the roof I had made the sign as good as new. Pleased with myself I got careless and swung onto the sill without looking, and almost got caught.

Once again it was a dumb, innocent thing that almost got me: a worker with a clipboard walking along the line of waste gas tanks and taking night readings. I saw him just as I was about to slide off the roof. I froze. As soon as I saw his head turn away from the building, I dropped back behind the sill as fast as I could. He hadn't seen me, but had I come all the way over and dropped to the ground, there was no way he would not have noticed me. I lay on the roof for another half an hour peeking around and making sure that no one was near, then I was over in a trice. Paint equipment returned to its hiding place and me to the bathroom to clean up. That oil worker had scared the bejesus out of me. I chided myself for being so careless.

Once again the lesson of being a prisoner was reinforced. Never ever, *ever* let your guard down.

Early in October, Germany was formally reunified, and the Germans among us asked Abdul Karim for some beer to celebrate. Not surprisingly he gave it to us and we had a Germany "reunification" party. I was surprised at how emotional Manfred, Ingo, and Herbert got about it. Rolf was more taciturn, but we could see that he was pleased. The others got sloppy drunk and quite maudlin. *"Deutschland Uber Alles"* was sung numerous times as well as many other German songs. Ingo especially got fired-up drunk. He rang in the reunited Germany by beating on a metal trash can lid until it was a question of who was going to kill him first, the minders or us. Finally Dave and John McCollah wrestled him into bed, and the remainder of German unification night (or morning by then) passed without incident. I was happy for my German friends. It was obvious they were very proud of being one country again. They all expressed hopes that now they could contribute forces to the coalition. It was a nifty thought: the Afrika Korps, take two. Manfred was especially pleased with the concept.

Other than the bright spot of German reunification, the world news during the first two weeks of October continued to be grim. Some Israeli lunatics who called themselves the Temple Mount Faithful gunned down a large number of Palestinians in Jerusalem without any provocation, and the Arab world reacted with disgust and horror. Saddam Hussein made the most of it, of course, and did his best to renew the call for "linkage" of the Gulf and the Arab-Israeli conflicts. Fortunately, saner heads in the Arab world prevailed. I could only wonder at our "friends" the Israelis. They weren't making this any easier for us. Various has-been western political figures such as Jesse Jackson and Edward Heath showed up with peace delegations and friendship groups during this period of time. They received a lot of coverage on the Iraqi news and helped contribute to the disinformation campaign being fed the Iraqi people. Each left with a handful of old, sick hostages after having given Saddam Hussein grist for his propaganda mill.

Watching Iraqi TV would have angered Mother Teresa; most of us found other pastimes. Our favorite one was walking the perimeter fence. This was useful for several reasons. First, the perimeter fence was long—more than two kilometers when you added up the lengths of each side. Walking it consumed time, and a prisoner has a lot of that. Second, it provided exercise. Spending four to five hours a day walking the fence meant being tired and sleeping well at night. Third, and probably most important, it got the guards used to seeing us by the fence. We could look for weaknesses and (if we were careful) create some. We could also get a good idea of what was outside the fence within our field of vision: where the guards were, and what posts were occupied when, and activities of the antiaircraft defenses. We could also monitor the frequency and type of traffic on the roads, aircraft overflights, and so forth. It also got us away from the minders, who, after the first few days, stopped trying to monitor our exercise periods. Walking was an activity that was conducive to thinking or daydreaming, and we could put ourselves on autopilot and go somewhere else for a time. Nowhere in my life has my "C student" ability to sit in class and daydream stood me in better stead than in captivity.

One day Schochi Hasegawa asked me for the picture of Donna that I kept in my wallet. Mystified, I gave it to him; he said he would return it in a day or so. He then disappeared back into his room. I was curious, but Sho was a sensible guy and I supposed he had his reasons, so I just went for a walk. Two days later all of us were in the TV room playing games or watching the awful Iraqi news in English when I noticed everyone glancing at me and smiling. As if on cue, Sho came in playing "Happy Birthday to you" on his flute and everyone was congratulating me. Sho then handed me two drawings, one a cartoon caricature of myself walking the perimeter fence and the other a pencil portrait of Donna made from my wallet photo. I was surprised and touched. I had forgotten that it was my birthday. How they found out I had no clue. I thanked Sho profusely and tacked up the portrait of Donna next to my bed.

We continued to watch the news for every scrap of televised information we could get. Occasionally the transparency of Iraqi propaganda was readily apparent. We were watching TV a couple of days after my birthday when the newscaster described large riots in London in opposition to the British government's "senseless and aggressive" policy against Iraq. The film clip of a protest came on: a few dozen no-minds chanting "no blood for oil" and other such drivel. Suddenly that clip transitioned into another one showing a huge riot. Thousands of struggling people, cars being turned over, policemen in riot gear whacking people, and tear gas all over the place. I sat up in my chair. Holy shit, I thought. This is serious. Everyone watched the clip in stunned silence. It was long, about forty-five seconds. The Brits watched it with particular interest. John mentioned that something was "not quite right" about the film footage. Dave and Mick also thought it looked strange. Just before it ended, Mick straightened up and said, "That's Arthur Scargill!" All the Brits suddenly burst out laughing. John explained that the film clip we had seen was from the coal miner's strike in the early 1980s and had been grafted onto the film clip of the little group of protesters we had seen earlier. Our minders were mystified at our laughter. We explained to them that the whole thing was a fraud, but they would have none of it. "Our news never lies," Mohammed told me.

It was sobering to realize that although the news clip was laughable to us, the Iraqis were taking it as the gospel truth. According to these newscasts, the will of the British and American people was already beginning to crack. Faced with Iraqi resolve, the Zionist American West was coming apart. Our minders, at least, believed it fully. Maybe the man in the street didn't, but he didn't have a vote. I wondered whether the protesters in Britain and the United States knew how much they were helping the Iraqi propaganda machine convince the Iraqi leadership of their own lies.

Not only was there a constant emphasis on TV about the difficulties and civil disturbances within coalition nations, this was played up in all newspapers. We were periodically given the English version of the Baghdad newspaper. Antiwar editorials from U.S. or British papers always made the news and were also translated into Arabic as further proof that the coalition was dissolving. I remember one letter from some malcontent named Alex (I won't give his last name; I'm cutting his kid some slack) that hysterically attacked President Bush and swore eternal enmity if Alex's Marine son were injured. Alex made the paper in two different editorials and became famous in Iraq. I'm surprised he wasn't asked to visit. I felt sorry for his kid. Can you imagine being forward deployed and having someone in your family write stuff like that? I thought about writing to Alex and offering to get him a place in our little hostage group. Seeing as he was so against the deployment of U.S. forces, what better way to protest this than to come and take Chuck Tinch's place? He could be a human shield and protect Iraq from the evil United States. We could have gotten Chuck to a hospital, and Alex could have made a statement. Unfortunately, no mail was getting out, so I just had to grimace when Khalid gleefully showed me Alex's editorial. I had to be content with pleasant thoughts of physically savaging Alex. For the first time, I began to understand how most Vietnam veterans felt about Jane Fonda.

To relieve the tension and boredom, we took to playing practical jokes on one another. John McCollah was the best at it with his good nature and wicked sense of humor. He caught a hedgehog and showed it to me. The British have an affinity for these little animals; Mick, Dave, and Reg inspected it in turn and pronounced it a large one. John explained to me that they were quite tasty. Seeing the disbelief on my face, he described how it could be cooked in coals, then the spines removed before eating. You have to wonder about the Brits sometimes.

John took the hedgehog and put it in Etienne Boussineau's bed. We were all sitting in Etienne and Phillipe's room talking and waiting for Etienne to notice the small bump moving under the covers. He almost sat on it and was oblivious to its struggle. He couldn't figure out what we were all grinning and giggling about until he noticed the lump. He threw off the covers, and the hedgehog was looking right up at him. I swear it was smiling. Etienne jumped about three feet in the air. *"Sacre merde!"* We collapsed into laughter. I guess you had to be there.

Dave Freeman took charge of signing for the cigarettes that the Iraqis would periodically bring. (After the Germany reunification incident, there was no more beer, but they brought two packs of cigarettes per man per day.) Once, Dave was not in the building and the Iraqis wanted one of us to take the daily ration. Unthinkingly I said I would do it. I took the cigarettes and put them on Dave's bed. He came back and counted and went marching straight down to our minders demanding the four packs of cigarettes we had been shorted. He then gave me a first sergeant's lecture about not letting the Iraqis gyp us out of our rations. It was no more than I deserved. At the end of it Dave grinned and shook his head. "Idle American git, I'll bet your supply sergeant loved you." I left it to him from then on. Never try to do a company sergeant major's work for him, even in captivity.

Most of our guards were wounded veterans of the Iran-Iraq war. Most were in their thirties or forties, and more than a few had noticeable limps. They were clearly not the sharpest troops in the world, or the most motivated. On the other hand, the guard mounts were pretty workmanlike, and they didn't sleep on post nearly as much as had the guards in the Baiji refinery or the power plant. For the most part they were not unfriendly, only distant. A few of them would attempt conversation but not many. The language gap combined with the natural gulf between a prisoner and a guard saw to that. There were a few characters, though, the most notable a guy named Muneef. He was in his early twenties and tall and thin, with the gawky stance of Ichabod Crane. One look at him in the guard formation was enough to peg him as a member of the awkward squad. He stood at attention with his rifle held like a broom and at a crooked angle. His shirttail was often out, his belt frequently missed loops, and his shoes were often untied. What was interesting was the reaction of his NCOs and the other Iraqi guards. They never tried to spot-correct him or reprimand him in an upbraiding manner. Whereas the sergeant would inspect everyone else in the guard mount, he just stopped in front of Muneef, shook his head, and continued to the next man. I realized that we had come in at the middle of this relationship and the officers and sergeants of the Iraqi guard force had long since written this guy off as immune to instruction. They treated him kindly, as sort of a mascot, and after a few contacts with him it was clear that he was not all there in the head.

We fascinated him, though, and he tagged along with us on our walks whenever he was put on roving patrol around the perimeter. This could have been annoying, but it was only about every fourth day so it wasn't too bad. At first I was suspicious that Muneef was just another attempt to plant a close observer within our group, but after spending a few days watching him I dismissed that thought. No one is that good an actor. He wanted badly to learn English, which was ambitious of him because he couldn't make himself understood in Arabic very well. Muneef was a Kurd and spoke some hill-dialect Arabic; on more than one occasion I saw one of the guards ask another, "What did he say?" But Muneef would try. He never got beyond the "Hello, how are you?" stage except for one glorious occasion that I relate later.

We could see that he was one of Saddam's 100,000 (an Iraqi version of Gomer Pyle), though, because he was incapable of performing even the simplest soldier task. He couldn't wear the uniform; the weapon he carried was always dirty; and he didn't understand his role in relation to us. This last lapse came home to me one afternoon when Muneef was walking beside me as I did my laps of the perimeter fence. He was strolling along, chattering happily to me in a language that only he understood, when he noticed that his shoes were untied. Why exactly he noticed it then, I have no idea; his shoes had been untied all day. Making a "tsk-tsk" sound, he bent down to tie them. His rifle clanged against his head as he tried to balance it against his shoulder. Annoyed, he handed me the weapon as he struggled to tie his shoes.

Now, this was not my golden opportunity. First off, it was about two in the afternoon on a glorious October day at the natural gas plant, so I would still have had to fight my way past the guards. Second, Muneef as a hostage was probably of less value than a barnyard animal. Last, the weapon itself was rusty and dirty beyond measure. I suspected that the sergeant of the guard (if he had any brains and was safety conscious) had removed the firing pin without Muneef's knowledge. He never cleaned his rifle, so he would never know. Muneef was the kind of troop that had "accidental discharge" written all over him.

I could see, though, as Muneef struggled for almost a minute to tie his shoes, that he had no idea what he had done. I thought about the TV show *Hogan's Heroes* and how no one would believe me if I mentioned this. So I returned Muneef's rifle when he was finally done tying his shoes. He thanked me in his pidgin Arabic and we resumed our walk. I couldn't resist saying to him, though, "This whole prisoner-guard thing is just over your head, isn't it, Muneef?" He smiled at me and said *"n'aam"* (yes), which was his answer to everything I said that he didn't understand. So we kept walking, me piling up the laps and Muneef following me like a happy, confused puppy, jabbering away with fine abandon. There were worse ways to spend the day.

I continued to get messages over the radio, and one day in late October I got a message from Donna that I will remember as long as I live. I was sitting by the radio listening to everyone's messages and wondering whether there would be any for me on this program. All of a sudden I heard Donna's beautiful voice. She wasn't on long, but what she said changed my life: "Martin, this is Donna. I miss you and hope you are all right. I've thought about it and I will marry you. Please take care of yourself and hurry home to me. All my love, Donna."

I sat stunned. The sheer joy of her words flooded through me like a strong, intoxicating drug. I almost leapt up and shouted for the absolute happiness I felt. My life has had its share of good moments, but sitting there in that dirty, little TV room and realizing in full what I had just heard over the radio will always be one of my fondest recollections. Donna would marry me. I was going to get married—as soon as I got out of captivity. But even that reality couldn't entirely quench my happiness. I went for a walk and thought of Donna.

It was during this period that I discovered the common bond between Kiyoshi Odagane (Doug) and me. We both loved movies. He was an inexhaustible fountain of knowledge about the movies and should have gone on *Jeopardy* or some other game show. I asked him who his favorite actress was and he replied without hesitation, "Audrey Hepburn." He then proceeded to wax enthusiastic about her. This intrigued and amused me. Here I was, a prisoner in Iraq, spending hours walking the fence with a little Japanese movie buff who had a *thang* for Audrey Hepburn. Crazy. So I asked him what Audrey Hepburn movies he had seen. Of course, he had seen them all, but his favorite was *My Fair Lady* and to my amazement he started to sing "I Could Have Danced All Night" as we were walking.

Now, it's not the kind of thing an infantry officer would readily confess, but I had always liked the movie *My Fair Lady* and I knew the words to most of the songs myself. To Doug's delight, I joined in on the second verse of "I Could Have Danced All Night" and we both sang the song together walking along the fence. We were so successful at that, we immediately launched into "Ascot Opening Day," with Doug stumbling along in his heavily accented English, "Evvy dook an erl an peeer iss here... evvy won who shood be here iss here . . ." and I trying to sing along with him between fits of laughter. We went through most of the songs that day and repeated our performance on several other occasions. We got into singing alternate lines, with one of us picking up where the other left off. Once, Muneef walked around with us and we halfway managed to teach him some words from "Wouldn't It Be Loverly," which he then joined us in singing. We must have presented a strange sight: a tall American, a short Japanese, and a gangly Iraqi walking along the fence singing songs from a Lerner and Loewe musical. A Kodak moment any way you look at it.

All during this time I continued with my preparations to escape. I had picked up enough water bottles and blankets and now it was time to seriously start preparing my equipment. I started by modifying my suit bag into a rucksack. I found a discarded pair of blue jeans in a rubbish pile and cut two large sections from the one good leg (the other was covered with dried paint) and used these to make the straps for my rucksack. To make a strap I first doubled over the material and sewed it together. Then I sewed the straps to my suit bag so that the large, outside pocket was facing my back and the two smaller pockets were facing out. I figured that putting blankets or clothing in the large pocket would act as padding to keep the rucksack from chafing my back. Food and water I could keep in the smaller pockets that faced out so they would be easily available on the march. Additional food, water, and clothing could go inside the bag. My seamstress work was poor at first. I didn't appreciate how much sewing had to go into something before it could bear weight. I tested it several times before I finally got it right. Sitting there sewing my rucksack (and jabbing myself repeatedly) I was surprised at the amount of time such a simple task took and the attention it required. I would not have made a very good pioneer. The rucksack took me a couple of days to finish. I didn't want to drop out of sight during this time, so I forced myself to continue my regime of walking for hours and playing a few games of backgammon. I hoped that during the time I was gone from the crowd, people thought I was just reading.

My next step was to make a camouflage cover and blanket. I made a large bedroll by sewing together a sheet and both of the orange blankets I had stolen. The sheet I could quickly turn brown with dirt when the time came. I wanted the bright international orange of the blankets quickly available to use as signaling panels. A dual-use item would work out well to save space and weight. I also obtained a large piece of plastic sheeting to make into a rain cape.

I figured it would be getting cold soon so I had better make some gloves as well. This became my next project. I made a pair of what looked like oven mitts out of a sheet, a blanket, and a towel, first making a large outline of my hand, then cutting from the fabric. The end product fit my hand roughly and had an opposable thumb. With all the practice I'd had making the other items, I was actually getting pretty good at sewing. Both of the mittens looked fairly uniform. I was very pleased with myself when I finally slipped them on and could actually pick things up.

In addition to sewing, I continued to accrue other escape gear. I was always on the lookout for anything that could be used for a water container that did not leak. I also continued to add to my store of tools, and on one notable occasion found four hacksaw blades, which I quickly secreted in my stash. My biggest concern was carrying enough food to allow me to walk for a week without having to forage. I started saving bread, but it didn't store well and after a week was too moldy to eat. At any given time I had only three to four days' supply on hand that was edible. Water I could get from streams, I was sure.

I selected the clothes I would wear. I planned to keep about half of what I owned and ditch the rest. I was very concerned about the condition of my sneakers. I had put a lot of miles on them, and the sole of my left sneaker was starting to flap. The last thing I needed as I tried to escape across country by night through northern Iraq was a bad pair of shoes. Reluctantly, I decided to stop running and limited myself to walking for exercise.

The other issue was who to bring with me. Most of my compatriots were not in favor of escaping. I talked to John McCollah and he was for going with me. Mick Finan wanted to take his chances alone. Dave felt a senior NCO's responsibility to stay and look after the group. Most of the others didn't fancy their chances out in the open. The exception to this was Manfred Locher. His desire to escape presented me with a problem. John McCollah was a trained soldier and was both younger and in as good a shape as I was. Manfred was over fifty and had years of good living on him, and he wanted to escape as soon as the bombing started. I never told him my fears about possibly being murdered by the Iraqis, but I think he came to the same conclusions I had. So I was faced with the dilemma of taking Manfred or ditching him. On the one hand, he would definitely slow us down and eat food. On the other hand, he was another set of eyes and another person to stand watch as we slept. In the end I decided to take him. I liked Manfred; unlike some of the others, he was not ready to passively accept his fate. He may have been out of shape, but he had a lot of guts and I wouldn't have felt right about leaving him. The guy I felt the worst about leaving was Chuck. There was no way he could make the trip and he knew it. He still helped me prepare to escape in any way he could, even though he knew that any of us leaving would decrease his own chances for survival.

Soon after German reunification we got electrifying news. Saddam Hussein announced that he was going to release all the French as a gesture for their "positive attitude towards resolving the crisis peacefully." The French guys were told to pack their bags and a bus would be by to get them tomorrow. They were stunned by the news; we could see tremendous conflict in their faces. They were ecstatic that they might be going home, but they suspected (and voiced the opinion) that this might be some sort of trick. Even when they became convinced that they would be leaving Kirkuk, we could see that they were uncomfortable with departing and leaving the rest of us here. We did our best to reassure them that we were happy that they were going (which was true; who in his right mind would begrudge his friends escape?) and wished them all the luck in the world. We pressed letters on them to be sent to our families, and I gave Jean Pierre and Etienne copies of all my notes from the observations I made since we had left Baiji to turn over to the nearest French and U.S. authorities. There were about a dozen pages of handwritten notes on military convoys I had observed, flight activities, antiaircraft defenses, guards around the site we were at, the conditions in which we were held, and a complete update on Chuck's condition. It was a lot of incriminating stuff that would get them into deep trouble if they were searched. They volunteered to carry it without hesitation.

The bus came for them the next day and we had an emotional farewell. It was clearly agony for them to leave us, and we were very sorry to lose them. They had been good comrades in adversity, humorous, brave, and dignified, men who could always be counted upon. They were a credit to La Belle France, and their nation has every right to be proud of their conduct.

After they left, we all shuffled back inside, feeling oddly empty and depressed. Even the Iraqi minders were strangely silent. It was as though we all sensed that this hostage crisis was entering a new phase. I walked by the Frenchmen's room and looked in. The emptiness of the place was new and disconcerting. I looked at the wall and saw that one of them had scrawled *"Vive le Resistance!"* before he left. I laughed, suddenly remembering Etienne hiding Saddam's portrait in the latrine. That's how I will always think of them: *"Vive le Resistance."* God bless you guys.

I got a little paranoid after the French left. I'd had no word from Josef, and here I had sent out a bunch of military information with my French friends. If any of those messages fell into Iraqi hands, I would be screwed. The Iraqis had hung a British citizen before the war for espionage, and I was sure that I was doing more than he ever did. The lack of word over the radio from the French for several days weighed heavily on me. What if they had been searched? Finally, to my immense relief, I heard Etienne's voice on the radio saying hello to all of us "roast beefs." Thank God they had gotten out.

Still, I was reevaluating my information-gathering campaign. Frankly, the thought of getting caught and being put on trial as a spy frightened me. I began to question the worth of what I was recording. Were my limited observations that valuable to the coalition? Were they valuable at all? Was it worth the trouble it would cause me and my companions if we were caught? We had been lucky so far, but I felt like a guy at a blackjack table who had won a pile but was uneasy about getting up and cashing in while he was ahead. That's what the house is banking on, I thought. Casinos make money because everyone's luck runs out sometime. Only a few people are smart enough to quit while they're winners. Here though, I was betting my life. So I had these cowardly thoughts and might have even acted on them (or rather done nothing from then on), but fortunately circumstance again came to my rescue.

The Iraqis brought us to church by a different route that passed by a large military motor pool with several hundred trucks in it, some of them under sunshades. I wasn't looking at it, but Manfred Locher was and suddenly gave out a low curse under his breath and tapped me discreetly on the arm. I turned and he whispered to me, "Look under the far sunshade. It's a Roland!" I didn't see it and we passed out of view. I understood Manfred's urgency, however. A Roland was a European antiaircraft missile and one of the most modern antiaircraft weapons possessed by the Iraqis. Manfred, the old Luftwaffe pilot, would instantly recognize one and see it for the threat it was. I asked him whether he was sure and he nodded. "No question about it," he said. All I could do was hope that the Iraqis would bring us back from church the same way we had come.

While I was sitting in church I tried to remember everything I had ever read about the Roland. It was a modern, second- or third-generation, radar-guided heat seeker that could also be optically tracked. Its presence was bad news for our pilots. I remembered that the radar and firing unit were normally on one mobile vehicle and the thing could quickly displace. I knew that the Iraqis didn't have a lot of them and wondered what was close enough to the truck park to be protected by it.

Fortunately the bus went back the same way and I got a good look at the Roland, thanks to Manfred. There it was, all right. The Iraqis had cleverly hidden it underneath a sunshade in a large truck park so it looked like just another vehicle (hide a stone among stones). We would never get any satellite imagery on it, and the system could stay hidden until called to come out and shoot at our planes.

All of my previous wavering thoughts vanished instantly. The enormity of the Roland's presence shamed me back into duty. I took as detailed a set of notes on it as I could. I also continued to keep notes on everything else I observed. The Roland had been a wakeup call, and a fortunately timed one at that. We all must do what we can. The only thing I could do at the moment was continue to take notes and prepare to escape. I couldn't get the notes about the Roland out right away, but when I could, by God I'd be ready. Seeing the Roland galvanized me, and I never wavered again.

As the days wore on into November, I walked the perimeter for longer durations. Some days I would walk for three hours before lunch and three hours after. I did this for exercise but also to keep myself occupied. There wasn't anything new to say to anyone, and at times we started to get on one another's nerves. Dave Freeman would walk the perimeter as well. Sometimes we would talk, but sometimes he'd just tell me he was feeling "a bit bloody" that day and wanted to be left alone. I understood what he meant and went the other way. Even Kiyoshi Odagane didn't want to sing the way he used to. We weren't withdrawing into ourselves, and everyone was still friendly, but more of us were going off by ourselves for a few hours than had been true at the beginning of our captivity together. It was under-standable; we had run out of stories, and talking about family only re-minded people of the fact that none of us might ever see family again. So we walked. It burned energy, it gave us exercise, it allowed time to think, and I believe it helped keep us all sane.

The only real relief was listening to the radio: BBC, VOA, Deutsche Wella, whatever. The Germans would translate the news they heard, and we would compare notes on the day's events. The Russian envoy Primakov going to talk to Saddam raised some hopes. Suddenly my fellow captives, especially Manfred, were talking about Primakov as though he was the Mighty Casey at bat, describing everything they had heard about the man. "He was the Russians' chief representative in the Middle East and is very well known in Iraq." Privately, I knew that it was all lies, but I expressed my hopes that maybe the Russian envoy could defuse the crisis. What did we know about Primakov? I doubt whether any of us could have picked him out of a police lineup. But when you're in a hopeless position, you tend to grab at straws.

During this time, Chuck was maintaining his composure and his friendly, outward appearance, but we could see that he was suffering physically. The Tagement and other medicines the Iraqis had given him were not helping. He was taken to the hospital several times and returned with additional medicines, but he continued to weaken. I appealed to the Iraqis frequently to evacuate him and suggested to them that Chuck might be a good guy for the Reverend Jesse Jackson or another one of these supplicants from the American left to take with them out of Iraq. I didn't like the fact that these guys were here making propaganda hay for our kidnappers; but because they were here, they could at least take Chuck out. None of my efforts was effective, however.

Watching Chuck's wan face as he tried to eat was painful to see. He knew he was in trouble, but he didn't want a repeat of the Baiji refinery incident so he acted as though he felt better than he really did. I think he was more scared for us than himself. Chuck had a lot of guts.

The Iraqis brought us winter clothes, which was definitely a bad sign. On the other hand, it solved my problem of having appropriate clothes to wear while escaping. I got several pairs of pants, socks, long-sleeved shirts, and a sweater. Best of all was a new pair of shoes, although where they got the size 13s I had no idea. They were normal street shoes, but after being broken in they would serve in a pinch. Another bonus was the generally neutral brown and black earth-tone color of the clothes. Only actual camouflage would have been better.

I developed daily rituals. Every day before breakfast I would go to the same spot by the big fuel tank in the back corner of the refinery. I would climb into the gap in the blast wall and look out onto the Kirkuk-Baiji highway in the distance. This was my alone spot. It was shady most of the day and off the beaten track of our walking path. Although I could be seen from the walking path, the fact that I was sitting in the shade by myself was a signal that everyone respected. I would go there in the morning and pray. I'd pray for my family and Donna and my fellow hostages. I'd also pray for my friends who were now almost certainly deploying for what looked to be a real knock-out of a war. I also prayed for the brigade and wondered where Bob Quinn and my Vinnell crowd were and how they were doing. I was concerned about Turki and felt bad about not being with the brigade. The last word had been that they were deploying to the border. Probably they were still there.

Prayer took on a heartfelt if rote aspect, and it wasn't long before I included everyone. From prayer my mind would wander. This was especially true in the afternoons, where after a day's walking I would sit on the steps in the shade of the blast wall. I would look out at the guard positions and the antiaircraft guns to see whether anything was unusual but would soon begin to daydream about different and more pleasant times in my life. I was surprised at what I remembered when I just sat down tired at the end of the day and thought about it.

I would sometimes think about being a kid in Fort Monmouth, New Jersey. Things I hadn't thought about for decades would come back to me. Our house on Gosselin Avenue and the big tree right outside that we used to climb. Playing army with my friends (I had imprinted at an early age). Walking to the library with my mother and sister and getting a sticker for every book I had read that summer. Going to Cape Cod to visit my cousins. Coming in dead last in the pinewood derby and playing with my toy soldiers. Breaking a lamp with a Superball. Sometimes I would think about previous tours in the military and the successes and failures I'd had. I remembered being a fat, out-of-shape butterball of a private. I remembered my dad's special, knowing smile when I got on the bus to go to basic training. What a shock basic training had been. In retrospect, it had not been a particularly difficult experience, but at the time it seemed like climbing Mount Everest. I was in terrible shape, and South Carolina in August had been like a steam bath. I was completely unprepared for the rigor of it and suffered accordingly. Even having been brought up on army bases, I didn't know what being in the military was like. My dad the sergeant major was a far cry from that caricature of military fathers, the Great Santini. He was no more of a strict disciplinarian than Ward Cleaver, and my mother had doted on me. In 1974 at Fort Jackson, South Carolina, I encountered unsympathetic people who seemed to take exceptional delight in pointing out my numerous shortcomings as a human being. They did this while at the same time making me reach levels of physical exertion of which I thought myself incapable. Fear is a wonderful motivator. I had lived almost eighteen years without it and was badly in need of some. A fat boy, failing the physical training (PT) test. Drill sergeant Ray would look at me and snarl, "Gonna send your ass home, fat boy. You can't hang." The thought of going home to my parents a failure haunted me and drove me to greater exertion. Drill sergeant Nalder (the good cop) would always be on me: "C'mon, Stanton, you can do it, get up there." I went to church there, too, the cool of the post chapel a sanctuary on Sunday morning, with details and extra training after lunch to look forward to. Weight poured off me, so much so that I had to return to the issue facility to get new clothes. I shaped up and sol-diered, not spectacularly but well enough to graduate. My parents didn't even recognize me at first when drill sergeant Nalder told me they were in the parking lot of the barracks and I would have twenty minutes with them before the parade formation. My mother was shocked and concerned at the weight I had lost. My dad was highly amused. You could see it in his eyes. It was as though he had just played the best practical joke in the world on me and now saw that I had "gotten it." I graduated from basic training in October 1974 with my parents watching me pass in review. For the first time in my relatively aimless young life, I felt as though I had accomplished something.

Later that day in packing out to go to advanced individual train-ing, drill sergeant Ray watched me make a rough job of properly packing my duffel bag and asked with mild disgust, "What have you learned here, Stanton?" I mumbled something about how to be a sol-dier, and Ray grunted and walked off. I really couldn't answer him then because I couldn't articulate it. Now I knew the answer. What I had learned that summer of 1974 at the hands of Staff Sergeants Ray and Nalder and other fine NCOs of B Company, 6th Battalion, 1st Basic Training Brigade, was perseverance.

Shortly after the Roland sighting, we received startling news over the radio. President Bush was sending the entire VII Corps from Germany to the desert. At first I thought I had misheard the an-nouncement. Then it dawned on me that the newscast was serious. The radio was abuzz with details of more than 100,000 additional U.S. troops and two armored divisions coming to the Gulf. This raised the number of divisions on hand that I knew of to six. The Brits looked at me, and their faces lit up as I explained the news to them. This meant that almost half the U.S. Army would be in the desert. There was no way that I and my compatriots were going to sit here for months or years. What was coming from Germany was a go-to-Baghdad force! I knew that it would take a few months for it to get to the Gulf, but once it was here, that was it. I was almost giddy with happiness. Now I knew that we were serious about winning this war. Whatever else occurred, at least I wouldn't be stuck in this camp for years waiting for something to happen. I told Khalid the dick about the new American divisions coming, and he simply shrugged and said there would just be more of us to kill. Oh well, there's no getting through to some people. We could see that he wasn't happy about it, though. For all my delight about the new forces, the news heightened my sense of missing out. Half the army was coming to the Gulf, and I was stuck in this camp.

As it turned out I didn't have long to wait before the opportunity to smuggle out information presented itself. The Iraqis announced that they would be releasing all Germans on 21 November. Instantly I gathered up all my notes and gave them to Manfred. I was glad they were being released, especially Manfred, because I doubted that he could have survived the overland trip to Turkey. But I was equally sure that he would have tried.

The remaining hostages saw the same scenes of mixed feelings and regret in the Germans as we had seen in our French comrades. Those leaving were finding themselves being reassured by those who were staying in captivity. Everyone pressed letters onto the Germans, and Manfred grimly promised me that he would do everything possible to get my notes through and inform the U.S. forces in Germany about "our friend Roland." I felt a lot better about this. The presence of that potent air defense system bothered me. At least now the air force would be warned about it.

There was a snag in the Germans leaving, though. Only Manfred, Ingo, and Herbert were to go. For some reason, Rolf Wachter was not included on the list. We all were upset and tried our best to get Rolf onto the bus, but to no avail. The other Germans then wanted to stay and could only with difficulty be talked out of it. I told Manfred that it was some typical Iraqi bureaucratic screwup and to press the German diplomats in Baghdad to get Rolf released. Rolf himself was upset but in full control of himself and insisted that his countrymen go without him. The look on his face as the bus pulled away was tragic. Why did it have to be Rolf, the one German who spoke almost no English? We hoped that he would be released in the next few days, but nothing happened. We all made sure that we took turns playing chess with him and otherwise looking in on him. He seemed to bear up well, but the question of why he hadn't been released with the other Germans gnawed at him. We never did find out the reason.

To replace the Germans, we received several new faces—all Brits. They had been hiding in Kuwait City and only recently had been captured. Their stories of evasion and hairbreadth escapes painted a grim picture of Kuwait City. One of them, a Scotsman named Owen, had dyed his flaming red hair black in an attempt to blend in with the Kuwaitis. The job was inexpertly done, and the red roots showed up clearly on the half inch of hair closest to his scalp. He took a lot of kidding about it.

The new guys were able to update us on what they had seen of conditions in Kuwait. The Kuwaiti people were definitely suffering under the Iraqi occupation, and there were constant incidents between the Kuwaiti resistance and the Iraqi occupiers. Most of the Kuwaitis went out of their way to hide westerners and help them escape, and the new guys were very complimentary of that. One of them was an especially valuable addition to the group because he was a resident of Malta and spoke fluent Arabic. We now had someone who could sit next to the minders and tell us exactly what they were talking about.

Shortly after the new arrivals showed up, the Iraqis brought a large duffel bag filled with items that had been sent by the British and German embassies to their people being held in hostage sites. The package contained books, writing paper, and all sorts of food and condiments as well as German army rations. The condiments we used (ketchup was particularly welcome), but the German army rations we set aside for emergency food supplies. I looked on them with a feeling of wonder and relief. In one fell swoop a lot of the food problems I would encounter on escape had disappeared. Eating one meal a day, I could carry two weeks' worth of food easily. The German rations were literally manna from heaven.

After the hostage package arrived, the Iraqis said they would take letters back to our embassies for us. I was skeptical but figured it was worth a shot. I sent letters to my family and to Donna. I told them not to worry, that I would be all right. I didn't dare include any military information because I was sure that the letters would be read. I couldn't resist sending out one other card, though. I made a homespun Christmas card for the U.S. embassy with a set of colored pencils. On the front I drew a Christmas tree and wrote in colored letters, "Merry Christmas." On the inside I wrote "FUCK IRAQ" and signed it Marty and Chuck. I sealed all three envelopes and gave them to the guy who brought the duffel bag.

Around the middle of November, the Iraqis hit us with yet another weird attempt at hospitality. They said we would be allowed to phone home. I had thought, no way, but sure enough the next day, one at a time, we were allowed to call our family. It took everyone a while to get through, and we were allowed to talk for only about ten minutes, but it was worth the effort. The ability to talk to our loved ones was wonderful and awful at the same time. My mom kept asking me if I was all right and did I need anything. My dad told me to take care of myself. It's odd, but when I actually got the opportunity to talk to my parents in this circumstance, I didn't know what to say. Then my dad laid a bombshell on me. My sister was looking to get her visa to Iraq to come and ask for my release. If he had been able to reach through the phone and punch me in the face, he couldn't have staggered me more. I almost made the minder leap out of his seat in surprise when I screamed, "Noooo!" into the phone. All of a sudden I was talking at a hundred miles an hour. "You can't let Peggy do it, Dad. Keep her out of here. Don't let her come." My father replied somewhat testily that he was doing his best (as I should have known he was), but Peggy was worried sick about me and thought she might be able to get me out. Others had done it. The thought of my sister coming as a supplicant to these jerks sickened and enraged me. I told Dad that she would be placing herself in danger, and if hostilities started while she was in the country we would both be prisoners. Besides, I didn't want members of my family being used by the Iraqis for propaganda. So the trip was definitely out. On this cheerful note we were disconnected.

Far from being an uplifting experience, the phone call terrified me. I knew Peggy, and she was as headstrong as she was brave. She also loved me unconditionally and would not hesitate to enter any lion's den necessary to get her little brother out of a jam. The fact that it would be of propaganda value to the enemy wouldn't enter her mind. Family ties cut all other boundaries. I was genuinely scared for her welfare. There was no guarantee that she could get out of Iraq if she ever got into it. Then Mom and Dad would be facing the loss of two children.

I had about a week to fret over this before we were allowed to make another phone call. Miraculously, Peggy and Donna were both there and I told Peggy in precise terms that she and her husband, Al, were under no circumstances to come to Iraq. She was unhappy with this (they, in fact, had visas and were working on getting plane tickets) but acquiesced to my wishes. I was tongue tied and awkward with Donna, but I tried to keep the conversation light. It didn't seem like the moment for impassioned "I love you, wait for me" speeches. We were cut off again in mid-sentence. I felt a lot better after this phone call. Thank God my father had told me about Peggy's plans. I had dodged another bullet. The more I thought about it, the funnier it got. I would have been the only U.S. Army officer in history whose big sister came to get him out of a POW camp. How would I have ever lived that down? Being captured on vacation seemed almost dignified by comparison.

Oddly enough, though, one of us did leave through the direct efforts of a family member. A large group of British wives, including several military wives, came to Iraq to plead for the release of their husbands and brothers. Among them was John McCollah's wife, Heidi. Just before the end of the month, John was suddenly told that he would be taken to Baghdad and released. He had no prior knowledge of this and was shocked when he got the news. I could sympathize with him, because I had found out about my own sister's efforts only by chance. He was at sea as to whether or not he should go. As the senior coalition officer present, I told him in no uncertain terms to go. My reasons again were fairly selfish. Since the Germans had left we had been out of (unmonitored) contact with our embassies. He could smuggle out almost two weeks' worth of notes and observations for me, as well as an updated list of the hostages here and detailed information about conditions at the site.

John displayed the separation anxiety that we had all seen in the French, but his fellow British NCOs and everyone else were unanimous in urging him to go. The quicker he and his wife got out of Iraq, the better it would be for their little girl. So we lost John McCollah. I found out later that he and his wife spent a few days in Baghdad, then were released to go home through a gauntlet of TV cameras. I was relieved to hear on the radio that he had gotten out. That meant more information reached the coalition, along with letters to Donna and my family. I was especially sad to see John go, however. He was one of those humorous people who had kept everyone going.

So now it was December, and northern Iraq was definitely getting cold. I took to wearing pants on my walks for the first time but resisted wearing a sweater in order to build up my resistance to the cold. The weather was bracing, and it took me a while to work up a sweat. We were all completely resigned to being here when the war started. Aside from the hope that we could get Rolf out (when the Iraqis were finally convinced that a German remained here), no one expected any more releases.

Surprisingly, escape planning fell off. Many of my fellow captives now said that they would wait out captivity and look for release after the war. I could accept their wishes and asked only for their assistance in helping me escape when the time came. With John and Manfred gone, my little escape group was back to just me, and I doggedly continued my preparations. Having sewn a poncho, a rucksack, and a pair of mittens, I went to work on a bag for all my stolen tools. It kept me busy. The news consisted of more posturing and troop deployments. We weren't saying much by this point. Everyone was withdrawn into his own thoughts. We played backgammon and walked the fence like automatons.

On 6 December we were watching television in the common room. There was no warning that anything of import was going to be announced, and we watched the news without anticipation. To get a glimpse of what was really going on, we kept an eye out for the western news clips that were periodically played. The newscaster read over a story about soldiers in Kuwait, and the film clips showed the normal troops sitting on antiaircraft weapons and chanting the "Saddam chant." Suddenly the newscaster announced in the same, bored, English-as-a-second-language monotone that the revolutionary council had approved the departure of all foreign "guests," and all the guests of Saddam would be leaving Iraq within the next few days.

We all stopped what they were doing and stared at the TV. "What was that?" Dave said. *Do they mean us?* I wondered. We all looked at one another with disbelief and confusion. They're going to release us just like that, after all this? It didn't make any sense. I could read the same look on all of my compatriots' faces and almost hear their exact same thoughts. None of us believed it for a second. We had been hopeful too many times before. Now we were mentally hardened to captivity. This had to be some kind of trick, some kind of Lucy-with-the-football trick that Saddam was going to pull on the coalition Charlie Brown. Get all our hopes up, then jerk the football away by asking for some last-minute concession. So we disdained to hope and looked at one another with knowing, hard faces. "Bullshit," I heard Chuck mutter as he went back to his room.

I was worried that this talk of release merely presaged another movement of hostages, and I was determined to pack and bring as much of my escape gear as I could. I went back to my room and folded up my poncho and camouflage blankets and put them into my suit bag along with my water bottles and mittens. The map and compass I would leave hidden until the last moment. I wondered about packing the German rations but decided against it. There would be time later to divvy them up.

We were all sure in the back of our minds that the news of release was a lie, but at the same time it started that little worm of hope. Possibly, just possibly, could this be it? Hope like this is a damnable thing, and I resolved to keep my countenance and not show my disappointment when it was dashed again. But the hope was there, in me and amongst my friends. We were all derisive of the announcement, and our outward face to one another was something along the lines of, They're getting ready to let us go? Yeah, right. Pull the other one, why don't you. At the same time, I noticed that we all gravitated to the radio as soon as the BBC news came on to get any confirmation of this report. Sure enough, the BBC announced that the revolutionary council had approved the release of all western hostages, and transportation for them was being arranged.

Later, Abdul Karim came by and confirmed what we had already heard. We were to be released, but he could not say when. He did mention that sick "guests" would be given priority. My immediate reaction was to press him for Chuck's release due to his illness. I was afraid that the whole thing was a propaganda ploy and the window of opportunity from this "release of guests" would be brief.

The thought of leaving Chuck was one of the grimmer aspects of escape. Getting him out of the country would relieve me of a considerable psychological burden. I wanted to help Chuck, but I would be dishonest if I did not admit to at least some selfish motivation. Abdul Karim said that he would ask permission to get Chuck to Baghdad early. And he told us all to be patient, that it could take a day or so before we could leave but we were definitely going. He must have read the sheer disbelief in our faces as he reiterated this last point several times. Our reaction must have been extremely odd to him. I think he expected us to jump for joy. Instead, he ended up trying to convince us that he was serious. "You're being released," he said. "Really, I mean it."

The hope monster ate at all of our hearts that night. I could especially see it in the face of Rolf, who had already gone through a cruel false hope once when he had been missed in the release of the Germans. He and I played our usual game of chess, and I beat him, which was unusual. Like all of us, he kept his countenance and did not show joy or fear. The hope in his eyes betrayed him, though, like the hunger it was.

The Japanese believed Abdul Karim and, being practical, set about choosing what they would bring with them and what they would leave. They recognized our skepticism and did nothing to set themselves apart from us. I warned Sho that this could all be another political maneuver by Saddam. Sho conceded I might be right but said there wasn't any harm in preparing. The Brits played backgammon and read, all the while keeping an ear cocked to the radio and TV.

I walked six laps of the perimeter that night and went to my spot near the big oil tank. It was cold and I shivered in my light coat, but I needed to be alone. My shoes had almost completely come apart, and I realized that I had better start breaking in the new ones if I was going to use them in an escape. Even with all the news of release, I still couldn't think in terms of going home. I knew that the promise of mass release was just another trick. I thought that at best they would send out a few more ill hostages. I prayed hard that night, for Chuck's release and for my family. I felt that whatever small group was released would be the last. Anyone who didn't get out of country this time would be stuck here for the war. If I could just get Chuck out, I could escape with a clear conscience. I felt like a runner at the starting blocks, waiting for the gun. I had everything as ready as I could get it. Mentally, I was wound as tight as a watch spring.

The disappointment over a last-second non-release of hostages would add a new and unstable element to the overall situation. I was certain that the bombing was going to begin before the January deadline. Sitting here in the cold, I made peace with God and thought about my family and everyone I had ever loved. The hugeness of escaping lay before me with a clarity as cold as the moonlight I sat in. It was a desperate thing. I could go missing and never be heard of again. I could break a leg in the mountains and starve to death. But escape still provided better odds than staying here. I accepted that and felt oddly at peace with myself, as though I was doing exactly what I should be doing. I went back to the building late, and most of my companions were already in bed. Chuck lay on his bunk and was still, although well into the night I could see his eyes open. I knew better than to talk to him. He would deal with his hope in his own phlegmatic way. Anything I said would be useless.

Abdul Karim was, as usual, as good as his word. The next morning a car showed up after breakfast to collect Chuck and take him to Baghdad. We were all surprised by this turn of events, which added a lot of credibility to the notion of going home. I still didn't believe it. I was just thankful that Chuck was getting out of Iraq. He packed his belongings in short order. Being much less of a pack rat than I, he had a lot less stuff. The car pulled up to the building and he shook hands and hugged all of us. The Iraqi minder Abdullah gave Chuck back his passport. The sight of this more than anything else convinced me that Chuck was really being sent home. Before he left he gave all of his Iraqi-supplied clothes to Yusef the Kurd from the mess hall. I thought that the gesture was a fine thing, that he could be so sick and in such peril while in captivity yet still think to show a kindness to the kitchen staff people who had done their best to be pleasant to us. No big emotional "thank you" or anything like that, just a practical gift of good clothes, given without fanfare. The gesture summed up Chuck's personality in a nutshell. He climbed into the back of the black Mercedes sedan along with two minders and was gone. I watched him looking back at us and waving until the car turned the corner. Then I went back to my room and wrote in my notebook: *"Dec 8, 2000, Chuck Tinch taken in Mercedes Sedan License # 76528. Destination Baghdad, no way to confirm this."*

After Chuck's departure we all stood around and looked at one another, but no one said much. Finally, Dave Freeman went back inside the building and one by one we filed in after him. Some guys went to watch TV or listen to the news. Others set up their backgammon sets as though nothing had happened. I played chess with Rolf, but my mind wasn't on the game and he beat me mercilessly. I shook my head and smiled. He looked back understandingly and nodded. I went for a walk to think. Chuck was gone—please God, to be released. We were supposed to go "soon." The next forty-eight hours would tell. If we were still here at the end of that time, it was all lies and we would be here for the war. Any way you looked at it, it was going to be another long night. I walked a lot that evening, my mind a race of thoughts and emotions. I did remember to stop at my "spot" and give thanks to God for Chuck's release, but I was numb.

The television that night showed groups of hostages being brought into a hotel in Baghdad that I did not recognize. The Brits said it was the Monsour Melia, the hotel they had been kept in before they were brought to the hostage sites. There were a lot of reporters, "guests," and Iraqis milling about in chaos. The BBC announced that flights from Iraq would take place on chartered Iraqi airliners within the next forty-eight hours. Abdul Karim came in and informed us that a bus would be coming in the morning to pick us up and take us all to Baghdad. He expressed his relief that our "stay" was almost over, then wished us all a pleasant evening. We stared at one another dumbly.

Even now it was hard to believe. We did nothing remotely like men about to be liberated. No one touched the German rations we had hoarded. No one did cartwheels down the hall or shouted with glee. We all stared at one another blankly. Then, one by one, we shuffled off to pack our bags.

I took out my suit bag/rucksack and laid it on the bed. I looked at my stuff; not much was left of my few personal possessions, just a few shirts, socks, and pairs of shorts. I decided not to pack any of the clothes the Iraqis gave me. I would give them to the Kurds as Chuck had done. I looked at my picture of Donna on the wall and at the letters and pictures I had received. I felt strange. I looked at all of my escape gear and realized I couldn't fit it in the bag. I had been planning to strap it on the outside of the bag, but I didn't want the Iraqis to see all the painstaking work I had done in preparation for escape.

Actually I didn't want to pack anything just then. I looked at my little corner of the room, and Chuck's bed already stripped on the other wall. I looked at my American flag and picture of President Bush next to Donna. I could pack in about ten minutes; there would be time in the morning. Somehow it didn't seem right to be taking down my little corner now. Besides, I wasn't bringing anything out of its hiding place until I absolutely had to. If we were not released at the last second, I was determined to save as much of my escape equipment as I could. So I left everything up and walked down the hall. The Japanese were busy sorting through their things, and Mick Finan sat in his room with the door open reading a book. He wasn't packing yet either. We talked a bit and repeated the don't-get-your-hopes-up mantra like a couple of parrots. Our hopes were absolutely soaring at this point, accompanied by the equally rising dread of last-minute disappointment. It was a weird time.

The rest of the day we spent listening to the radio and standing around on pins and needles. I walked and walked, with the loose sole of my sneaker flapping and the cold creeping through my thin windbreaker. I was so jumbled with conflicting emotions that coherent thought was difficult. One determination shone through all of it, though. Whatever happened, I would keep iron control of my emotions. I would not say anything and I would be there to help my friends.

That night we barely touched our supper, and for once there were no conversations and no backgammon games. Even the minders seemed changed, their faces jubilant that this long, annoying detail would soon be over and they would be rid of us. The optimist in me saw this as another reason to hope. The realist understood that they could be happy simply at a change of shift versus an end of detail. The pessimist thought they simply could be good actors and this was all a plot. Captivity had made me suspicious to the point of being a little goofy.

I packed the next morning after breakfast. The pathetically few things I owned disappeared easily into the suit bag/rucksack. I decided to fold up the poncho and bedroll to be ready to take them but not show them until the last minute. The compass and map I gingerly took from their hiding places along with all of the notes of activities I had written down since the release of John McCollah. Then we all moved our bags into the hall and waited.

The bus came around 11:30. Late enough to make us anxious. We uploaded it in record speed. We each gave our Iraqi clothing and all the German rations and other goodies to the Kurdish kitchen staff, who received them with gratitude. Yusef and Michael—Little Kurd and Big Kurd—seemed especially sad to see us go. No doubt they had been eating well off our rations, but I like to think that at least some of their friendliness and generosity was genuine. Abdullah and Khalid the minders came with us. They had our passports in a box. I asked for mine, and Abdullah initially refused. I insisted, saying that it was my property. With a shrug he gave all of us our passports. We said our good-byes to Abdul Karim. He was not a bad soul. I told him that if it ever came to a war-crimes trial, I would testify to our good treatment. That made him blink. Abdullah frowned.

A what-the-hell mood seized me. I didn't have my bedroll, but suddenly I felt that I wouldn't be needing it. So I boarded the bus in my light clothes with my sneaker sole flapping as I went up the steps. The bus pulled out of the compound, and I could see the guards and minders and Abdul Karim staring after us. Maybe it occurred to them that we were being set free but they still had to live there. Probably not. We had just been a blip in their day-to-day routine. Now they could go back to what passed for normal life in Iraq.

The bus trip to Baghdad took about four hours. The first thing I noticed was that we did not have our usual chase cars of minders that we'd had on every other trip to a new location. The only Iraqi officials were the two guys detailed to get on the bus with us. This gave even more credence to the fact that they really were taking us to Baghdad to turn us over to our embassies. I was still wary, however, and kept on the lookout for an escort to join us. None did.

The car turned onto a main highway headed south, and we entered territory I hadn't seen before. The scenery south of Kirkuk was bleak and mostly flat. We stopped once to take a piss break. We passed several military compounds bustling with activity and numerous convoys heading south toward Baghdad. I tried to remember as many of these details as possible to write down in my notebook. For the most part there was little vegetation, just endless scrub and occasional red dirt-colored hills. On the left we could see the mountains that led to Iran. I was still jumpy and waited for the bus to make an unexpected turn, but it never did.

The bus itself was an old Tatra that wheezed and clattered as the speedometer wound up to a hundred kilometers per hour. The driver seemed determined to change gears without depressing the clutch pedal, but the thing ran, and every minute got us closer to the Monsour Melia and the movement home. We passed an old police station that had been left over since British times. It looked like a small fort and was clearly placed with defense against brigands in mind. A lot had happened since bandits ran the country. I watched the imposing structure go by and wondered whether any of the men who served there were still alive and, if so, what they would say about the current state of affairs.

We passed a convoy of tanks on transporters, and I counted thirty-four ratty looking T-55s on various types of flatbeds. The tanks looked like fugitives from the boneyard. I could only shake my head in wonderment at people who would use museum-piece armor such as that against us. The old tanks would simply be slaughtered. An M1/Bradley task force would go through them like a rottweiler attacking a sack full of kittens. I remembered the big M1s rolling down the Drinkwater Valley in Fort Irwin at forty miles per hour, engaging targets more than two kilometers away. The panel targets were barely visible to the naked eye, but they would be hit almost before they finished coming up. A T-55 couldn't even fire on the move. It had to fire from the short halt. Its gun was badly outranged by the M1, but that didn't matter because it couldn't penetrate an M1 anyway. Even the 25mm cannon on a Bradley could get a mobility kill on a T-55. The TOW missiles a Bradley carried could eviscerate a T-55. I remembered Abdullah the minder and how proud he was of being a tanker and how he liked the T-55 better than the newer T-72s. He said they were easier to maintain. Which I suppose was true, in the same sense that a little red wagon is easier to maintain than a car. I remembered the Republican Guards sitting for two days on their T-72s without once doing any kind of operator's maintenance. I thought about the training that Abdullah had described to me and how few rounds they had shot. I thought of our own massive gunnery qualifications and live fires. I looked at the soldiers riding in bovine contentment in the cabs of the tractors or sitting on the tanks themselves (another unsafe and unprofessional indicator from the Iraqi army). A few noticed us as we passed them slowly on the left, but most were oblivious. They looked like any other troops talking or sleeping or peering out the window. I wondered whether they realized what was about to happen to them, that they and their 1950s-generation rust bucket tanks were like livestock being led to the slaughter. I wondered whether they knew their guns were ineffective against M1s and that they couldn't see us at night but we could see them, and that night was when we would come. It was eerie looking at these men because I knew that most of them would die. We passed them and I watched the convoy recede behind us. The person who sent them to war in those antiques belonged in jail.

We passed other convoys and military compounds and I surreptitiously took notes on as much as I could. I had no idea of miles traveled, so I recorded events in so many hours and minutes along the main highway going south. The trip seemed interminable and we did not talk much. We made the bus driver stop for another bladder call, and the twelve of us stood by the road pissing on Iraq while military traffic passed us wide eyed. Then we continued on.

Baghdad appeared first as suburbs of low houses typical of an Arab city. The highway became four lane and the traffic picked up. I was fascinated by Baghdad. It would be an interesting place to visit in peacetime. Now I was determined to drink in every detail I could of the enemy capital to note any changes in the past four months. My companions must have thought me obsessive as I sat there with my pencil and paper. No one was saying much as the bus worked through traffic toward the center of town.

The bus started across a bridge over the river, and the Brits perked up and pointed to a large hotel on the opposite bank that they said was the Monsour Melia. Sure enough, as we got closer I could read the letters on the side of the building. It was a large, modern place about thirty stories tall right along the river. We crossed the bridge and almost immediately made a right turn into the parking lot. We had to creep through a lot of traffic to get close to the door. Hundreds of people, maybe even a thousand, were milling about outside the hotel, and I could see even more inside the lobby. A lot of buses were in the parking lot and more kept coming in behind us. There wasn't any order or traffic control. Finally our minders just opened the door and told us to walk to the lobby, that someone would meet us there. That was it. That was how we left captivity—dropped off at the hotel like kids being returned from summer camp.

I was last off the bus. I looked at the driver and the two minders, who stared blankly back at me. It was one of those moments when I was truly at a loss for words. It wasn't in me to say anything pithy or cutting to these guys. My previous impulses to do so seemed childish. Finally I just grinned and shook my head as I turned from them. Most of the others were already well toward the door, and I hurried to catch them.

RELEASE

Pandemonium reigned inside the lobby. There is no other word to describe the scene. Embassy officials were trying to corral all newcomers, but there was no order to it. Hostages were coming in and seeing others from whom they had been separated. It was like a big reunion and old home week, with the embassy people and the hotel staff desperately trying to impose some sort of order.

As soon as we entered the lobby, the little Kirkuk group was seized by this maelstrom and separated. Before I got in the door, the Japanese embassy people (superefficient, as always) had seized Sho, Doug, and Toshio and whisked them away. The Brits had gone to sign for rooms, and Rolf was patiently canvasing every Caucasian person to find someone from the German embassy. I just stood there like a bumpkin fresh in from the north forty and took it all in for some minutes. There were several hundred people in the lobby. Some were clearly hostages by the look of their ratty clothes and ragamuffin carry bags. A few looked like relatives who had come to beg the release of their loved ones, now reunited. Some were obviously embassy staff. Ominously, there were also a lot of news teams, with reporters and their cameramen frantically running about. In one sweep of the room, I counted three separate interviews taking place.

I had already decided to give all reporters as wide a berth as possible, just in case some Iraqi government official figured I was worth holding onto after all. I didn't want anyone saying on TV, "Hey, look, there was a real U.S. Army major as a hostage!" So far I had been treated just like one of the civilians captured in Kuwait. The last thing I needed at this stage of the game was to call attention to myself.

Suddenly I saw Paul Eliopoulos with a woman hanging on him and I went over to him. Paul saw me and jumped up and we embraced each other with a lot of pounding on the back and "How the hell are you?" The woman was his wife, Angelica, who had come over to get him out but was now going to just come home with the rest of us. I asked him where the U.S. embassy people were. He pointed toward a pretty brunette woman about my age standing by the reception desk. Some of the other originals from the Al-Rashid and Al Quaim/Baiji saw us and came over, and we spent a few minutes with "What happened to you?" and catching up, which seemed to be the standard topic of conversation all around us. Most of them had similar stories. Paul had been taken north to Mosul; a few others had gone south to Nasariyah or Kut. Some had an easy captivity; others had been held in unsanitary conditions and ill fed. None looked truly the worse for wear, although all had lost weight. I could have stood there all day and talked with them, but I figured I had better check in, so I excused myself and went to talk to the young woman from the State Department. Her name was Barbara Bodine, and her face lit up when I introduced myself. "*You're* the guy who sent us the Christmas card!" she said. "We loved it! We put it up on the wall." I don't know whether that was true, but flattery from a pretty young American woman was easy to take at this point (with mental apologies to my fiancée). I asked Barbara if we would get out today and she said they were working on it but to get a room just in case it wasn't until tomorrow. She said to come back and check with her in about an hour or so.

The fact that we might not leave that night didn't really bother me. There was such a carnival atmosphere in the Monsour Melia that I was thoroughly enjoying myself just being there. In a surprisingly short time I had a room key. The reception staff was passing them out to anyone who asked for one. I put my belongings in my room and went to get something to eat.

The main dining room held a vast and sumptuous buffet for the hostages and other members of the carnival. After our limited diet of the past few months, the variety was a treat and I got some of every-thing. I looked for people from my group but couldn't find anyone. I was almost finished with lunch when I heard that all Americans would be leaving in a few hours and should bring our bags down to the lobby.

This disconcerted me because I thought I'd be able to find mem-bers of my group later that evening and say my good-byes and maybe drink a beer or two. Now I had only an hour or so to grab my stuff and make the bus. I hurried to find Dave and Mick, because I wanted to say good-bye to them most of all. I found Mick on a hotel floor full of Brits. He said he would be flying out the next day, as would Dave and the rest of the Germans. I couldn't find Dave, so I told Mick to say good-bye for me and to stay in touch. It seemed such an odd and haphazard way to leave them.

I headed back to my room, pausing to pick up a paperback book out of boxes of them that had appeared in the hallway where the Brits were staying. Now we get books, I thought. I remembered the New York City guide in my bag and smiled. I stopped briefly by the dining room again to stock up on buns, just in case. On the way out I passed a waiter's station that had very large, sharp steak knives sitting with the cutlery. Instinctively I took one and dropped it hilt first into my pocket. Stealing stuff that might be useful was a reflex action by now. The steak knife felt very useful in my pocket as I went back into the lobby.

Barbara Bodine proved to be as ruthlessly efficient as she was ef-fervescent. The buses showed up only about ten minutes after they were scheduled (a small miracle for Iraq). We were filmed getting onto the buses by what must have been a dozen camera crews. I'm sure we looked like a bunch of tired and bewildered tourists going home. As we left the Monsour Melia parking lot, there were a few scattered cheers and waves to people watching us. Most, though, just gazed out the window, still looking a little numbed by it all.

Baghdad airport was outside of town, and we had to go through a lot of traffic to get there. There was no police escort or official desig-nation of any kind. Ours was just another bus making its way down a crowded highway. I looked at the Iraqis in traffic beside us and felt a surge of pity for them. What a way to go through life, watching what you said and scared of your own shadow. Living in a place where men like Khalid the minder really could come in and take you away. Looking at pictures of Saddam everywhere, forever.

As we approached Baghdad airport, which was smaller and less modern than I expected, I saw several military aircraft at a side installation, including an IL-76 AWACS (airborne warning and control system) aircraft. I knew that the Iraqis had only one of those, and here it was. I studied it in detail as we passed, but there was no activity nearby; it sat there unattended. For once I didn't make notes. I figured I would remember it.

We pulled up to another crowd of newsmen, many of the same ones from the hotel. The reporters actually got in the way and crowded us as we came off the bus and tried to get through the terminal doors. Few if any of us stopped to talk. At the airport the feeling of imminent release was palpable, and suddenly everyone wanted to be inside the building, as if being closer to the gate would somehow get them nearer to home.

As I got off the bus I looked at the throng of reporters and took my place in the line patiently filing through the halfway-blocked terminal doors. I was still determined not to say a word to them, but their presence annoyed me. *Just let us go, why don't you?* I thought. Suddenly, I remembered the buns I had in my bag and in an instant I had them out. Putting my bags down for a second, I took careful aim and began pelting the newsmen with buns from the Monsour Melia Hotel. My aim was a little off and I hit with only one out of four, but it was enough for several of them to look around in confusion to see where the projectiles were coming from. Several of the hostages in line with me saw it and laughed. Feeling much better, I picked up my bags and rejoined the queue.

Inside we had to go through immigration. It made sense in a warped sort of way. I remembered my "Disney World interrogator" and shook my head. It seemed a hundred years ago. The immigration control lines were slow, and it took me a good hour to get to them. Finally it was my turn. I presented my diplomatic U.S. passport to a thin, young man who had mastered the jaded air of an immigration official on duty. He asked me a few questions about my nationality, then floored me by asking the purpose of my trip to Iraq. The bastard. I answered "sight-seeing," and he looked up at me for a second, then smiled. He stamped my passport with a triangular exit stamp and told me to have a good flight.

We were assembled in a large waiting area by one of the gates. It took about three hours to get the aircraft ready, but nobody minded. This was one layover that no one was going to complain about. We occupied our time by continuing to catch up on one another's experiences. Several of the oil workers came up to me and reported times and dates of military activities they had witnessed. I took down all their observations in my notebook and thanked them for their efforts. It was gratifying to see that many of them had taken an active interest in the military goings-on around them and had done their best to remember what they saw. I told them they would be debriefed when they got back and to be as thorough and detailed as they could in their descriptions of what they saw. They were pleased that their efforts mattered and were appreciated. Although they could not express it to me in so many words, I could see that it validated their own efforts at resistance.

Many people had heard Donna's acceptance of my proposal of marriage on the radio, and I received quite a few congratulations. I also spent a lot of time talking to some of the guys I had last seen in Al Quaim. They were relieved that I had made it through captivity, which surprised me until I remembered that the last time they saw me I was well on the way to becoming unglued because of my disappointment over the missed escape opportunity. As it turned out, they had been moved from the workers' camp a week or so after that into a factory that was more heavily guarded. (I found out later that it was a chemical weapons plant.) So my window for escape had been limited anyway.

Mixed with us actual hostages were people from the U.S. embassies in Kuwait and Baghdad who had been detained on embassy grounds since August. Their experience had been different in that they were in constant contact with the United States but were unable to leave the crowded embassy compounds. There were several military types, whom I talked with briefly. Colonel Ritchie, the Iraq defense attaché, was still in the embassy and would not leave until the last plane. There was so much to catch up on with everyone that, although we spent hours waiting for the plane to be readied, I didn't get bored or impatient.

Finally an old Iraqi Air 747 pulled up to the gate, and shortly thereafter boarding was announced. It was quite orderly, with no one pushing or shoving to be first. People didn't seem to care where they sat, and carry-on baggage (all that any of us had) was stowed in record time. The Iraqi aircrew was plainly uncomfortable with us, but no one gave them a hard time. The aircraft door stayed open for what seemed inordinately long as the Iraqis and the State Department people checked names and details. At last the door was closed. When the plane pushed back from the ramp, there was an audible sigh of relief.

As we taxied out I studied the interior of the plane. The seats were fraying in places, and there were no new conveniences such as seat audio systems. I suspected that the plane was one of the first 747s made, and wondered vaguely what the maintenance record was as it squeaked onto the taxiway. I checked my route to the nearest exit, fortunately right behind me. I hoped that the old guy sitting next to the door was quick, because if not he would have my footprints down his back. It would be ironic to have lived through all this only to die in the honest air crash of a 747 that was old enough to vote (and drink). I almost immediately dismissed these thoughts, though. White-knuckle flyer that I was, if this thing was really going to get us out of Iraq, I would get out and push if I had to.

The mood in the aircraft as we moved was hushed. Conversation was limited and whispered. Looking at the faces around me, I saw only blank expression, but there was a sea of emotions in everyone's eyes. The plane sat at the end of the runway for a few minutes. There were always these little delays, right until the very end. I looked out the window for the last time at Iraq. I wondered how many of these airfield facilities would be standing when it was all over. Finally we started rolling—slowly at first, then building up speed, with the wheels of the plane going clacka-clacka-clacka like a Lionel train set. Baghdad airport rushed by, then the nose lifted and seconds later we were airborne.

That was when everyone let loose. A yell of triumph the likes of which I have never heard before or since erupted in the cabin. More than 350 souls yelling their heads off in that confined space. The cheering lasted a good three minutes and let up only when people were exhausted from sheer, repetitious yelling. People who were total strangers embraced and pounded one another on the back. Everyone was up walking around the cabin and visiting. All the tension and shattered hopes of the past four months broke from us in a vast wave of palpable relief. As a moment of pure satisfaction, it approached the sublime.

The flight was long but unremarkable. We were served a gross airline meal of two hotdogs in some kind of yellow sauce. (I suspected there were few takers for the Iraqi Air's frequent flyer program.) I spent a lot of time walking around and visiting my friends. While I was doing this I noticed bottles being passed, beverages from

Beefeater gin to the local version of date brandy and arak to stuff I couldn't even recognize. Apparently several of my compatriots had secreted away a stash for hard times and now it was all coming out. The passenger compartment started to look like a charter flight to Vegas.

I wondered what I would say when we got off the plane. I wanted to make sure the cameras saw me so that everyone would know I was all right. But after that? I wanted to shout out things to the world, but I couldn't. The problem was, if I said what I wanted to say on TV, I would be famous. The last thing I wanted was to go back to the States. We were flying to Germany, and once I got there I would immediately want to go back to Saudi Arabia; my brigade was right on the border and sure to be in the thick of it. Donna was in Saudi Arabia as well. Through no fault of my own I had missed Grenada and Panama; I was damned if I was going to miss the action this time. My best chance for getting back to Saudi Arabia as soon as possible was to keep a low profile. So I reluctantly concluded that I would just walk by the cameras, making sure they saw me but saying nothing. I would hold up my homemade American flag, though. I retrieved it from the bowels of my bag to make sure it was handy.

If the flight to Germany was happy and uneventful, landing was a true white-knuckle event. We approached Frankfurt through fog at 2 A.M. and missed our first approach. We had wheels down and were well into the landing process when the pilot suddenly poured on the coals and climbed sharply out of the approach. I thought, Jesus, we really are going to get killed on this flight, but there was nothing to do but hang on.

We made a second approach, descending through the fog with everyone in the plane extremely quiet. I looked out the window but could see nothing until the runway lights were beside the aircraft and we touched down seconds later. A second yell of triumph went up as we rolled down the runway and rapidly decelerated. Guys were up dancing in the aisles as the plane turned onto the taxiway. Entreaties of the Iraqi aircrew to sit down were ignored. The plane pulled up to the gate and stopped. The door opened and a man came into the aircraft and said something to the effect of, On behalf of the United States of America welcome back to freedom. He was drowned out by our cheers and nearly trampled. The Iraqi aircrew didn't stand at the door and do the usual "Good-bye and thank you for flying Iraqi Air." It would have been a nice touch.

Giddy and buoyant, we walked down the long ramp into the terminal. It was the middle of the night and we should have been dragging, but we were energized. The State Department people tried to keep us together, but from the outset it was a lost cause. The ramp exited into a room where a pitifully few State Department people attempted to get us into some type of order. A huge crowd of reporters could be seen through the sliding doors, and I took out my flag. Apparently the State Department people were frantic to get us under control because we would be flying out to the United States in a few hours. Unfortunately they hadn't reckoned with a planeload of people who were not only mildly drunk but possessed of an independent streak. Many of my compatriots had already brushed past the few frantic State Department staffers at the door and were wading past the cameramen outside, looking for a bar that was still open. Observing the lineup of rowdy hostages at the tables manned by a half-dozen harassed State Department employees, I decided that this was where I would check out. I scooted under a crowd-control line and headed for the door. A tall, thin State Department guy tried to stop me, and I told him to get bent. The sliding doors opened and I marched out of the Frankfurt airport terminal; others followed me. The shine of lights hit me instantly, and dozens of cameras were trained on me. Hordes of reporters screamed questions at me, but the police held them back behind crowd-control lines. I had already decided not to say anything, but I smiled, gave a thumbs-up, and held up my American flag as I walked past. I knew exactly what I wanted to say, but I had the presence of mind to remember that the most important thing was to get back to my unit. I figure now, though, after all these years, it won't hurt, so here goes. What I wanted to say was this:

"God bless President Bush."

"God bless every serviceman in the Gulf."

And

"Fuck Ramsey Clark."

There, I feel much better.

Part Four

HALFTIME

11

GERMANY

WE MUST HAVE PRESENTED a strange sight to the graveyard shift workers in Frankfurt airport. Dozens of newly released and pleasantly out of control hostages were wandering around looking for a bar or just a place to sleep, with no one was telling them what to do for once. Frankfurt airport is cavernous, and at 2 A.M. mostly empty. My right sneaker sole's "flap-flap-flap" sound echoed in the big, vacant hallways. I thought first to go down to the United Service Organization (USO) to see if I could catch a ride to the 3d Armored Division and report to Major General Funk, but the USO was closed. I decided to hell with it; the army could wait until morning. I was going to get some rest. I walked back through the airport and across to the big hotel. The clerk eyed me warily as I flapped my way up to the counter. I couldn't blame him. I looked like a vagrant, with my home-sewn suit bag, beat-up summer clothes, and flapping shoe. Just like in the commercials, though, my American Express card opened doors and soon I had my room key. Some of the other guys were coming in just as I left the registration desk, and I reflected that the clerk was going to have an interesting night. I promised to meet my friends in the coffee shop for a drink, then went up to my room.

First things first, I called OPM-SANG to let the boss know I had gotten out. At first the sleepy operator did not want to connect me to Brigadier General Taylor's house, but eventually I prevailed on him. Taylor came on the line sounding a bit testy. I shouted, "Sir! This is Marty!" He digested this for a moment, then said in that marvelous deadpan voice of his, "Okay, where are you *now?*" I quickly filled him in on the details and told him I would be back as soon as I could get a flight. He told me to call my parents immediately. "They've had a bad time of it, Marty. Been worried sick." He said to get back as soon as I could—"No more side trips, okay?"

I called my parents, and my mom's shout of elation when she found out I had been released was one of the most beautiful things I'd ever heard. My dad came on the line, and the joy in his voice was wonderful. True to character, after his initial congratulations, he said, "You dumb ass! What were you doing up there to begin with?" To which I had no good reply, but Mom shushed him up anyway. I promised to be home as soon as I could but told them I had to go back to Saudi Arabia first and probably wouldn't be able to make it back until the hostilities were over. They took it well, like the old army couple they were. They were just happy for me to be out of captivity.

I called my sister and her husband. Peggy was ebullient at my release and told me funny and hair-raising stories of her efforts to come to Iraq. She had come close to doing it, too. Thank God that Dad and I had foiled her. Al sounded greatly relieved that it hadn't come to that, and I understood the emotion completely.

I saved my call for Donna until last. I caught her asleep, and she had never been one to wake up quickly, but after a while I convinced her that I was, in fact, Martin, and I was in Germany. To this she perked up considerably, and we talked until I couldn't think of another thing to say. I was loath to hang up on her, though, and she finally had to tell me to go to bed. I put down the phone; to my shock I saw that I had been talking for more than an hour. I was a little too keyed so I went down to the coffee shop. Peanuts, Rodenbush, and a couple of the other oil workers were there and I joined them. We talked for a while trading stories of captivity. They were all happy to see that I had made out okay; the last time they saw me was at Al Quaim, and I was very agitated. "You just gotta learn to take it a day at a time, Marty. No point in getting upset about stuff," Peanuts told me. Truer words have never been spoken. These men would go back to the States. But, unlike some of the other hostages I had talked to, none was surprised that I was going back to Saudi Arabia. Maybe that reflected the kind of people they were. Americans who never shirked responsibility and always stood ready to help. All had been through military service and many were Vietnam veterans. They nodded their heads in approval when I said I was going back to military control the next day. As I left they said, "You go kick their asses now." It was touching and, in a way, one of the greatest compliments I've ever received. I said my good nights to those fine men and finally went to bed. The comfort of my room enfolded me and I slept like the dead.

Around 10 A.M. the next morning I got my wakeup call and quickly showered. I looked at my threadbare clothes and my holey shoe. Hell of a way to report back, but I didn't have anything else to wear. I called the duty officer at the 3d Armored Division and managed to get hold of my buddy John Scudder, General Funk's aide. Scuds was incredulous at my being there. Like most of my friends in the NTC Mafia, he had known I was a captive and now I was on his doorstep. He sent a car with a couple of counterintelligence sergeants to meet me. They were suspicious and requested an ID card and asked some questions about Captain Scudder (wife's name, son's name, et cetera) to make positive identification. After I passed those tests, they brought me to division headquarters (HQ). It was cold outside and I shivered in my light clothes, but I was feeling too good to really mind.

The 3d Armored Division was on full alert. I doubt I would have gotten into the headquarters without my two escorts. As it was I received a lot of strange looks from the military police. I guess I couldn't blame them. It's not every day that a long-haired rag picker in bad shoes comes to see the commanding general.

My arrival in the command group area stopped all conversation. Fortunately, Scudder took me under his wing and introduced me as the "guy from Iraq," then sat me down and plied me with a dozen questions. It was great to see my old friend again. We spent a few minutes talking about Iraq and the 3d Armored Division's deployment. Then General Funk came out. I straightened and reported to him: "Major Stanton returning to duty after a hundred and twenty-four days in captivity, sir."

What else was I supposed to say?

General Funk grinned and shook my hand. I spent about half an hour outlining what had happened to me. He instructed his G2 to organize a debriefing and inform the intelligence community that I was here. He also asked me to brief his divisional intelligence section and other key staff members, which I of course agreed to. Then he took a good look at me and said, "Jesus, Marty, you need some new clothes." I had to laugh at that one, because I did look like one of the homeless. As busy as they were, trying to outload the division, General Funk directed John Scudder to get me some warm clothes and take care of me. I didn't want any uniforms; all of mine were back in Saudi

Arabia and I could debrief just as well in civvies. I told John to drop me off at the PX and I could find my own way back to the headquarters. He was skeptical, but I could see that he had a ton of work to do and I didn't want to be a bother. So he dropped me off and promised to send a car if I called for one.

Just after he left I stepped in a big puddle of slush, which instantly went through the hole in my shoe. So I entered the PX with my shoe making a "squish-squish-squish" sound and getting the usual stink eye from the person at the entrance desk because of my appearance. Shopping for clothes was like something out of a commercial (MasterCard, clothe me), and I soon found a warm coat and other clothes as well as a good pair of sneakers. The PX Nazis would not let me change in the store, though, and they made sure they verified my charge card before they would accept it. Clothes really do make the man. So I stumped across the wet parking lot to the pizza place and changed in the rest room, to curious looks from some of the patrons. I didn't give a damn. The warmth of the new clothes was wonderful, and the pizza wasn't bad either. I decided that this western civilization stuff was all right. I made a quick stop at the bookstore for the latest news magazines, then got a haircut (can't go walking around like a ragman). I caught a cab back to division HQ.

I spent the rest of the afternoon debriefing various members of the 3d Armored Division staff on what I had observed about the Iraqi army and the Republican Guards in those first days in Kuwait City. My general impression of all of the staff officers was that they were grossly overestimating the capabilities of the Iraqi military. They were surprised at my assessment that the Iraqis exhibited only a moderate standard of training and that their overall combat efficiency was probably low. Like most people they didn't know that much about the Iraqis and were just counting numbers. Mathematactics. I told them I hadn't seen the entire Iraqi military, but if what I saw was any true indicator, we would tear them apart. I could see that they were heartened by my assessment, if a bit skeptical about it.

Scudder took me to his home that night and I spent the evening in their guest bedroom. Cindy Scudder didn't know how to treat me at first—had captivity weirded me out?—but once I assured her that I was fine we got on like old times at Fort Irwin. Tomorrow I would debrief some more people who had flown in to see me, then I would work on getting back to Saudi Arabia. The lack of sleep got to me fairly early in the evening and I crashed heavily.

They let me sleep in the next morning, so John had to come back from work to get me. I spent the rest of the morning debriefing some intelligence officers and NCOs on what I had seen in Iraq. I showed them the notes I had taken, and they made copies of them. They were very interested in my observations of life in Iraq and asked a lot of questions. After lunch I began briefing the same group again when an odd incident occurred. A man wearing sterile fatigues (sterile means no name tags or unit identification markings, rank, or brass of any kind) came into the room, flashed an ID, and said that they were to cease questioning me immediately, that I was now an asset belonging to his intelligence agency (not the CIA). My interrogators looked surprised and put out. I noticed that although they left in a huff, they did leave. The man had another guy come in and they both asked me simple questions that I had already answered. Then the other guy really scared me by asking whether I had any suppressed rage or felt suicidal. In one instant I went from being annoyed to scared. They were asking me questions to see whether or not I was a mental case. I took great pains to assure them that I was fine. My mystery man compounded my anxiety by telling me that I was not to relate my experiences to anyone and that he and I would fly to Washington the day after tomorrow.

I was appalled by this news. I was frightened that if I were taken back to the States, I would not be able to return to Saudi Arabia. The thought of my brigade going to war and me being held in some obscure intelligence debrief tank was intolerable. I had come so close and now I might miss the war after all. I inwardly cursed myself for reporting to military control in Germany. I should have just bought a plane ticket with my American Express card and flown back to Saudi Arabia on my own. Now this jerk was going to take me back to the States.

Wait a minute. Why not just get the ticket now?

The whole thing fell into place in a split second. Ditch these guys, make a beeline for the airline ticket office, and buy a ticket. Then fly out before they were scheduled to see me again. Perfect.

First things first. Break contact. I managed my best wan smile and told both of my mystery men that I was very tired and would like to spend the rest of the day with my friend Scudder. I would meet them back here tomorrow after lunch. The guy who asked me about my feelings put his hand on mine and said he understood (this was creeping me out bad). Mystery man number one grumbled a bit but agreed. I had them both drop me off at the division HQ, after which they no doubt left to make arrangements for my repatriation, maybe with visions of sugarplums in their heads. Sorry, guys, I've got other plans.

I raced into the division command group and told Scudder the whole thing. He was sufficiently alarmed to get me in to see General Funk. The general was surprised at the story but nonplussed. He looked at me quizzically and asked me what I wanted to do.

"Sir, I'm going AWOL," I replied. This raised his eyebrows a little. I related to him my plan to buy a plane ticket to Saudi Arabia. Would they cover for me until tomorrow afternoon? General Funk laughed. "Sure, Marty, we'll see you there in a few weeks." He directed Scudder to get me to the airline ticket office, then asked if I would brief his primary division staff officers after I had gotten my ticket. I thought about mystery man one's injunction to not talk to anyone. Fuck him. These people were my friends and they were going to fight alongside me. I told General Funk I would gladly brief the officers.

As it turned out, the only ticket I could get to Riyadh before I was supposed to link back up with agent 007 (and his sidekick empathy man) was a Lufthansa flight that was booked except for first class: $2,600 one way. I didn't even hesitate. I reflected on the fact that I was probably the only son of a bitch in the U.S. Army who ever had to pay to go to war. I spent the rest of the afternoon briefing General Funk's staff and preparing to return to Saudi Arabia. I kept as low a profile as I could, because I didn't want my mystery men, Colonel Flagg and his pal, running into me.

Cindy Scudder gave me a delicious breakfast and a big hug the next morning, then Scuds took me to the airport. Being your average toad of an economy-class flyer, I was unprepared for the degree of service that awaited me. I was fairly whisked along through airport in-processing and given a chit to get into a plush lounge where people were already drinking at 10 A.M. I laid low just in case (paranoia is a hard habit to break) and spent a pleasant hour reading the papers: more dire predictions of Armageddon in the desert. Cheerful stuff. I watched the high rollers knocking them back way too early, then went to get another blueberry muffin and more orange juice. Oh well, at least I'd be transported back to the cannon's mouth in comfort.

The flight back was one long picnic. First class is definitely the way to travel. Another bottle of wine, Mr. Stanton? More venison pate,

Mr. Stanton? Another filet mignon, Mr. Stanton? Let me fix your pillow for you. Oh baby! This was the life. The flight was eight hours long, and it seemed as though I consumed food for five of those hours. I also helped myself to the excellent red wine that the flight crew was so free with. By the time I reached Riyadh I was feeling no pain. At this point I had an almost devil-may-care attitude. Sure I was AWOL, and God only knew what kind of fit Colonel Flagg and his assistant were pitching, but to hell with it. Life would sort itself out.

We landed at Riyadh around 11 P.M. My reception was fairly comic. I had gotten word to OPM that I was coming, but they had no idea of my condition. Brigadier General Taylor and Colonel Noble probably figured that I was being modest when I had said I was fine over the phone. No doubt they both had visions of me being starved and tortured. They sent my friend Maj. Jim Good with a medic and an ambulance to get me, which I found hilarious. I came reeling off the plane stuffed to bursting with good food and smelling strongly of red wine. I greeted Jim like a long-lost brother, loudly and gracelessly. "Hi, Jim! How the hell are ya?" He looked at me and shook his head. "Clearly, you've survived captivity." Jim dismissed the ambulance crew, and I rode back to the OPM-SANG quarters with him. Brigadier General Taylor wanted to see me no matter what time I got in, so we went to his house first. He probably expected a lot of things, but not a happy drunk. He took it in stride, though, welcoming me effusively and commending me for the job I had done. This last filled me with relief, because I honestly didn't know whether or not I was in trouble, and I still felt bad about losing the truck. Even with the drunken state I was in, to learn that the big boss looked upon my actions with approbation was no small relief. Taylor didn't keep me long, though. He said there was a surprise for me at my apartment and I needed to get to bed anyway. Jim Good grinned as though he were in on the joke. He brought me to my place and opened the door.

Donna was waiting for me. There are a few rare, perfect moments in a person's life; this was one of mine. Of all the homecomings in my life, this was by far the sweetest.

RIYADH

The next day Jim took me to OPM-SANG headquarters, and everyone came up to shake my hand or just look out of their offices at me. Half the people wanted to mob me with questions and the other half treated me as though I were made of porcelain. I was a little uncomfortable with my new celebrity status. I hadn't changed on the inside, and for all the approval and "way to go" comments I got, I still felt dumb for going to Kuwait to begin with.

I learned that Colonel Noble was up with the brigade along with many of the OPM headquarters staff officers. The brigade no longer had just me as an active duty advisor. Bob Quinn and his guys had been up with the brigade the whole time. Just hearing of them made me ache to go back to the brigade. I felt even more useless for not having been there to help them deploy to the border. I had an office call with Brigadier General Taylor and spent an hour telling him of the high points of everything I had seen. He made some phone calls and arranged for me to debrief CENTCOM J2 (intelligence) staff personnel starting the next day. Then I went to get a physical, driving myself for the first time in four months. First, though, I had to change out my uniform because it was too big for me. The physical confirmed that I had gone from 215 to 187 pounds. Otherwise, I was in good shape. Law of unintended consequences: the Saddam Hussein weight-loss clinic. I could just see the advertisements: "Be our guest and we guarantee you'll lose weight." Move over, Richard Simmons. Saddam Hussein, sweatin' to the oldies.

I did a lot of debriefing over the next few days. The interrogators knew what they were about and asked very specific and detailed questions. They were particularly interested in the blast mitigation fortifications around the Baiji oil refineries and the Jambur and Al Hassan project. How high were the blast walls? How thick? What other facilities on the site were hardened against bombing, and what was the purpose of specific buildings? The power plant was of particular interest, and I was able to provide details of where the generators were in the building and where some of the other major control facilities were. A chill went through me as I realized that the people talking to me were target analysts and would use my information to develop the optimum attacks on the sites at which I had been held. I thought of Ra'ad and the people in the control room when we were taken on a tour of the plant. The treated us for all the world like a visiting group from the Better Business Bureau or the Kiwanis. I remember how proud Ra'ad was of his power plant and the embarrassed smiles of the workers. They felt bad about us being there. Now I was helping to engineer their destruction. What a cruel and useless waste it was, one insane son of a bitch and his ambitions and now Ra'ad and his people would pay the price. I hoped that the attack would come at night when there weren't as many people on shift. I also didn't delude myself that some people I had met would probably die as a result of information I brought back. The phrase "fish in a barrel" came to mind. Divulging full intelligence about each site was necessary, of course. It might even help the target planners figure out safer attack profiles for our aircraft. It was a strange feeling just the same. The war was no longer as impersonal as it once had seemed.

The debriefers were also fairly exhaustive in their questions about the antiaircraft defenses I had seen. What kind of training did they do, and what did I think of their crew proficiency? They were very interested in the Roland at Kirkuk. I was dismayed to learn that they hadn't gotten anything from the debriefs of the French or the Germans. Just goes to show that intelligence acquired is only half the battle. Intelligence disseminated to the user is just as important. I quickly filled them in on as much as I knew about the Roland and its hide techniques. I also told them to check with whoever was debriefing in Europe, because there was a lot of intelligence to be gathered from all the other released hostages as well.

Other sections of the J2 were interested in my impressions of the effectiveness of the Iraqi army. I related in detail my observations of their invasion of Kuwait and their training in Iraq. I also told them of my conversations with former Iraqi soldiers who were our minders. I could see that a lot of these officers were falling into the old mathematactics trap of thinking that because the enemy had a big force, it logically followed that it was a *good* force. They were surprised at my stories about no maintenance and starving soldiers in Kuwait City. I told them I thought we would slaughter the Iraqis and the ground war would be over in two to three weeks. I could see the skepticism in some of them, but they took down everything I had to say.

I also debriefed senior members of the Saudi National Guard, including Prince Meteb, the son of Crown Prince Abdullah. They were naturally more interested in the impact of the invasion on Kuwait and the Kuwaitis than in the hostage story itself, so I concentrated on my observations of Kuwait City in those first few days. They were clearly appalled by what I described and were resolved to fight the Iraqis.

Prince Meteb invited the officers and wives of OPM-SANG to dinner at his estate outside Riyadh. It was a lavish affair, and the prince was the perfect host. He was charmed by Donna and made me relate the whole story of how we met in Saudi Arabia. He also demanded to hear the hostage story in detail. I told him some of the more humorous stuff. He thought my story of escape from Germany was immensely funny and told Brigadier General Taylor to be sure and pay me back for the plane ticket I'd had to buy (Taylor had already authorized this anyway). I asked Prince Meteb later that night whether he thought the Iraqis would see reason and withdraw at the last minute. His face took on a sad expression and he shook his head. He was convinced at this stage that there was no way to avoid war. I had thought as much, but hearing it from a senior member of the Saudi government put the whole subject to bed for me. We were going to war.

After about four days of debriefings and physicals, I went to Brigadier General Taylor and asked to be released to return to the 2d Brigade. I wasn't there to help them deploy to the border, but I could still be there for the war. Taylor smiled and told me I would go back to the brigade, but he wanted me to take leave first. "Your family has had a rough time, Marty. You need to go see them. And you should marry Donna while you're at it." It was typical of Taylor. I was hesitant. If I went on leave, I was afraid that after all that had happened, I might miss the start of the action. Brigadier General Taylor smiled and shook his head. "Don't worry about it, Marty. I know that when the war starts, you'll be back in plenty of time. You're going home." He said it with a tone of friendly, authoritarian finality that brooked no discussion. So on 20 December 1990, Donna and I flew back to the States.

LEAVE

I had to go to Washington to brief Brigadier General Taylor's boss on everything that had happened to me. Not that it was necessary. I think it was Taylor's way of paying for the trip.

Donna and I woke up to DC 101 and the Greaseman railing about Mayor Barry. The more things change . . . I did my briefing, then we loafed around Washington waiting for our plane to Orlando. The news was full of the Gulf buildup and dire warnings to President Bush by the Democrats in Congress that he had better receive congressional authorization before taking action.

Now that I was back in the States, I could not help but be struck by the normality with which everyone conducted their lives and the contrasting hysterical tone of the news. I knew it would come to war; there was no way we could send half a million souls to the Gulf and not do something. People in general seemed to be taking it in stride, though.

We set out for Orlando, having completed my small official chore. I was eager to see my parents. Brigadier General Taylor's words on how my captivity had affected them made me nervous. Not for the first time did I realize that they had suffered much more from the captivity than I had. For them it really had been an ordeal.

To say it was an emotional homecoming would be an understatement. My mother was almost crying with joy, and my sister and brother-in-law, Albert, were all over me with questions. Only my dad remained his normal, composed self. I knew he had a lot to say to me but would choose his time. Donna and I told them that we were going to be married, which further added to the festive atmosphere of the arrival. They spent the rest of the day almost driving us crazy with consideration and solicitude. They showed me all the newspaper clippings they had kept and how they had tracked me through Iraq by way of the messages I smuggled out. It was here that I learned that everything I had given Josef got to them within a few weeks of my handing it over. I mentally blessed that good man again and prayed for his safe deliverance from Iraq. My mom also showed a tape of me walking through Frankfurt airport that had been sent to her by Jean Burch, one of my friend's wives. There I was with my American flag. God, did I look skinny.

My parents had kept my whereabouts a tight secret. No media interviews and no fanfare. No one in the army talked either. My friends knew; so did the NTC Mafia, which spread the word within its circles, but that was it. Even though I had been in plain sight, the potentially newsworthy fact that I was a U.S. soldier in Iraqi captivity went unrecorded. This gave me an insight into reporters and the media that has stood me in good stead to this day: Reporters cannot plague you if you refuse to talk to them. The whole news apparatus depends on people who volunteer information to the guys with the cameras. If you don't play, there's nothing they can do. If you have loyal friends who know you're in a bad situation and they had better keep their mouths shut, you're safe. One of my biggest fears throughout my captivity was that somehow the media would get hold of the fact that I was a prisoner and blast it all over the news. I had disturbing mental images of camera trucks besieging our house and rude people bothering my parents. Publicity would also have made me different and special to the Iraqis. (The only U.S. soldier? Hmmm, what were you doing in Kuwait, Major Stanton? Really?) It didn't happen because everyone who cared about me knew enough not to talk about it. I also learned just how close Peggy and Al were to going to Iraq to secure my release. The thought gave me the willies. The propaganda value of it to the Iraqis and the image of my sister as a supplicant to them made my blood boil. I couldn't get mad at Peg, though. Brave big sister would have gone and parleyed with the devil himself to get me back. I was glad that their passport documentation had been delayed until it was too late. I think my dad might have had something to do with that. He showed me cards he'd had made announcing my arrival back home. They looked like wedding invitations. Reading them, I had to laugh. Neatly inscribed on the fine paper was the following paragraph: "Charles R. Stanton takes great pleasure in announcing that on December 9, 1990, his son, Major Martin N. Stanton, got the hell out of Iraq."

Dad finally got to talk to me alone after dinner. It was a different side of my father. He told me that the past four months had been a great strain on him and my mother and that for a while he had steeled himself to consoling my mother about my death. He asked about Kuwait and what I was doing there. I told him the truth, but I was surprised to see him nod as though he didn't believe me. I didn't press the point. (Which would be more disquieting to a parent: that their kid is sent on secret missions into the teeth of the enemy, or that he's so stupid that he goes on vacation to a country that's about to be invaded?) We never discussed it again. His relief at my being back was overwhelming and a bit unsettling to me. He was never a demonstrative person, just always there when I needed him. I stressed to him that I was fine and nothing bad had happened to me in captivity. He seemed reassured by this. We talked about the upcoming war and what I thought would happen, and about the risks I would face. Oddly, he did not seem unduly worried that I was returning to an infantry brigade at war. It was my capture and incarceration in Iraq that had frightened him. Battle, and the fact that—like everyone else—I must take my soldier's chance, he understood. We talked long past everyone else's bedtime. That evening in his study is one of the most pleasant memories I have of my father. I helped him to bed, then turned in myself. Donna nestled up to me, silent and understanding.

I lay on my back and thought of my parents and our home and how lucky I was. It had been a wonderful, giddy, strange day.

The next few days went by in a blur. Donna and I went Christmas shopping and confirmed our flight for Toronto on 27 December. We also made arrangements to be married on the twenty-sixth. I wanted to marry Donna before I went back to the impending war. We didn't know how long the war would last, and neither of us felt like waiting any more. So on the day after Christmas 1990, Donna O'Shaughnessy and I were married at the courthouse in Winter Park, Florida. My parents, sister Peggy, and brother-in-law Albert witnessed the ceremony. Donna was an enchantingly beautiful bride. We spent our short (one-night) honeymoon in the Park Avenue Hotel, then flew up to Toronto to meet my new in-laws.

It was snowing when we got to Toronto. Donna's sister, Louise, who was excited at the news of big sis getting married, picked us up. It must have been a somewhat disorienting experience for my new relations to meet me. "Hi! I'm your new American son-in-law. I just got out of an Iraqi jail and now I'm going back to fight in the Gulf War." This wasn't part of their very normal Canadian lives. They were gracious people, however, and took it all in with aplomb.

Donna and I spent a wonderful five days in Toronto seeing the sights and visiting her friends. We rang in the New Year together and prepared for my return to the Gulf. I went back on 2 January. We had decided that Donna would stay out of the Gulf for a few more weeks on leave until we had a better picture of what would happen. Leaving Donna was hard, and I felt a surge of loneliness as I watched her and Louise walk from the departure area in Toronto airport. Then I turned to the job at hand. After twelve years as an officer in the army, I was going to war.

Part Five

SHIELD'N' AND STORMIN'

12

Back to Brigade

ON MY RETURN TO RIYADH, Brigadier General Taylor congratulated me on my marriage, then told me to get to work. I spent a few days drawing a new vehicle and equipment and being briefed on the latest happenings. I did some last-minute debriefing to a few more people who hadn't gotten a crack at me before Christmas, but I was eager to get back to the brigade. Finally on 5 January I began my journey north. It was time to get on with it.

The drive north was impressive. Military traffic on the road was heavy, and I was constantly passing convoys from various coalition forces, mostly American, but Brit and Saudi as well. Columns of American Bradley fighting vehicles and M1 tanks were moving in the desert on the left-hand side of the road. It seemed as though an unbeatable force was building up in the desert. From the briefings I had gotten at OPM-SANG headquarters in Riyadh, I realized that I was seeing only a fraction of what was here. As I wove in and out of the convoys and saw all the vehicles newly downloaded from VII Corps in Germany, I was hit by the enormity of the buildup.

Periodically I came upon checkpoints manned by Saudi guardsmen, but I was usually waived through. On the odd occasion I was stopped, I identified myself as an advisor to the National Guard. I had the impression that they were more on the lookout for reporters than anything else.

I noticed how friendly and helpful everyone was. Stopping at a transportation fueling station, I got a meal at the Wolfburger and gassed up without anyone asking me who I was or what organization I was with. The morale of the soldiers I chatted with seemed high. Some had been in the desert for months, others only a few days. All had a sense that something would be happening soon and were keyed up about it. Seeing this level of motivation in the usually mellow support troops was encouraging. It made me wonder how my Saudis were doing.

So, late in the afternoon of 5 January 1991, I returned to the King Abdul Aziz Brigade after a five-month absence. The brigade welcomed me back with good humor. They threw a large dinner in the officers' meeting tent, and we all sat on the rugs and cushions and ate goat far into the night. Everyone wanted to know what had happened to me, and I told them the funny stories. Turki looked at me and shook his head. "Didn't I tell you not to go?" he said. In fact, he hadn't, but I just smiled and said that next time I would listen to him. It doesn't cost anything to be polite. Later that night I sat down with Colonel Noble and Bob Quinn, and they brought me back up to speed on what had happened to the brigade in my absence.

Shortly after I had finished talking to Bob Quinn from Kuwait City in August, the brigade had been alerted and given orders to move to the Saudi-Kuwait border with all possible speed. Bob described a hectic all-night effort in which the brigade loaded out all its vehicles and ammunition and drove hell-bent for leather up the highway for Khafji, negotiating refugee traffic as it went. The lead elements of the King Abdul Aziz arrived at the border on 4 August, about the time I was being taken into captivity in Kuwait City—a fact that made me feel even more like a jerk. For more than a week the brigade was the only force facing the Iraqis across the border. The battalions of the brigade were stretched out on a long screen line from the Gulf north of Khafji to almost the heel of Kuwait. They would be able to provide early warning of an invasion and delay the Iraqi advance for a bit, but that was about it. The Ministry of Defense and Aviation (MODA) armored brigades (made up of M60A1 and French AMX 30 tanks) did not get up to the border until the second week of August. Even with them in place, the Saudi forces on the border were only a fraction of the size of the Iraqi army they faced.

Of course, Bob Quinn and the whole Vinnell team went with them. Although this was a gray area in terms of legalities, Quinn and the guys didn't hesitate for a second. They might be civilian contractors, but they were also retired soldiers of long service. Their aid in the next few weeks was invaluable, not only in helping the Saudis get to the border but helping to coordinate the brigade's actions with incoming American forces.

Bob was proud of the Saudis and what they had accomplished. He spoke enthusiastically of the effort they had made to get to the border. He stressed that members of the King Abdul Aziz had done this largely themselves without American aid. He contrasted their move from Al Hofuf to the much slower movement of the MODA brigades, emphasizing with pride that the SANG brigade had moved and supported itself without any contract third country nationals for mechanics and logisticians. I felt his pride as well. The brigade was not perfect, but it had so far performed creditably.

I learned that the next few months were spent training alongside the MODA and the U.S. Marines and that the sector of the border for which the brigade was responsible got smaller, eventually confining itself to the area around Khafji. The brigade's units practiced breaching and assault techniques and did live fires alongside the Marines. As the months dragged on, the King Abdul Aziz instituted a leave policy that let a good number of the troops go back to their homes in Al Hofuf. As a result there was a large parking lot at the rear of the brigade's sector at Saffiniyah for the troops' privately owned cars, creating a large assembly of autos in the middle of the desert. Strange.

The OPM-SANG staff had grown considerably. Initially Colonel Noble had come up to replace me, then subsequently brought other officers from the SANG staff in Riyadh. Officers who had recently departed OPM-SANG were brought back, most notably Bob Sullivan, who came back to the Abdul Aziz to assist Colonel Noble, and Jim Good, who returned to be the intelligence advisor to the eastern province SANG headquarters. As the crisis dragged into the fall, OPM-SANG managed to task the army for additional personnel to flesh out the advisory teams. Unfortunately, once the personnel system started it was difficult to stop, and by the middle of February we had received more officers attached to OPM-SANG than we actually needed. The Saudis were gracious hosts, but toward the end they became somewhat exasperated with the number of American advisors in their midst. Fortunately this did not become a problem until near the end of the war.

Besides the OPM-SANG advisors to the King Abdul Aziz Brigade there were two other groups of Americans: a twelve-man Special Forces team under Capt. Steve Bonk, which was there for liaison purposes, and a Marine ANGLICO (Air Naval Gunfire Liaison Company) team under Captain Braden, which was attached to the brigade in order to provide direction for U.S. naval gunfire and air support. The AN-

GLICO team was a thoroughly professional bunch whose help was to be critical to the brigade in the coming fight. Although there was no formal command relationship between the three teams, Colonel Noble managed to get everyone on the same sheet of music in support of the Saudis. There was little duplicated effort, and the three organizations actually complemented each other well.

This was fortunate, because the weakest part of the brigade was probably its command and control. In spite of the best efforts of Bob Quinn and everyone else during my absence, the brigade tactical operations center (TOC) looked the same way it did the last time I had seen it on exercises: one radio truck with a bunch of maps on the walls and a few people answering radios. Brigade-level command and control was still completely inadequate. We had done everything we could: brought the Saudi staff officers to a U.S. Marine Corps brigade TOC to show them what one looked like, held classes, made map boards and charts for them. You name it, we had tried it. Nothing took. The Saudis were comfortable doing things their way, and only a significant emotional event (such as combat) would change them.

Faced with this, Colonel Noble set up a shadow brigade TOC in another C2 truck that had been allocated to us. We kept our own status and updated locations on all the Saudi units as well as intelligence maps and situation updates. The Saudi staff officers would come to our "advisor TOC" to update their maps and situation boards and discuss actions with us. In effect, the advisor TOC became a detriment to training the real TOC, because we were doing most of the work. The administration and support of the brigade were still being handled by the Saudis in their own informal way. The entire apparatus was creaking along, but Colonel Noble, Bob Quinn, and the rest of us were somewhat apprehensive as to how it would hold up in contact with the enemy.

Colonel Noble gave me an orientation of the brigade's deployment shortly after I returned. The 5th Battalion was screening just south of the border, and the rest of the brigade was about twenty kilometers to the south, in the vicinity of Ras Mishab. A small brigade from the Qatari army was attached to us as well; it consisted of a tank battalion and a mechanized infantry battalion equipped with French tanks and armored personnel carriers (APCs) as well as artillery and support units. The rest of the Arab coalition forces in sector consisted of the 20th and 10th MODA Brigades, a Kuwaiti brigade, and smaller units from Oman, Bahrain, and the UAE. The Eastern Coalition Forces headquarters was located almost twenty kilometers farther south than our brigade headquarters. It was guarded by a battalion of Bangladeshi infantrymen (against what, is beyond me). There was an American advisory team under a Colonel Petri with the eastern headquarters.

On 15 January I went up to Khafji to take a shower and check out the Iraqis from a border observation post (OP). We knew the war would start soon; this would be the last chance to get cleaned up and do laundry for some time. Noble let a few of us at a time travel to the town because it was easier than trying to use the overcrowded facilities in Ras Mishab and Saffiniyah, to the south. I remembered the journey into Khafji from my drive to Kuwait before the war. Then it had been a busy little border town full of traffic. Now it was practically deserted. The Saudis had evacuated the populace, and I saw only a few Saudi guardsmen on the streets as I drove through. I went past the desalinization plant and up to the observation post at the Saudi border crossing station. The Iraqis were clearly visible on the Kuwaiti side about two kilometers away. They appeared to be manning an OP, as we were. Farther back I could just make out what looked like field fortifications and obstacles of their first defensive belt. It was too far away to see much. I studied the closer Iraqis through the binoculars. They did not seem particularly alert or motivated, displaying the same lackadaisical attitude I had seen in many Iraqi soldiers in Kuwait and Iraq. I almost felt sorry for them.

Our observation posts were better organized than those of the Iraqis but still sparsely manned. It doesn't take much to keep eyes on the other side, and there was no point in putting a lot of people forward to be targets. The OPs were made up largely of U.S. and Saudi Special Forces and U.S. Marine Corps recon teams. The 5th Battalion of the King Abdul Aziz was the only combat unit forward in the eastern forces sector. It was set up in a screen line between Khafji and Wakra, a few kilometers behind the border. I talked with the guys at the OP for a few minutes, and they said that it was just another dull day so far. They were happy with the duty, because they were billeted in the workers' quarters of the desalinization plant, which still had power. Other than taking turns to man the OP, they were living a lot better than we were.

After taking my tourist look at the Iraqis, I drove to the Khafji Beach Hotel, a small but pleasant and clean establishment in the northeastern part of town. Although deserted, all of its facilities still worked and the advisors used it to take showers, do laundry, and cook. I spent a fine few hours getting myself and my clothes clean, then cooked myself lunch in the kitchen. I took my food onto the porch and sat looking north with my binoculars into Kuwait. I was able to clearly make out the red-and-white-striped smokestacks of the power station at Mina Saud, but I couldn't see anything useful.

Suddenly I had the happy inspiration to call Donna. Everything else in the hotel worked; why not the phones? Sure enough, after some trial and error and various operators I was able to bill the call to my calling card and got through to Donna. It was about seven in the morning Canada time and she was just getting up. She was surprised to hear from me, and her voice sounded wonderful. We were both talking so fast that neither of us was intelligible. She stopped and I stopped and there was a pause and I tried again. "So how are *you?*" Pause. She let the pause hang for a few seconds to make sure I wasn't going to ask anything else, then answered clearly and resoundingly, "Pregnant!" I was speechless for a good five seconds. "Did you hear me?" she asked. I said yes and was she sure? She was. We talked for about ten minutes about what she should do. I wasn't nearly as keen for her to come back to Saudi Arabia now that she was "with child." She told me I was being silly and of course she would go back to her job. I managed to get her to agree to wait a few more weeks. We talked over names and other practical matters, then she asked how I felt about it all. In truth I was a bit stunned. That we would have children I never doubted; that we would have them this soon was surprising. Then again, marry an Irish Catholic girl from a family of six kids and what did I expect? I told her this and she laughed. We talked a bit longer, but I had to get back before dark. So I said good-bye to my pregnant wife, knowing that the war would start that night. I left the deserted hotel a little dazed and overwhelmed. Kidnapped, held prisoner, released, debriefed, married, going to war, and now this. Any way you look at it, this had been an eventful six months.

I of course shared the news with everyone as soon as I got back to brigade. They were full of congratulations and good-natured kidding. We were geared up for the start of hostilities, which we were certain would begin that night once the ultimatum expired. So that's how I spent my countdown to war, wondering about parenthood and listening to my married buddies' children-and-pregnant-wife war stories.

13

HOSTILITIES

THAT NIGHT THE WAR STARTED. The radio code word for the commencement of hostilities that would go out over the advisor net was Prairie Fire. Toward midnight I lay down on my cot for a few minutes and fell asleep. I awoke to the words, "Prairie Fire, Prairie Fire, Prairie Fire, all stations. . . . Hostilities with Iraq have commenced." I looked at some of the other officers in the tent with me. One turned on the radio and tuned in to the BBC. There were reports of bombings throughout Iraq, of armadas of planes heading north. Some of us went outside and could hear jet engines in the distance as aircraft flew past. The noise of the planes was constant. Suddenly one of us started whistling the theme music to the movie *The Longest Day*. There were a few giggles and several others joined in. For a minute we stood there whistling like idiots, then broke up into loud guffaws. Life imitates art.

Other than the sound of the airplanes in the distance and the news reports, the first night of the war was dull. We didn't hear any explosions or action, and we were already in our dispersed and hunkered-down posture, so there was no movement required. For the most part, the brigade learned about the war the way the rest of the world did, by listening to the radio news. Everyone crowded around battery-powered shortwave radios getting the blow by blow like avid sports fans listening to a playoff game. The only parts of the brigade that were actually forward enough to see into Kuwait were the 5th Battalion and the joint observation posts along the border. None of them reported any enemy activity, although all reported observing the bombing in Kuwait. As the night wore on, people slowly drifted away from the radios and trickled off to bed. The first night of the war ended with a yawn, not a whimper.

The Iraqis retaliated by shelling Khafji the next day. No one was killed, but a Special Forces soldier on one of the observation posts was wounded and the refinery tanks at Khafji were set alight. We could see the large plume of black smoke from our base camp. The Iraqis also began to shell the elements of the 5th Battalion that were screening at the border. None of the Saudi guardsmen was hit, but the order was passed for the 5th Battalion to withdraw out of sight of the Iraqi observation posts. It made sense; there was no point in sitting up there letting the Iraqis shell you. Unfortunately the withdrawal was seen by some reporters and subsequently characterized as a "precipitous retreat," giving the impression that the 5th Battalion was running. Had the reporters asked me, I would have told them that the Saudis just drove like hell everywhere they went. Using that standard, I had been on a bunch of "precipitous" convoy movements with them as well. After pulling back about five to seven kilometers, the 5th Battalion reestablished its screen. The Iraqis kept throwing shells southward, but it was just random, unaimed fire.

We spent the next ten days doing more of the same: conducting training and precombat checks on our equipment, trying to get the brigade commander interested in improving his brigade command post, maintaining awareness of the current situation by receiving updates from the division operations and intelligence advisors and OPM- SANG headquarters itself, and in general being spectators of the war. Every night we heard the planes go by in the distance and in the daytime could see the contrails of the B-52s going north, then heading back to Diego Garcia.

We had one incident of a "chemical attack" false alarm. Some Iraqi long-range artillery hit in the desert a few kilometers from one of our units, and a few of our people reporting feeling sick. By the time this news reached the brigade, it had been exaggerated into a chemical attack. The panic that ensued when this word got out was indescribable. The guardsmen had never become disciplined to always wearing their protective masks, and word of a chemical attack sent the entire brigade headquarters scrambling over the encampment to retrieve their masks. Colonel Noble, who was in the bunker with Turki, later described how a lieutenant had run in screaming and everyone had frantically tried to find a mask. Noble just sat amazed and watched Turki try to open his protective suit, become frustrated with the package, then frantically attack it with a knife. What a sight that must have been. I could see Noble trying to keep a straight face and calm everyone. In the advisor TOC, everyone wore his mask for a few minutes, but then unmasked after observing the goats at the mess truck unconcernedly munching their hay and showing no effects of chemical agent poisoning. None of our M8 alarms had gone off either. It took a good half hour to calm everyone down. An investigation of the cause of the incident revealed that it was food poisoning. None of the troops was permanently incapacitated.

The incident was humorous but did have one benefit. The Saudis wore their protective masks from then on. The few hard-core Islamists who refused to shave their beards or wear boots (as opposed to sandals) we would probably lose on the first real chemical attack. (Another training point: We could say to the Saudis, "You see why you need to shave your beard, so your mask will fit properly.") I was concerned about their ability to survive in a chemical environment. I hoped we didn't get hit with anything but a nonpersistent agent. As it turned out, the Iraqis never did use a chemical agent, so maybe those frizzy-bearded guardsmen were right all along: God really does protect them.

For the most part, though, the first ten days had us sitting around, wondering when we would get our chance with the enemy. It was to come sooner than we thought, in a manner we didn't suspect.

The field artillery battalion of the 2d Brigade was the first Saudi ground unit to strike a blow against the Iraqis. The Marines in the adjacent sector had begun conducting artillery raids against the Iraqis about a week after hostilities began. These raids were typically done by a single battery of 155 howitzers, with ground maneuver forces for security. The batteries would move to firing locations close to the Kuwaiti border, then attack preselected targets in the Iraqis' first defensive belt. Their targets had been previously identified by intelligence and were selected for their relatively stationary nature. The overall impact of these raids on the Iraqis was minimal in and of itself; however, the raids gave the Iraqis yet another way of being attacked that they had to worry about while at the same time providing valuable experience to the Marine artillery units and the forces that secured them. As a shakedown exercise to units that were still new to war, the raids were very valuable.

Colonel Noble coordinated through the ANGLICO team to have some of the Marine officers who had conducted the raids come and talk to the SANG brigade headquarters, in hopes of getting them interested in conducting similar operations in our sector. The briefings went well. Colonel Muthi was all for conducting the raids and wanted to begin as soon as possible. Colonel Turki was less enthusiastic. I'm sure he was aware that no other Saudi ground units had yet engaged the Iraqis in the war, and he was hesitant to be first. The idea was shelved for a couple of days, but Colonel Noble finally talked Colonel Turki into letting the artillery battalion conduct a raid into Kuwait.

Once Colonel Turki assented to conduct the mission, he allowed the brigade staff to work with us and the eastern division headquarters to plan the raid. We set the raid's date for the night of 27–28 January. The targets for the raid (two air defense sites behind the first defensive belt) were based on intelligence received by the eastern division HQ from CENTCOM.

The raid would consist of two artillery batteries, each with a line company escort from the 6th Battalion. The batteries would go to two separate firing points and each engage their respective Iraqi air defense site. The method of attack would be rocket-assisted projectile, or RAP. This would give the M198 howitzers a maximum range of thirty kilometers. The actual distance to target from the selected firing positions was twenty-six and twenty-seven kilometers, respectively—long shots but not impossible ones. Each battery would fire five rounds per gun, then displace. Ideally, within the space of a few minutes each of the targets would receive forty 155 high-explosive rounds—enough to ruin your day. More importantly, the Saudis would be on the scoreboard in terms of ground combat. We hoped that this action would presage even further Saudi offensive operations.

The day of the raid, the batteries and their escorting forces practiced getting into position several times. The Saudis could occupy their firing positions fairly quickly. They were more concerned with quick displacement. As had many of the units in the coalition, the Saudis had been given briefings on Iraqi capabilities and believed what they had been told. They were concerned that the Iraqi's South African G6 howitzers could outrange them for counterbattery fire in spite of the fact that none had been reported to be supporting the Iraqis' first defensive belt, and the Iraqis possessed relatively few counterbattery radars. The Saudis' fear of possible Iraqi counterfire was overblown, but we allowed them to factor it into their overall scheme of maneuver because it was good practice. Besides, we did not want to do anything to discourage their preparations for the mission.

While the brigade staff and artillery battalion were preparing for the mission, there was a series of confusing messages from the eastern division that either rescinded permission for the raid or granted final permission for it. We could tell that the Saudi higher command was not too enamored of the idea but couldn't cancel it for fear of losing face in front of us. Finally we got the word on the morning of 27 January allowing the brigade to conduct artillery raids but warning that the permission could be rescinded at any time.

All Colonel Muthi needed was the go-ahead. He quickly organized his forces for the raid on the night of 27–28 January. The 1st Battery and 2d Battery would actually participate in the raid and 6th Battalion would provide security. The final locations for targets were given and plotted in the battery's fire direction centers. The firing points were confirmed as safe by reconnaissance elements. We would ensure accurate after-dark arrival at these locations by the use of global positioning systems (GPS). It was to be a mainly Saudi show.

Majors Newton and Wallace would accompany the artillery batteries as advisors to provide technical expertise if needed. Major Dunn would accompany the escorting infantry companies from the 6th Battalion. I would go along to observe the operations to recommend training modifications and capture lessons learned from the raid. My position was the most superfluous of the four Americans accompanying the raid, and I was afraid that Colonel Noble would cut me from the mission. To my delight he accepted without comment my rationale for going. I had been with the brigade longer than any of the other advisors, so I might provide insights that others may miss. But more than that, I think he sensed in me a need to go on the brigade's first combat mission. Reacting to his permission with more overt happiness than I should have shown, I went to get my gear.

I linked up with the brigade headquarters element traveling with the raid, and we subsequently joined the artillery batteries and their escorts in the assembly area. We left at dusk; the movement out to the firing positions was slow and cautious. The Saudis did not possess as many night vision devices as did U.S. forces, so most of their drivers were without night vision goggles. The column traveled about twenty kilometers per hour and halted several times to confirm direction of travel and ensure that we did not inadvertently bump into one of the coalition outposts along the border, or cross the border it-self. These fears were overblown, because it was a fairly clear night and the GPS showed us to be traveling right on track. I found it to be a forgivable show of caution. The Saudis were as nervous as any troops conducting their first real combat operation. They wanted to do the job right.

There was only one difficulty—communications. The raid forces lost radio contact with brigade around 2100, but because we had communications with the 6th Battalion throughout the course of the raid I didn't worry too much. If anything of true import happened, the raid forces could reach us through the 6th Battalion. As it turned out, this loss of communications with brigade was more critical than I thought.

We finally arrived at our firing positions around 2330. After spend-ing a few minutes to confirm that we were indeed at the right loca-tions, the word went out to establish battery positions and prepare to fire the missions. The Saudis went to work with a will. The V-150s of the escorting infantry took up defensive positions around the two batteries, and the batteries themselves went through a textbook night occupation. I watched the Saudi artillerymen in the moonlight as they pulled their trucks into position, dismounted, and emplaced the guns while others set up aiming circles and aiming stakes for the weapons. Trucks disgorged ammunition at each gun position, and the fire direction center (FDC) was established to the rear of the battery. I was impressed; it was the best night occupation I had ever seen them do. Newton and Wallace went from gun to gun, then to the FDC, checking, observing, and conferring with the Saudi officers. Wallace told me that there wasn't much for them to do in the way of advising because the Saudis had done a good job. The only fly in the ointment was that Colonel Muthi had arbitrarily cut the number of rounds to be fired from five to four. That old bugbear of the imag-inary Iraqi counterbattery capability was rearing its head again. I told my compatriots that it wasn't worth arguing about at this point, that it was more important that the Saudis shot—period—as opposed to how much they shot.

In short order, all was in readiness. Colonel Muthi tried to contact brigade to tell them he was about to shoot, but he could not estab-lish communications. He relayed the message to 6th Battalion and gave the word for his guns to load, then stand by. The Saudi ar-tillerymen at each gun grabbed the first 155 round on its tray and lifted it to the breach. Other artillerymen shoved it into the gun with a rammer, then followed the projectile with powder bags. The gun was then craned to its proper azimuth and elevation. One by one the big M198 barrels crept steeply skyward pointing into Kuwait. Each gun reported its readiness, and the lanyard was held by the sergeant in charge of the piece in anticipation of the fire command. When every gun was ready, Colonel Muthi gave the command.

The eruption of sixteen 155 howitzers was shocking in the quiet night, not only because of the noise but the large fireball that came from firing a rocket-assisted projectile. Feverishly the Saudi gunners worked to get their second projectile loaded. Some guns were faster than others; instead of repeating the first perfect volley, the subsequent rounds went out in a fever pitch of activity, with the Saudi artillerymen loading and ramming the projectiles and powder as though their lives depended on it. In less than two minutes all rounds were complete and the trucks were already backing up to the guns, whose crews were working frantically to restore them to travel configuration. I stood to the side and watched them with interest. If there really were an Iraqi counterbattery capability, we should be seeing return fire soon. The Saudis continued to break down their battery position in record time. Some trucks were loaded faster than others and disappeared to the south into the darkness.

I then realized that a control measure had been omitted in our planning. Unlike the Marines, who had radios in practically every vehicle, the Saudis had only a few radios in the battery. We had neglected to designate a rally point. A sensible control measure would have been to designate a location that was four to five kilometers south of the battery positions where all trucks could assemble and count noses. This would have gotten us out of the possible impact area for unobserved counterbattery fire more quickly. As it was, most of the trucks and guns waited for the last of their compatriots to finish before they moved out. The others who had gone off on their own took a while to round up. At any rate, this was one lesson learned. We had treated the raid as just another fire mission. Even done with indirect fire, all the control measures for a raid should be used, including a withdrawal plan and rally points. It didn't matter that much this time, because there was no Iraqi counterfire. But you might as well do things correctly.

The Saudis were pleased with their efforts. The brigade team with me was all smiles, and Colonel Muthi looked especially happy. He had a right to be. His battalion had performed its first mission better than anyone had expected and made history in the bargain. They had fired the first Saudi shots of the Gulf War.

The drive back took almost as long as the drive out. I returned to brigade at dawn. Somehow the long ride back didn't chafe as much as going out had. Everyone was happy, Americans as well as Saudis. Newton told me later that he was concerned about the accuracy of the subsequent RAP shells, because the Saudis had rammed them in when the guns were still superelevated (as opposed to being brought down to loading elevation). But he was sure that the rounds had cleared the border and gone into enemy territory, so no harm was done to friendlies. The SANG gunners would get their technique down better in subsequent missions. For now, it was enough that they had shot. As for the Saudi artillerymen themselves, they were pumped.

Colonel Muthi was hardly prepared for the reception he received when he arrived at brigade headquarters after the raid. Colonel Turki was furious. Apparently at the last minute the eastern division had sent down orders putting the raid on hold, and Colonel Turki had been unable to call them back. That the Saudi eastern division commander would get cold feet about this was not surprising. Although the coalition was conducting massive air operations out of Saudi Arabian territory (operations in which the Saudi air force was participating in a large scale), no Saudi ground forces had been yet engaged. I questioned Colonel Noble as to any possible tactical reasons for canceling the raid, but he shook his head. He was exasperated with the Eastern Coalition Forces commander. Clearly the cat was out of the bag in terms of hostilities. There was nothing to be gained by holding back. It was just the old Saudi mentality of not wanting to be first.

Unfortunately this mix-up had serious repercussions within the brigade's chain of command. Colonel Turki ripped Muthi, and for a while we were afraid that he was going to relieve him. Colonel Noble called Brigadier General Taylor in Riyadh to brief him on the situation and prepare him to intercede with the National Guard's leadership on Muthi's behalf should this become necessary. Fortunately it wasn't. Noble was able to calm Turki and make him realize that the raid was a done deal and nothing would be gained by savaging the artillery battalion commander. The thing to work on was improving communications. Once again the inadequacy of using high-frequency

(HF) radios as a primary means of communication was made apparent. Major Pancoast, the communications advisor, and the Saudis went to work on the fixes.

But before we could implement any lessons learned from the artillery raid, the Iraqis attacked Khafji. In the most unexpected way possible, the King Abdul Aziz was about to be involved in its biggest fight of the war.

14

KHAFJI

THE IRAQI ATTACK ON KHAFJI surprised everyone. Not so much because we didn't think the Iraqis had the capability to do it, just because it didn't make any sense to try it. At first, reports were incredibly confused and we had a great deal of difficulty making out that this was in fact a tactical emergency and not just another border skirmish. In truth we didn't get a good grasp of what was going on until well over a day into the fight, and then it took us almost two days to finish it. Khafji was in many ways a revelation to me. It was the first real battle I had ever participated in; and for sheer "Who's on first?" confusion, I've never seen the like, before or since.

Like most great events, it began subtly. I was in the advisor TOC van and had just finished writing my statement about Colonel Muthi's artillery raid for Colonel Noble. He had spent most of the afternoon talking to Turki and calming him down. Colonel Noble thought that Muthi was out of the woods in terms of danger of being relieved, but he wanted statements about the raid from those of us who participated in case it did get bloody. There was no doubt in my mind that Noble and Bob Quinn would fight for Muthi, and no doubt that they should. The idea that a commander could be in trouble for attacking the enemy under such circumstances seemed silly. Noble was in the bunker now, schmoozing with Turki. Although at first I had been resentful of having my title as senior advisor to the brigade taken from me by all these interlopers, now I was grateful. Noble was better at cajoling Turki than I ever could be, although I knew that having to do it grated on him. I was still preoccupied by these thoughts when we started getting reports from 5th Battalion about contact on the border.

The Iraqi attack on Khafji began in the late evening of 29 January. Because the observation posts along the border sensibly withdrew when the first Iraqi echelons came into sight, initial reports about the strength and composition of the Iraqi forces were confused. It took almost until the end of the battle to obtain a good appreciation of the enemy we faced. The Iraqis who attacked Khafji had come from the 5th Mechanized Infantry Division, a unit that had been in reserve behind the Iraqi forward defensive belts. The division moved south, passing through these defenses, and split into two columns. One column went toward the Wakra oil fields and the other headed down the main highway to Saudi Arabia and Khafji itself. By 1:30 in the morning of 30 January, all the observation posts along the border north of Khafji had reported the Iraqi advance and begun to withdraw.

During this withdrawal, a team of Marines was cut off from escaping and went to ground in the town. Although this caused great consternation and concern for the welfare of the trapped Marines, it turned out to be fortunate, because the reports from the hidden men were the only accurate intelligence that the brigade had on the enemy's movements in Khafji on that first day of the battle. Despite the trapped Marines' best efforts, however, they could see only a portion of the town, and the intelligence picture was still vague. Throughout the morning and early afternoon, the 2d Brigade continued to get conflicting and erroneous reports of what was happening in Khafji.

At approximately 1300 on 30 January, the brigade was given the order from the Eastern Coalition Forces commander to detach a battalion and establish a screen south of Khafji. At 1500 the 7th Battalion was given the mission. For the purposes of this mission, two Qatari tank companies would also be attached to the 7th Battalion. The battalion commander (Lieutenant Colonel Matar) was given no useful intelligence other than "the enemy is in Khafji" and no time to conduct any reconnaissance. At approximately 1600, the battalion moved out from its defensive positions in the vicinity of Ras Mishab and advanced up the coast highway toward Khafji. Two American advisors, battalion advisor Lt. Col. Mike Taylor and Master Sergeant Middleton, traveled with the 7th Combined Arms Battalion (CAB).

When the battalion reached the gas station three kilometers south of Khafji, it encountered elements of the 3-3 Marines from Task Force Taro. The Marines had been sent up to keep Khafji under observation and facilitate the rescue of their trapped teams. Lieutenant

Colonel Taylor began to conduct coordination with them when word came that the mission of the 7th Battalion had been changed. The battalion was no longer to establish a screen south of Khafji; instead, it was to retake Khafji. Colonel Matar digested this, then called his company commanders forward to be briefed. Meanwhile, Lieutenant Colonel Taylor continued to coordinate with the Marines and succeeded in getting artillery and attack helicopter support for the attack. The Marines also directed a small unit made up of TOW and .50-caliber machine gun-armed Humvees to follow the 7th Battalion. These elements were to move in and recover the Marine recon teams when the moment was right.

It took a while to sort this out, and the attack was delayed by the necessity of waiting for two Qatari tank companies that were cross attached to the 7th Battalion. Further delays were experienced trying to clear preparatory fires on Khafji. The Marine artillery was reticent to shoot preparatory fires into Khafji because of the presence of friendlies (the recon teams). This, in spite of the fact that those same recon teams had been reporting and directing artillery fires for the better part of eighteen hours already. Finally a fifteen-minute preparatory fire was shot by the Marine artillery on the southern half of Khafji. At 2300 the 7th Battalion moved forward from its positions south of town toward Khafji.

As the 7th Battalion advanced toward town, it was met by an extremely heavy volume of fire. Lieutenant Colonel Taylor, a veteran of infantry combat in Vietnam, described the volume of enemy fire as "flabbergasting." The initial Saudi attack was halted outside Khafji, with the National Guard companies and the Qatari tanks exchanging fire with the Iraqis for the better part of two hours. Finally at 0320, Colonel Matar ordered a withdrawal to behind the National Guard barracks compound adjacent to Khafji. En route to the compound, the battalion encountered a large fence that blocked its movement. The 7th Battalion had to breach this fence using grappling hooks while continuing to suppress the enemy with fire. Shortly thereafter, the guardsmen withdrew behind the SANG compound, temporarily breaking direct fire contact with the enemy (although intermittent tracer fire could still be seen coming from Khafji).

A large amount of ammunition had been expended in the battle, and an ammunition resupply convoy (called a logistics package, or LOGPAC) was sent forward to replenish the 7th Battalion's ammunition load. This LOGPAC somehow missed its linkup and instead

drove past the battalion toward Khafji. Two of the vehicles in the LOGPAC were destroyed, and only good luck prevented the Saudis from taking casualties or losing more vehicles. The remainder of the LOGPAC quickly reversed out of Khafji; it eventually linked up with the 7th Battalion and transferred its ammunition.

Throughout the engagement, communications between brigade and the 7th Battalion were inadequate. This was due in large part to the unwillingness of the brigade commander to move his headquarters forward. The only reliable communications between the 7th Battalion and the brigade was over advisor nets using civilian citizens band radios that were left over from the prewar advisory group. The advisors talked over the long distances through the relay/retrans station (call sign Cherokee) set up by the communications advisor, Major Pancoast, and the Vinnell contractors. This station was the most reliable communications node available to the coalition forces during the battle. What little intelligence the 7th Battalion received was given to it before the battalion moved forward, sent over the advisor net, or obtained from the Marines at the gas station. As a result, the battalion had attacked blind into a much larger force than it anticipated. Only the fact that the Iraqis were as disorganized as the Saudis prevented the 7th Battalion from taking many more casualties.

At the advisor TOC that first night, the frustration was palpable. It was clear early on that the 7th Battalion, instead of rounding up a company-sized element, was in a fight with something significantly larger. Colonel Noble repeatedly tried to get Colonel Turki to move his tactical command post (TAC-CP) forward that night, but the brigade commander refused. Turki would not leave his bunker, although there were no communications in the bunker other than the single telephone. He would have to get officers sitting in Pinzgauer radio vehicles outside the bunker to tell him what was happening. The communications from the Pinzgauers was spotty, though, and Turki relied primarily on the American advisors to learn what was going on. Colonel Noble stayed in the bunker that first night to try to get Turki to act. Noble periodically called us on his Motorola brick radio for updates or quickly left the bunker to come to the advisor TOC to find out what was going on. However, he could never stay for long, because Colonel Turki kept sending runners asking for Colonel Noble to return to the bunker. Noble became exasperated. He couldn't track the fight from Turki's bunker very well, but at the

same time he couldn't persuade Turki to come out of his hole in the ground. Noble was dependent upon us to feed him information. Finally he told Lieutenant Colonel Sun to go into the bunker and take "Turki watch" for a while. The name stuck instantly, and Noble and Lieutenant Colonel Sun spent the better part of the next thirty-six hours conducting Turki watch, occasionally relieved by myself or Major Tidler. Turki didn't like us mere majors, though, so for the most part the onerous duty of holding Turki's hand fell on Colonel Noble and, later in the battle when Noble and I were forward, Lieutenant Colonel Sun. I did not envy them the duty, because the air in the bunker was barely breathable. The woodstove upon which they heated their tea, combined with the sweat of crowded bodies, made for a stygian atmosphere.

Colonel Turki clung to John Noble like a life preserver. I remember coming in to give Noble an update on what was happening in Khafji and watching Turki hang on Noble's every word. I could not help but contrast Turki with Matar in the 7th Battalion, Hamud in the 8th, or indeed any of his subordinate commanders. They might have had their shortcomings as officers, but at least they *commanded* their battalions. As I watched Turki dither in his bunker this first night, I reflected on what a pity it was that Meteb Jawal had been replaced in June. Meteb was at least aggressive. If he had been in charge, he would have been up at Khafji already getting a firsthand appraisal of what was going on. The biggest problem we would have had with Meteb Jawal was keeping him from attacking the enemy personally.

Another problem we had was a lack of maps of the town proper. Each battalion team had only one, and there was one in the advisor TOC. We had map sheets of adjoining areas but not enough of Khafji proper. These map sheets were on order, but there was a shortage of them theaterwide. So we went into the first night's fight with insufficient maps. This was a classic case of sitting on the solution and not seeing it. The American NCO working in the advisor TOC the first night was Sergeant First Class Desjardins, a cavalryman who had been sent to OPM-SANG from the States. A master gunner and all-around brilliant NCO, he had been invaluable in helping the Saudis improve their training on the 90mm gun. Now his common sense was coming to the fore again. Hearing me tell the 7th Battalion advisors that we had no more maps to give, he shook his head. "Hell of a way to fight a war," he said. Half an hour later he exclaimed, "Jesus

Christ!" and removed the map from the wall. I thought he'd gone nuts and asked him what he was doing. "The copier!" he yelled. I saw the solution at once. We could make black-and-white copies of the map, which would be a whole lot better than nothing. We all set to work making copies of the map and sent them forward with Sergeant Desjardins. Lieutenant Colonel Sun and I looked sheepishly at each other. I reflected on the fact that there was probably a hundred years' worth of college education among the officers who had looked at the map issue, and it took a master gunner with some common sense to finally solve the problem. NCOs truly are the gold of the army.

After the initial setback, the 2d Brigade ordered 6th Battalion and 8th Battalion to cross attach one company each to 7th Battalion, and ordered 7th Battalion to attack again at 0730. Although the brigade commander still refused to send his TAC-CP forward to control the fight, the brigade did send forward one communications vehicle and Capt. Mohammed Al Gharni to "coordinate" efforts. The 7th Battalion attack was to be coordinated with an attack by the 5th Battalion and a MODA tank battalion; the attack would take place to the northwest of town. It was decided that the 7th Battalion would attack the southeastern part of Khafji with three companies, keeping the two attached companies in reserve. The MODA forces were to take the western part of Khafji. From these initial footholds, the Saudis planned to move south to north to secure the town. As it turned out, the MODA battalion was not able to get into position quickly enough, and the National Guard attacked alone.

This plan of attack was based on no real reconnaissance other than the initial contact with the Iraqis. It was uncoordinated by brigade in all but the most general terms. What coordination was done was accomplished by the Saudi battalion commanders, Capt. Mohammed Al Gharni, Colonel Noble, Bob Quinn, and Captain Braden's ANGLICO. The ANGLICO was especially useful in relaying reports from the trapped Marine recon teams and assisted the advisors and the Saudis by relaying radio messages for them.

By 0830 the 7th Battalion had commenced its attack into town, meeting heavy resistance, losing several V-150s, and taking numerous personnel casualties. The battalion's casualties would have been even greater but for the fact that the Iraqi fire, although heavy in volume, was inaccurate. Because the MODA battalion was not in position in time, the 7th Battalion had to use the attached two companies from the 6th and 8th Battalions to attack in the MODA sector. The 7th

Battalion and its attachments made good progress into the town and knocked out numerous Iraqi APCs and tanks. Because of the lateness of the MODA forces, the brigade (on Noble's urging) ordered the 8th Battalion with several attached antitank platoons from the 6th Battalion forward at 1000 to assist the 7th Battalion in its attack. The 8th Battalion displaced forward to the gas station south of Khafji accompanied by Lieutenant Colonel Bowers, Major Sampson, Major Lockett, and Sergeant First Class Melby.

Meanwhile the 5th Battalion was conducting a separate action to the north of town. There had been tremendous confusion early in the morning when Iraqi tanks approached the 5th Battalion and the crews dismounted. The Saudis called on them to surrender, but after a few minutes the Iraqis remounted and drove off. No shots were fired. At about 1000 the 5th Battalion, under Lieutenant Colonel Naif, had moved to engage and destroy an Iraqi company in the vicinity of the main road north of Khafji. It knocked out thirteen tanks and APCs (with one TOW gunner personally knocking out four Iraqi armored vehicles) and captured several more along with 116 prisoners for the loss of two killed in action (KIA) and five wounded in action (WIA). A MODA tank battalion with M60A1s was supposed to join in this action, but its commander was afraid of moving to the north of Khafji and becoming a victim of possible fratricide. The battalion positioned itself to the northwest of town and didn't move for the rest of the battle. The senior advisor with the 5th Battalion, Lieutenant Colonel Laage, tried to reason with the MODA tank battalion commander, but it was no use. The tank battalion stayed in place for more than two days. Meanwhile, after destroying all the Iraqi vehicles in sight and securing their prisoners, the 5th Battalion withdrew four kilometers to positions north of the SANG compound. This withdrawal was a tactical error, because even though the tank battalion was not moving forward to support them, the 5th Battalion had been in a good position to block the Iraqis' escape route from Khafji. Now, because it had pulled back, it left the road open and a few Iraqi vehicles managed to escape.

The 7th Battalion continued the attack in the town, with the attached company of the 8th Battalion making contact with and relieving one Marine recon team at 1200. (The other recon team evacuated the town on its own during an opportune moment in the fighting.) The remainder of the 8th Battalion later linked up with the 7th Battalion and took over the northeastern sector of town. The at-

tack continued with the two battalions abreast clearing most of the southern and eastern parts of town. In these engagements, the Saudi V-150 armored cars proved to be much more agile in street fighting than the Iraqi armor, in some cases wheeling quickly around the block to engage a tank from the rear before it could turn.

The volume of fire continued to be heavy (if largely inaccurate), and the damage to the town of Khafji was increasing rapidly. The Saudi guardsmen did, however, knock out about a dozen more Iraqi tanks and APCs and largely destroyed what little tactical cohesion the Iraqis had left. Unfortunately, pockets of Iraqis were bypassed throughout the town. The battalion advisors were concerned about fratricide if we stayed in the town after dark. Around 1830 (dusk) the attack was discontinued, with the 7th Battalion traveling back to the SANG compound to rearm and refit and the 8th Battalion remaining in place at the edge of town. Later we learned that at this point the Iraqi remnants, consisting of approximately 20 armored vehicles and 150 to 200 troops, were still in the northeastern portion of town. Isolated Iraqi vehicles made it out of Khafji on the night of 31 January, but no organized attempt was made to withdraw from the city, in spite of the fact that the road to the north was open. Although at the time I was dismayed when I learned that the 7th Battalion was withdrawing out of town, later I came to see the sense in it. The last thing we needed was to stay intermixed with the Iraqis in the town during hours of darkness. The chances for fratricide were too great. We had caused the Iraqis a lot of losses, and even though we still didn't have a good handle on the size of the Iraqi forces in Khafji, interrogation of prisoners taken indicated that the Iraqis had suffered considerable losses and were shaken and demoralized. If we stayed among the remaining Iraqis, the chances were greater that we would shoot one another in the dark. The prevailing thought was that we would finish the battle the next day, and it wasn't worth risking casualties to the battalion by staying in town.

In addition to the drama going on at Khafji that night, there were some nutty things as well. Bob Quinn and Colonel Noble were near the gas station with the SANG brigade TAC-CP under Captain Al Gharni collecting reports from the battalions and coordinating resupply. There was still sporadic firing coming from the town, and the smoke and cordite smell of battle was everywhere. Some Marine Hummers came up behind the TAC-CP, and in the darkness a Marine officer came over and asked for an update. Thinking that he was from

Task Force Taro to our rear, Quinn quickly updated the Marine on everything he knew, using his map and giving all the latitude-longitude coordinates he had. The Marine thanked Quinn and went back to his vehicles. Ten minutes later the guy was back asking for another update. Quinn was perplexed, but he updated the officer with what he knew. The man went away again and through the darkness Quinn could see him briefing a group of people. A bit later the officer came up again and asked what was going on. He also inquired about the location of any U.S. Marine units. This time Quinn got mad. "What the hell kind of liaison officer are you? You don't have a map, you don't even know where your own people are." Somewhat abashed, the Marine answered that he was a public affairs officer escorting a reporter pool. Colonel Noble told him to get the hell out of there and stop bothering them.

Meanwhile there was a series of frightening false alarms in the brigade due to false intelligence reports received from Eastern Coalition Forces headquarters. The eastern forces advisory team had received word from Marine Forces Central Command (MARCENT) that J-Stars had picked up a fifteen-kilometer-long armored column heading south from Ahmadi in Kuwait to Khafji. This column was identified as the remainder of the 5th Mechanized Division and was supposed to consist of several hundred more tanks and APCs plus artillery. If taken at face value, this report presented the Saudi guardsmen with a quandary. The oncoming Iraqi force would vastly outnumber the guard forces currently engaged in Khafji. What made it even worse was that Khafji was on the north of the large, impassable Sabka (salt flats), and the only way out of town was the two-lane road through the center of the salt flats. There was no way we could get everyone out in time if the reports of what was coming down and its proximity were correct. An attempted withdrawal to the south of the salt flats would have turned into a disorganized mess. Besides, it would have been disastrous for the morale of the guardsmen, who so far had fought a successful, if somewhat disorganized, battle. A decision to withdraw would have given the Iraqis victory. I started formulating a plan to go into hasty defense around Khafji. The three battalions forward (5th, 7th, and 8th) could certainly move in and establish defenses in the parts of town we owned. Although the Iraqis would be on us before light, there was no reason to assume we couldn't last until past daylight. Then coalition aircraft could eat them up. I had this plan in my head when I briefed Colonel Noble a few minutes later.

It was here that I got a lesson in battle command and making decisions. I explained the report of the Iraqi column to Colonel Noble and started to explain my proposed hasty defense to him. I was anxious. We had to get the orders out to the battalions. With only about three hours before the first Iraqis were due to show up, time was of the essence. Colonel Noble politely told me to be quiet for a second. He pursed his lips and studied the map, looking at the distances, measuring, contemplating. He asked what the sources of this report were and I said J-Stars. (I didn't understand what J-Stars was except that it was supposed to be the newest early-warning and long-range reconnaissance and detection platform. Sort of like a ground AWACS. The limited briefings we'd had on its capabilities claimed that it was just short of infallible.) Noble digested this, then asked whether there was any second source of confirming intelligence. I told him no, not to my knowledge. I was concerned that he was going to sit on the information and reminded him that we were on a tight time line if we were going to get into hasty defensive positions to receive the attack. Still being polite, he held up his hand as if to order silence, then looked at the map again. Then he looked at me and said, "I don't believe it, I don't believe this report is true. We will continue to prepare to attack in the morning."

I was momentarily taken aback. I mentioned again that this was a J-Stars report and that division advisors had taken it seriously. He smiled at this. "Marty, we had a whole lot of electronic crap like this in Vietnam too," he said. "It was wrong more than it was right." He went on to explain that the key thing was to quickly verify reports such as this with second sources, preferably "eyes on." He further cautioned me about telling the Saudis about this. Noble would break it to Turki in his own way, to ensure that Turki would not panic and order a withdrawal. Noble said, "The battalions have done some good fighting. It would be a shame to lose this momentum we've built by withdrawing or going into defensive posture when we don't really need to."

The whole conversation took less than fifteen minutes, but it held a lot of lessons for me. Like many younger officers, I took on faith the infallibility of our new electronic warfare and surveillance capabilities and believed that everything they said must be gospel. Noble, the old veteran, instinctively distrusted them. But, typical of him, he turned the whole episode into a sort of one-on-one class to me. Not just "You're wrong, young major, here's what we're going to do" but "You're wrong and here's why and here's what you really need to be thinking about"—not only the enemy but the effect on friendly morale and the personality of the Saudi commander. Like the old blind Chinese monk in the TV series *Kung Fu*, Noble was always finding lessons to impart to his apprentices. ("Snatch the pebble from my hand, Grasshopper.")

After Noble was done talking to me, I felt foolish. I went back to talk to division advisors and tried to get an update on the Iraqi reinforcements. They didn't have any more news but said that a lot of air strikes were being diverted onto the road leading south from Ahmadi. This would atritt and slow whatever was coming down. I asked whether anyone could actually see anything on the road, but they replied negative knowledge. Basically, we knew all there was to know already. I thought about Noble and his decision to continue with our preparation to attack. He was already in the bunker talking to Turki and couching the J-Stars report in such terms as to not throw the jittery Saudi commander into a panic.

John Noble was taking a lot on himself with this decision. It came home to me that this was the true test of command: to take incomplete information, then use all your training and life's experience to come up with a quick decision. There was no way for Colonel Noble to know 100 percent for sure that he was right. But his intuition told him that the J-Stars report wasn't true, and he knew he had to do something. So he decided to advise Turki to continue the attack, and he never looked back. In doing so, he ensured the victory the next day.

As it turned out, the J-Stars reports had been erroneous. No additional Iraqi forces ever showed up, and I eventually found out that the J-Stars had mistaken long rows of barbed wire for vehicular movement. At least that was the story I got when I inquired after the war. Who knows? Gremlins in the night, maybe. Anyway, Noble had been right.

I went forward with Noble and the TAC the next morning. We resumed the attack on 1 February at 0730 with 7th and 8th Battalions initially attacking abreast into Khafji, with the 8th Battalion then swinging south to eliminate the last pockets of Iraqis in the southern part of town. Meanwhile the 5th Battalion would continue to provide security to the north, and the MODA tank battalion would ostensibly help them. At least this is what the MODA brigadier general told Colonel Noble. I could see that Noble didn't believe him, but he was polite about it and thanked the general. Noble then got back to coordinating the attack through Captains Mohammed Al Gharni and Ayash.

Colonel Noble briefed Lieutenant Colonels Taylor and Bowers on the attack, and they went off to see their counterparts. Bowers was his normal jocular self; Mike Taylor looked tired and somewhat overawed by what he had seen the previous day. "That's the most tracer bullets I've ever seen in my life," he said. I thought that if a solid Vietnam vet such as Taylor was impressed, this must be a big fight. He had actually been firing the .50-caliber machine gun in the commander's vehicle that first night, suppressing RPG gunners firing from the rooftops, while Lieutenant Colonel Matar had been commanding the battalion. What struck me, though, was the way, almost in the next breath, Taylor said that they would be going back in as soon as the 8th Battalion was up. Here he was admitting that it was the biggest fight he had ever seen, then preparing instantly to go back in. Mike Taylor had a lot of guts.

I spent the last day of the fight helping Colonel Noble and Bob Quinn coordinate the efforts of the 5th Battalion and MODA tanks with the main attack by the 7th and 8th Battalions. This was frustrating because of communications limitations. We had to relay through a lot of people to reach everyone. The lack of decent FM tactical radios was really being felt. Citizens band (CB) is not a good combat radio system. There were many times I couldn't talk to anyone. Once, while trying to get into a better position to talk to the battalions, I forgot where I was and moved my vehicle out from behind the cover of some buildings. I was bent down looking at my map when I heard firing that sounded closer than most. I looked up in time to see tracers zipping past the front of my vehicle. I automatically threw it into reverse, then stood on the accelerator. (Thank God no one was behind me. I would have run him over for sure.) The episode was scary and instructive (don't get so caught up in what you're doing that you forget basic stuff, such as staying out of enemy observation). I was a lot more cautious after that. I kept my vehicle behind some large buildings at the end of town and peeked around the corner only when the firing sounded closer. Mostly I just talked on the radio, relaying messages from the battalion teams, doing my best to keep track of where units were, and relaying situation reports to Colonel Noble. When you get right down to it, I was little more than a spectator.

From my position, I could see down the main street into town and gauge the progress of the two battalions. The crackle of machine-gun fire swelled and ebbed every few minutes in a sine curve pattern as the Saudis wrinkled out Iraqi resistance in the town. Periodically there were larger explosions as TOWs, mortars, and 90mm guns reduced more resolute pockets. There were still burning armored vehicles on the main street, both Saudi and Iraqi, and the smoke from them, combined with several building fires, left Khafji in a dirty haze of battle smoke. I was surprised at the damage that had been done to the town in such a short time, damage done mostly by us. The Saudi guardsmen had fired a lot of ammunition into the town, and scarcely a building was unscathed. For the first time I noticed Iraqi dead near one of their burning APCs. For a moment I had mistaken the bodies for duffel bags blown off the vehicle when it was hit.

In truth, the attack didn't need too much coordination; both battalions were doing fine. The 7th Battalion attacked to clear the town north of the Khafji Beach Hotel and up to the desalinization plant. Iraqi resistance was weak except for a few pockets that had to be reduced by TOW, 90mm, and mortar fire. The 8th Battalion completed its clearing of southern Khafji without much trouble (although both Major Sampson and Lieutenant Colonel Bowers told me they were concerned when the battalion had stopped to pray in the middle of the clearing operation). By 1500, pockets of resistance were reduced and all the Iraqi vehicles in town were either destroyed or captured. A few tried to make a run for it back to Kuwait but were destroyed either by Saudi TOWs or Marine attack helicopters. Some Iraqi fugitives hid in houses throughout Khafji, but most surrendered. The prisoners were taken back to a collection point south of town where they were lined up and counted, then served tea in the classic Arabic fashion. The Saudi soldiers moved easily among them to talk, and soon we could tell the difference between Saudi and Iraqi only by the fact that the Saudis still had guns. Everyone was chatting happily away without the slightest embarrassment. We could tell that the Saudis were proud of their treatment of prisoners. If anything, they went out of their way to be hospitable to the Iraqis they had captured. For their part, the Iraqis were just grateful to be out of it.

Eventually the Iraqis were moved to the rear by trucks and buses.

At 1200 Colonel Turki finally gave the order to move the brigade headquarters forward along with the remainder of the 6th Battalion. By darkness the battalions had closed on Khafji and were in hasty defensive positions. A few buildings still burned, and numerous Iraqi and Saudi vehicles still smoldered in the streets, but the battle for Khafji was over.

The Saudis finished their initial clearing of the town too late in the day to do major repositioning before it got dark, and Colonel Noble didn't want to take the chance that units would shoot one another by mistake. The next morning, however, he set about organizing the hasty defense of the city. The brigade headquarters was still en route to Khafji, and Noble was still, for all intents and purposes, in charge.

I spent most of 2 February moving from unit to unit and coordinating their place in the defense. I first visited Lieutenant Colonel Taylor in the 7th Battalion. I found him and Lieutenant Colonel Matar sitting on a carpet beside their vehicles and eating breakfast. Both had gotten some sleep but still looked haggard. Mike Taylor had seen more of the fight than any of us and was still a bit overawed by it. He was proud of the 7th Battalion and effusive in his praise of Lieutenant Colonel Matar's conduct during the battle. Although Matar would never say so to us, Taylor and I knew that he was very unhappy with brigade's command and control of the battle. He and Taylor thanked Colonel Noble for doing what he could and took their assigned sector in the proposed defense of Khafji without comment. It was moving to speak to them. Both were tired and dirty, but they had an air of satisfaction and triumph about them. They were winners and they knew it.

I also visited 5th Battalion and spoke with Lieutenant Colonels Laage and Naif. There was some confusion as to where the MODA tank battalion was, so I just told them they were the extreme western flank covering the SANG compound. I was concerned that this defensive scheme would put us well within range of the same Iraqi artillery from which we had withdrawn out of range at the beginning of the war, but there was no other choice save abandoning Khafji again. Even I could see that that option was a nonstarter.

The night of 2 February I spent with Lieutenant Colonel Bowers and Major Sampson in the 8th Battalion. It was pulled up at the desalinization plant, and we spent the night in the plant workers' apartments, where the plumbing still worked. All of us were dirty and took turns showering. Major Sampson had found some eggs that had not gone bad, and we made a huge omelet, which we shared. Sitting around this normal suburban-type apartment, in the light of our storm lanterns, laughing and joking about the day, I thought over what I had seen with a sense of wonder. After twelve and a half years as an officer, I had finally been in a battle. But I was disturbed by the way that communications had gone and frankly horrified at the command and control structure we'd had to cobble together. I hoped that we could get Turki and the brigade TAC-CP to go forward the next time.

15

AFTER THE BATTLE

THE BRIGADE HEADQUARTERS CAME FORWARD and established itself in the SANG compound. I thought it would be too conspicuous a place, but the Iraqis didn't have eyes on it so it wasn't that bad. Although we dug bunkers as a precaution against artillery strikes, we never had to use them.

The Saudis quickly made themselves as comfortable as they had been near Ras Mishab. Turki, of course, had transformed himself from his "Dugout Doug" role to that of the conquering hero. All and sundry VIPs came up to see the aftermath of this first real battle of the war. As a result, Turki was often pressing the flesh and left the more mundane details of positioning the brigade and organizing the defense to Noble and the brigade staff.

The aftermath of the battle left all sorts of strange debris, especially from Iraqi vehicles that had been knocked out trying to flee Khafji. One of the major reasons that the Iraqis had not organized a more creditable defense in those few critical hours they were in the town unmolested by coalition forces was that most soldiers had been too busy looting. As a result, many of their vehicles were overloaded, some to the point that it interfered with weapons function. A lot of this loot was what you'd expect from an army on a foraging expedition: all manner of foodstuffs, warm clothing and blankets, fuel. What was surprising was the stuff with no redeeming military value that was just plain loot. There were a lot of TVs and radios, VCRs, and other electronic gear, along with cassette tapes and movies. Strangely enough, there were a lot of air conditioners carried on the top decks of armored personnel carriers. On one particular APC, I saw two air conditioners and a barber's chair. They had been jarred loose by the impact of Saudi gunfire but were still hanging off the vehicle. It was as though we had surprised some twentieth-century Visigoths carrying their loot out of a plundered town. The other pathetic thing about the loot was that many of the Iraqi vehicles that had been knocked out trying to flee the town had some sort of toys on them: Big Wheels, stuffed animals, playground equipment. When the Iraqi vehicles were hit, the loot was blown all over the desert around the vehicle. It was disquieting to see a burning APC with a couple of burned bodies on the ground beside it with blankets, television sets, and scorched stuffed animals strewn all about. It wasn't what I had expected to see at all.

Many Iraqi vehicles had been abandoned, and in the end we captured about twenty APCs in serviceable condition as well as a couple of tanks. The Saudis had looted many of them for souvenirs already, but I still managed to get hold of an AK-47 and ammunition from one of the APCs, and an RPG with some rockets from another. I checked the rockets to make sure they were safe, then stashed the weapons in the back of my Jimmy. It certainly beat having only a pistol to go to war with.

I was surprised at the disorderliness of the Iraqi vehicles. Equipment had been thrown into them any old way. It didn't look as though the Iraqis had load plans or even knew how to properly stow weapons and ammunition. Many of the Iraqi APCs were literally stuffed with crates of RPGs and recoilless rifle rounds, some to the point that soldiers couldn't have fit into the passenger compartment. So this was why we had seen them advance on us sitting on the tops of their vehicles. We thought it was because they were afraid of mines. It also explained why some of the Iraqi APCs had literally vaporized when they had been hit.

All day on 2 February the Saudis rummaged through the knocked-out and abandoned Iraqi vehicles. Several American technical evaluation teams came up to look at the Iraqi armor, but in most cases they were not able to get the full benefit of intelligence, even from Iraqi vehicles that had been abandoned intact, because of the vandalism and souvenir taking inflicted on the enemy vehicles after the battle. Several of the intelligence officers complained to me, but I could only shrug. What did they want me to do, go up to the Saudis and say, "Give back your souvenirs"? I would have gotten laughed out of town.

The intelligence analysts were especially interested in the add-on armor the Iraqis had put on the T-59 Chinese tanks. They were disdainful of its effect, noting that the extra weight offered minimal protection and made it easy for the tank to get bogged down in wet sand. They were also surprised at some of the weapons we had captured, especially the SA-14 shoulder-fired antiaircraft missiles (a Russian "Stinger") and French Milan antitank missiles. What surprised them (and me) was the fact that the Iraqis had not used these weapons, instead relying on the simpler RPG-7s, recoilless rifles, and machine guns. The intelligence analysts were at a loss to explain this. I was just grateful.

The Saudi guardsmen collected every Iraqi vehicle that could still run and brought them to the SANG compound outside of town as trophies. By the end of the day we had a dozen type-63 APCs and two tanks. In addition there were seventy-six burned-out hulks of Iraqi vehicles south of the border, in and around Khafji. Many Saudis (and quite a few American advisors) had souvenir weapons. Small arms were one thing, but I was concerned with all the captured antitank rounds and explosives. Based on a recommendation from Colonel Noble, the Saudis began collecting every captured weapon bigger than a rifle and stockpiling it at the SANG compound.

It wasn't just Iraqi munitions we had to worry about. Khafji right after the battle was an extremely dangerous place. Unexploded munitions from both Iraqi and coalition forces were everywhere. Especially prevalent were rockeye bomblets—powerful, little grenade-sized bombs that had fallen in the hundreds from a single canister that burst open in midair north of town. The bomblets had a fairly high dud rate. After two casualties on 2 February from unexploded ordnance, the Saudi guardsmen of the King Abdul Aziz Brigade learned to leave duds alone. To their credit, the Saudi chain of command placed great emphasis on dud safety, and the brigade lost no more soldiers to duds.

Other Saudi units from MODA (army and Marine) were not as fortunate. In the two weeks following the battle, more than two dozen men were killed and injured by dud munitions in Khafji. There was a foolish and tragic incident in which a soldier threw a rockeye bomblet into a campfire as a joke; it killed or wounded nine men. All of this came from undisciplined souvenir hunting and the inability of commanders in these units to get the word out to their troops. In truth, several MODA units lost more men from these unexploded munition incidents than they did in either the battle for Khafji or the coalition offensive that would end the war. I was proud of the job the King Abdul Aziz Brigade did in protecting its soldiers from this menace.

With all the souvenir hunters, tourists, and intelligence weenies crawling around, Khafji was a busy place for a few days. On 4 February a group of reporters was brought up in a bus to tour Khafji. Noble and Turki took them around the battlefield. I chickened out on the opportunity to play what would have been one of the best practical jokes of the war. The reporters, mostly American and British men and women, were standing around looking at one of the knocked-out Iraqi tanks north of town when the Iraqis suddenly started shelling the desalinization plant across the road. They were using white phosphorus, and the shell impacts gave off puffs of brilliant white smoke. I knew they were firing blind from almost a mile away, so I wasn't too concerned. But as the *crump, crump, crump* of the falling shells registered, I could see on the reporters' faces that they were frightened by this sign that the Iraqis could, in fact, fight back. Then I noticed that only about a third of the reporters were carrying protective masks. More shells hit and many of the reporters looked at me as if to gauge how worried to be from my reaction.

All of a sudden I had the impulse to look at the shell explosions, exclaim, oh my God! and hurriedly put on my protective mask, running to my truck as I did so, then jump in and drive madly south. I can only imagine the panic among our fourth estate friends—fighting over the few protective masks or fleeing in terror behind me. Turki wouldn't know any better either. It would be fun to watch him panic. Then I saw Noble and reluctantly decided not to do it. The last thing the boss needed was a bunch of hysterical civilians convinced that they were going to be gassed. So I just let the little gaggle go in peace. Later that night at dinner I told Noble about what I had almost done. The look on his face was priceless. The more he remembered of the afternoon, the funnier it got. He laughed until his sides hurt. Finally he wiped a tear from his eye and said, "Goddamn, Marty, am I glad you didn't *do* that."

The artillery battalion also had moved forward and now began to shell Iraqi targets across the border on a fairly regular basis. Lieutenant Colonel Matar had been forgiven by Turki now that the brigade commander was flush with victory. The artillery positioned itself a few kilometers southwest of the SANG compound. The batteries received their targets from intelligence reports of enemy positions that came down from the Eastern Coalition Forces headquarters or, more often, from Captain Braden's ANGLICO, who were still with us and in direct communication with the Marine and Special Forces observation posts that had been reestablished along the border.

Khafji and its environs periodically came under Iraqi artillery fire in the three weeks leading up to the big coalition offensive. This fire was never directed at anything in particular, nor was the impact of it observed and adjusted onto target by Iraqis still hiding in town. Rather it was more of the same sort of "point-it-south-and-pull-the-lanyard" kind of fire that we had seen before the battle. It normally came a few rounds at a time, occasionally up to a dozen but never more than that. Mostly it impacted out in the desert; occasionally it would fall in town. I never heard of anyone being hurt by it.

It was still an odd experience to come under enemy artillery fire, even briefly. On one occasion I was driving north of town on the way to the desalinization plant when a series of shell bursts walked down the road for about twenty seconds at hundred-meter intervals. I looked at the new guy with me (a major named John Bombard) and turned south, driving about a kilometer, then stopping to see whether there were any more impacts. We waited about ten minutes, then continued where we were going like motorists who had just avoided a rain shower. Another time I was at the 8th Battalion with Lieutenant Colonel Bowers and Rich Sampson, eating lunch in the parking lot of a strip mall, when Iraqi artillery started landing across the street a few hundred meters away. Wordlessly we picked up our lunches and walked into a covered stairwell, then kept talking as though nothing had happened. The Saudis were equally nonplussed. Some would investigate the craters left by Iraqi artillery fires to get pieces of shrapnel for souvenirs. If the Iraqis' intent had been to intimidate us with this desultory fire, it failed completely.

In fact, we were almost eager for the Iraqis to fire artillery at us in this manner, because invariably we could locate their guns or rocket launchers in their act of firing and crush them with the resulting counterfire. Sometimes the ANGLICO would vector orbiting aircraft onto the firing unit locations. Other times, the 155 artillery of the SANG artillery battalion would fire the counterbattery missions based on data relayed by the ANGLICO. Toward the third week of February, the enemy artillery fire tapered off and stopped. I could understand why. The Iraqis must have known that their fires were of harassment value at best, and they were losing firing units every time they did it. Smarter from their perspective was to wait until we attacked, so they would have an observed target to shoot at. I was surprised it took them so long to figure that out.

On 7 February a member of the 5th Battalion stepped on a dud and was wounded. This act was initially attributed to Iraqi fire coming from a nearby apartment building, so the guardsmen riddled the building with fire, then cleared it and the buildings around it. No Iraqis were found, but several had surrendered earlier in different parts of town. This led the SANG to finally do a thorough sweep of the town, which netted a surprising number of Iraqis. By the end of the day we had rounded up more than thirty fugitives who had found empty houses and chosen to sit out the war. We couldn't blame them. The weather had been miserable, cold, and rainy for several days. There were soft beds and warm clothes along with plenty to eat left in the houses. Far from sniping or reporting back on our movements to the Iraqis up north, these guys were on a low-profile campout. All surrendered upon being discovered, and none offered the slightest resistance.

Although the sweep got most of the Iraqis, periodically over the next week a straggler would give himself up, or try to. I saw an Iraqi soldier trying to wave down a Saudi convoy, and it drove right by him. I called in to the advisor TOC and told them to inform the military police (MPs) that there was another Iraqi on Main Street. Presently a red-and-white MP jeep with one man came up to the Iraqi, who was sitting dejectedly on the curb. The Saudi MP leaned over and opened the passenger door. The Iraqi scrambled up obediently and handed the Saudi his rifle, then he got into the jeep and they drove off. I was reminded of Andy Griffith picking up the town drunk.

Not much went on once we got settled into our defensive positions. Ideally we should have sent strong combat patrols up north to maintain contact with the Iraqis and keep them off balance. However, we were under instructions not to go in that direction, because anything north of the border was regarded as hostile and could be engaged at will by coalition forces. So we had to be content with our line of observation posts at the border itself.

In truth, Turki and the brigade staff gladly accepted this limitation. I was sure that we could have coordinated limited offensive patrol action with the air missions being conducted in southern Kuwait. I drew up several concepts for reconnaissance in force up to the Iraqis' first line of defense that involved company-sized elements supported by the brigade's artillery and Captain Braden's ANGLICO. Colonel Noble floated the ideas to Turki but didn't get so much as a nibble. Turki understood how much he had abdicated the battle to Noble, and now he was trying to reassert himself. The brigade staff was also unwilling to consider the ideas. Outside of a few of the younger fire-eaters such as Mohammed Al Gharni, most were only too happy to assume their defensive role at Khafji. In a way they were like pleasantly surprised tourists who had won five hundred dollars at their first hand at blackjack in Vegas. They could quit winners now; they had the power of the entire coalition behind them. Why do anything above and beyond?

Looking back, it's too bad that coalition forces didn't do more to engage the Iraqi first belt in southern Kuwait after the Khafji battle. A series of raids that ultimately withdrew might have bolstered the confidence of the Iraqis into actually thinking they had repelled coalition assaults. They might have moved more forces to the south to bolster their "successful" defense. Probably something like this was considered but ultimately rejected as being too complex and risky of coalition casualties. It's a pity, though. I believe it would have worked.

The upshot was that after the first week in Khafji, there wasn't much to do. We were dug in pretty well, but our requests to build obstacles and lay minefields to defend Khafji were denied. I could see the reason behind this. The coalition was going to attack north soon and there was no point in building a set of obstacles that would have to be negotiated by the attacking forces. The intelligence we received was that the probability of another attack on Khafji was low. Of course we had heard that the first time, but there we were.

I spent some of each day checking in with the Saudis to see if anything new was happening and if they needed anything. I had to watch myself to avoid being a pest about the patrolling issue. In truth, it got kind of boring, the monotony of it broken only by the occasional counterfire mission being worked by the ANGLICO.

Noble recognized this and reinstituted the program of sending people back to Riyadh for a few days' rest. I was unenthusiastic about this and didn't go with the first or second groups of guys. It wasn't much of a war, but it was my only one and it didn't seem right to take a break only a month into it. Colonel Noble, however, was adamant about sending me in the third group, saying he wanted me to update the OPM-SANG rear in Riyadh about what the brigade was doing. Colonel Noble was still trying to get the 1st Brigade, or at least some of its units (particularly the artillery battalion), out of Riyadh to come up and join us. I didn't know how much weight I would carry as a pitchman, but I promised to talk to Brigadier General Taylor about it. So around 15 February I went back to Riyadh for a few days.

Riyadh was a happening place. American and Saudi troops were everywhere, and there was lots of activity. Numerous security checkpoints had sprung up, and everyone was checking everyone else's ID. I tried to stop at the PX on the way in but was halted at the gate by an MP Hummer mounting a machine gun and brusquely told to park outside. The MPs looked askance at my dirty truck with its broken window and shrapnel holes at the rear (which looked impressive, but I hadn't even noticed until someone pointed them out to me several days after the battle). It wasn't worth arguing that I was one of the permanent residents of this place. Besides, one look into the almost carnival-like atmosphere inside the PX was enough of a warning not to bother. I just went back to OPM-SANG and checked in.

As it turned out, Noble needn't have sent me on the mission to get the 1st Brigade sent forward (I suspect he knew this when he sent me; it was just his excuse to get me to the rear). Brigadier General Taylor had been pushing this exact subject for some weeks. His point was that even if the Saudis felt they needed to keep back the full infantry strength of the 1st Brigade to assist in internal security operations (which, considering all the other police they had, was a doubtful proposition), why shouldn't they at least send their supporting arms (such as artillery) to augment the King Abdul Aziz Brigade? The SANG leadership was adamant that the 1st Brigade stay near Riyadh. My friend Howard Swanson, the 1st Brigade advisor, was frustrated with this. Clearly, the Saudis could afford to send the units of the 1st Brigade to support the 2d Brigade. They just refused to do so. Later there was a plan to send two battalions and supporting units of the 1st Brigade to Ar Ar, on the western part of the trans-Arabian pipeline (TAPLINE) road, but the war ended before the plan could be implemented. My friend Howard was destined to spend his war dodging Scud missiles and helping the Saudis make movement plans that were never implemented.

I had a small taste of what life under the Scud threat was like that evening. After a pleasant dinner at the OPM-SANG adjutant's quarters, I turned in to bed. An hour or so later I heard the alarm go off. It took me a while to get fully awake; then I realized that this had to be one of the famous Scud alerts I had heard about on the radio. Muttering to myself, I pulled on my pants and walked out to the parking lot. I had no idea where the shelter was but figured I could ask someone. Unfortunately, no one was outside at first and I began to feel silly standing there in my pants and bare chested with a protective mask strapped to my hip. Then several people ran by me with cameras and disappeared into a house. I heard a lot of shouting and saw more people on the roof of their houses, setting up tripods and getting video cameras into position. I called up to them and asked what they were doing. One finally noticed me and looked down with something akin to pity. "We're getting Scud pictures," he said in a tone that implied that I was asking a stupid question. I said to hell with it and went back to bed, feeling like a rube. No explosions occurred, so I guess it was a false alarm.

I found out the next day that this was common practice. At first people had been scared of the Scuds. But as the novelty wore off and their negligible impact was plain for all to see, they became sort of a tourist attraction. People had "Scud parties" on their roof and everyone had a camera ready, hoping to get that perfect Patriot-hits-Scud picture or film clip that they could sell. I could have drawn some unfavorable comparisons between the rear echelon in Riyadh and the guys with the brigade at Khafji, but the truth was, except for the fight at Khafji we weren't in much more danger than they were.

I spent most of the next day picking up equipment we would need, getting my vehicle fixed, and briefing members of the OPM-SANG staff on operations. I talked to Donna and told her to come back around the end of February. I figured it would be safe enough by then.

Many of the guys at OPM-SANG headquarters were envious of those of us forward deployed, and after a couple of days in Riyadh I could see why. They were involved in important administrative and supply work, and the war had generated numerous requests for planned equipment fielding and upgrades to be accelerated. They were working long days and every weekend and no one looked to be having any fun. The old saying "There but for the grace of God go I" was never more true. I spent a second night in Riyadh, then headed back up to Khafji leading a convoy of several new advisors who had joined OPM-SANG in the interim.

Nothing much had changed during my brief absence. We'd had a few more artillery missions, and the observation posts at the border periodically reported seeing individual or small groups of Iraqis, which would then be shelled. But that was it. Turki and the brigade staff were more than comfortable with the status quo and mainly fulfilled their role as tour guides for the Khafji battlefield. Most of the more dangerous duds had been picked up from the high-traffic areas, and most of the burned-out wrecks of Saudi and Iraqi vehicles had been dragged off the street.

To kill time I would go to the tallest building in Khafji (a four-story school building) and look into Kuwait with my binoculars. I could never see much, but it was something to do. Once I saw the battleships *Missouri* and *Wisconsin* off the coast and to my great delight saw them fire into Kuwait. The roar of their huge guns was loud even at the great distance they were from me; the sound arrived like an express train about fifteen seconds after the flash of the guns themselves. Amateur historian that I was, I knew that I was probably witnessing the last actual involvement of battleships in combat. The huge ships were majestic to watch and gave the impression of massive power. I couldn't see where their shells were falling, but I wouldn't have wanted to be underneath them. The battleships were more tangible evidence of the power of the coalition forces. So I spent a few hours on a February afternoon sitting in my deck chair, drinking cold soda and eating MREs (meals ready to eat), watching the battleships and airplanes rain explosives on Kuwait. There are worse ways to spend an afternoon. We all knew the big coalition offensive was coming, and we wondered what our part in it would be.

16

THE GREAT OFFENSIVE

TOWARD THE THIRD WEEK OF FEBRUARY, the Eastern Coalition Forces forward CP moved up to Khafji along with its advisor TOC (sort of a larger version of our own shadow brigade TOC). This was convenient in that we wouldn't have long to travel to receive updates from our higher headquarters. The only downside was that they occupied the schoolhouse, and the roof was taken up with numerous communication antennas. I still had my favorite observation place, though. Shortly after the Eastern Coalition headquarters came to Khafji, they issued their order for the general offensive that would begin on 24 February. The OPM-SANG advisors were given an English-translated copy by the division advisor group, and we pored through it eagerly.

When we read the Eastern Coalition Forces order, we were surprised to learn that the 2d Brigade's part in the great offensive was a humble one. The brigade was to create breaches in the berm at the border and make lanes through the first obstacles. After this we were to pass the rest of the Eastern Coalition Forces through and remain in place to widen the main road with our engineers. We also had the "be prepared" mission to follow and reinforce the eastern division forces if necessary. None of us thought it would be.

The advisors were disappointed and surprised at the King Abdul Aziz Brigade's small role. The reconnaissance in force on 22 February had clearly indicated the enemy withdrawing from the southern defensive belt. The King Abdul Aziz was just the sort of armored cavalry-like organization that should have been leading the eastern division, moving quickly to reestablish contact with the Iraqis in divisional sector. However, word had trickled down that MODA was more than a little miffed at the central role played by the National

Guard at Khafji. The scheme of maneuver would ensure that the guard remained in a subservient role. A key indicator was the detachment of our direct support artillery battalion to division control. Had they meant for us to fight, we certainly would have maintained control of it. The American advisors were more annoyed by it than the Saudi guardsmen themselves. Their philosophy seemed to be that they had won their fight, and if someone else wanted to lead the next attack it was all right by them. For Noble and me, it was especially galling because clearly 2d Brigade should have led. However, there was nothing to do but help the brigade get ready to support the general offensive in its limited role.

The engineers, secured by V-150s from the 7th and 8th Battalions, would create a series of fifty-meter-wide breaches in the border berm using bulldozers with armor-plated cabs. Other engineers would widen the breach and mark lanes into it. Once an initial breach was created, still other engineers would move forward, breach, and mark lanes in the first minefield. This would be easy, because the mines were largely surface laid and easily identifiable. Upon creation of the minefield breach, the armor of the eastern division would begin moving through the breaches: the two MODA brigades, followed by the Kuwaitis and the remainder of the Gulf Arab forces from Bahrain, UAE, and Oman. The King Abdul Aziz would follow on as required. Our subsequent task once we passed the eastern division through was to clear five kilometers into Kuwait to widen and mark lanes in minefields, accept transfer of prisoners, and repair the main road to Kuwait. The brigade's engineers, having missed the fight at Khafji, were itching to show what they could do.

The rest of the day was spent by the brigade staff giving orders to all of its subordinate units for the coming attack. Reconnaissance of the breach sites was a simple task, and the engineers were able to plan their breaches by looking over the actual sites. The artillery was already emplaced and registered. It would be easy to shift from planned preparatory fires to fires in support of the breaching effort in the unlikely event that they ran into trouble.

In spite of our best efforts, though, we could not get Colonel Turki to move the brigade TAC out to personally overlook the breach. He reasoned that he could control his forces just as well from the SANG compound. In one sense he was correct; there wasn't nearly the distance between brigade headquarters and the forces conducting the operation that there had been at Khafji. On the other hand, a commander should never pass up the opportunity to have eyes on his forces if he has the chance.

Noble was philosophical about this failure. The infantry battalions and the engineer company were chomping at the bit to make the breaches and pass everyone through. Lord knew there would be enough OPM advisors keeping an eye on things. Noble would be on hand if anything did start to go wrong. Besides, the 2d Brigade's part in this was pretty cut and dried. It was just a pity that we couldn't get Turki out forward.

We spent the next day rehearsing and preparing to conduct the breaches. The preparation of targets in southern Kuwait continued spasmodically, but the volume of fire was not nearly as furious as it had been in the previous two days. It was clear that the Iraqis were moving out, and there was beginning to be a dearth of targets to shoot at. Periodically, though, the big 155s would hurl their projectiles north into Kuwait, making the ground shudder with their concussions. All the battalion teams reported their readiness and the status of the Saudi units to the advisor TOC. A sense of anticipation was building throughout the brigade, as though everyone could feel the power of hundreds of tanks and thousands of vehicles massing behind our brigade, waiting for the order to pass through us.

We detached Captain Braden and his ANGLICO team to move forward with the Saudi Marines. They were too valuable an asset to leave in reserve with our brigade. We were all sorry to see them go. The ANGLICO team had been brilliant in its support of the brigade. Its assistance had been a key factor in the brigade's success, both in the fight for Khafji and the artillery duels afterward. Colonel Noble said good-bye to Captain Braden and the ANGLICO troops outside the advisor TOC. I watched them with envy as they drove out the gate. At least they would get to accompany the advance to Kuwait City. Also leaving was Capt. Steve Bonk's Special Forces detachment. They had been reassigned to other elements within the eastern division. We would particularly miss their linguists.

The artillery battalion would support the initial breach from where it was, then displace to join the eastern division's artillery to add general support and reinforcing fires as necessary. The artillery advisors were all packed and prepared to follow their battalion. Colonel Noble had to put his foot down on last-minute volunteers to "augment" the field artillery battalion advisor team. There were no other artillerymen besides Major Janda, who was the brigade fire support advisor and had to stay with brigade headquarters. Anyone else added to the artillery team would just be unqualified baggage. We all had our roles to play advising the brigade. This was where we would stay.

At dawn on 24 February, the lead MODA brigade entered the breach. Sunrise saw the eastern division conducting an orderly movement through multiple gaps in the berm. A few minutes later, the Saudis reported that they had taken the customs station on the Kuwaiti side of the border. The day was heavily overcast with clouds and oil fire smoke, but visibility at ground level was good. I monitored the progress of the eastern division and the rest of the coalition from my location in the advisor TOC. I was eager to see the offensive for myself, but I had to wait until I was relieved of my shift. It was almost lunchtime before I could go out and see the progress of the advance.

The eastern division forces were still moving through the breaches. Their progress was steady but slow. Here and there a broken-down tank or support vehicle waited for recovery, with its crew sitting disgustedly on top watching the world drive by them. For the most part, however, the movement proceeded without any major complications. The breaches were well marked by the SANG engineers with pylons and red and white tape. The engineers sat off to the side watching the armada pass them, obviously proud of their handiwork. Periodically I could see multiple-launch rocket system (MLRS) batteries firing multiple volleys of long-range rockets off into the gloom, adding to the fantastic quality of the scene before me. There seemed to be armor as far as the eye could see moving up to the breaches. It was an awesome sight, made even more so with the realization that the entire eastern division was only a fraction of the overall coalition offensive.

I drove through town to the border post, passing the Saudi Marines who were formed up south of the desalinization plant. They would be driving up the coast and eliminating any Iraqi pockets of resistance. I felt envious of them. Sitting in place and watching the rest of the world pass through is a hard thing. I climbed up on the water tower at the desalinization plant and looked out into Kuwait. Even with the haze I could see a huge number of vehicles surging forward. It was an elating moment. Suddenly, more than anything else I wanted to stand on Kuwaiti soil. The 8th Battalion had secured the Kuwaiti customs post, so I went to visit them.

The actual road to the customs post was undamaged. The customs station itself (long a suspected Iraqi observation post) was a burned-out shell. However, I could recognize in its outline the buildings I had seen on 1 August, when I passed through there on my journey to Kuwait City. How long ago that seemed. I stopped under the sun-shade of the post and looked at the gutted offices and the blackened cashier's windows. I remembered the cheery customs officials and how surprisingly easy the transit of the border had been. I hoped that they made it out OK. Certainly it would have been easy for them to run into Saudi Arabia, but maybe they stayed to retrieve their families. Either way I would never know. War leaves a lot of loose ends.

The brigade had advanced about three kilometers into Kuwait to secure the initial breaches and was holding in place while other Arab coalition units moved through it. The difference in the landscape between Saudi Arabia and Kuwait was appalling. The road north in Kuwait had been completely destroyed by Iraqi engineers. The pavement was so dug up and fractured that it was actually easier for vehicles to travel in the sand beside it than for engineers to try to make it trafficable again. Instead the SANG engineers concentrated on widening the lanes in minefields and filling in the tank traps and oil-filled ditches that they encountered. The Saudi MODA brigades were already well ahead of the SANG units and apparently had made contact, because a Saudi army MLRS battalion (Brazilian-made AS-TROS) pulled into firing positions beside me on the other side of the road. The battalion fired several missions, each one sending hundreds of rockets north onto the retreating enemy. I previously had seen an MLRS firing off in the distance, but this was the closest I had ever been to an MLRS unit firing. The noise and volume of rockets they fired reminded me of newsreels of the Soviet's Katyusha rockets in World War II. It was an awesome sight.

Soon after the MLRS fired there were several large explosions close to me. I thought for a moment that we were receiving counter-battery fire, but then I saw that the SANG engineers were blowing up the mines (which were surface laid and easy to see) as part of clearing lanes in nearby minefields. Intrigued, I went over to watch. Their technique was direct to say the least. A SANG engineer would walk up to a mine and inspect it for anti-handling devices and booby traps. Finding none, he would emplace a small demolition charge on the mine, then pull the fuse igniter attached to the charge's time fuse. So far so good. However, I was alarmed to see that instead of running at least a hundred meters away and lying flat, the SANG engineer would walk about thirty meters away and squat down. These were fairly large Italian antitank mines that they were blowing up, and I saw a SANG engineer disappear in the dust cloud of the explosion. Cursing, I called for medics and ran forward to see if he was still alive. To my amazement, the soldier rolled out of the dust cloud like a rubber ball, shook his head, stood up and dusted himself off, then reached in his demolition bag for another charge and went on to the next mine. I told their lieutenant that they should move back more when they blew mines in place like that. He smiled and agreed, then proceeded to carry on just as before. The engineers succeeded in clearing the lane, and to my knowledge none of them was hurt. Allah really did protect them.

Being in divisional reserve after the breach had us sitting around and waiting for the next two days. During this time we got to look at some of the much-publicized Iraqi defenses in southern Kuwait. What we saw left us shaking our heads in disbelief. It is U.S. Army doctrine that a defense is never truly finished. Any unit in the defense continues to improve its positions and obstacles in any way possible as long as time permits. Soldiers dig fighting positions (foxholes); then, if more time permits, those holes are dug deeper with overhead cover. If there's still time, the holes are connected by trenches. Mines and obstacles are laid out to support the defense. The key phrase is "continue to improve." All during the buildup to war and the air war, we had kept in mind that the Iraqis had months to prepare their defenses in Kuwait. The intelligence we had been given confirmed that the Iraqis had massive defenses in southern Kuwait.

Now here we were, looking at what we had been so apprehensive about. The Iraqi positions were, to say the least, much less formidable than we expected. In fact, every defensive position I saw showed a startling lack of completion and shallowness. It wasn't the Maginot line, that was for sure. I'll never forget one set of trenches that we stopped to investigate. The bunkers were uncamouflaged and clearly visible from several kilometers away. The trench itself was shallow, only about waist deep. But the entire trench—floor and walls—was tiled. It was like a bathroom floor that extended for five hundred meters. I could only imagine what was going through their heads as they built this. "Have you continued to improve your positions?" asked Saddam. "Oh yes, Excellency, we've got half the trenches tiled already and next week we'll put in sunroofs." They should have dug latrines, because their trenches were foul with excrement and discarded food. There was also a lot of equipment left there: field phones, knapsacks, sleeping bags, gas masks, weapons, and ammunition. It was the detritus of an army in collapse.

None of the bunkers had overhead cover to keep out shrapnel, and few had fields of fire that actually covered the obstacles to their front. Each strongpoint's metal water cistern, half dug into the desert floor, stuck out like a sore thumb. Looking at the dregs of dirty water in the bottom of one cistern, I could only wonder what troops would live like this. The dissolution of the Iraqi units due to poor discipline was evident. Their officers obviously did not support their troops by providing them with decent food or supplies. They did not insist on field sanitation discipline, and their positions became unhealthy pestholes. No wonder their morale collapsed.

Another example of the Iraqis gang-that-couldn't-shoot-straight defensive preparations was their "fire trench" obstacles. Much had been made of these in the press before the war. Coalition forces were supposed to be met with deep trenches filled with Kuwaiti oil. At the appropriate moment the Iraqis would set the oil on fire and the coalition forces would be stopped by a sheet of flames and pummeled by preplanned artillery fires. That was the theory anyway. The actuality of it was almost comic. The trenches were there, and filled with oil all right. The trouble was that the Iraqis had placed the earth that they had dug out of the trench on the wrong side of the excavation. The excavated earth should have been on the defender's side of the trench, providing extra cover for the defenders and an additional obstacle to be breached by the attackers. Instead the earth was on the side the coalition forces would be approaching from. All the coalition engineers had to do was bring up bulldozers and push the earth back into the trench, extinguishing the fire and filling up the obstacle to allow movement at the same time. Not that they would need to bother, because the bypasses around the trenches had no positions covering them. As a professional effort, it was pitiful. It made you want to conduct remedial defensive preparations training.

Even when the Iraqis had a good idea, they didn't execute it correctly. They did try to construct deception positions near their actual positions. The theory behind this technique is for an attacker to go after the dummy position instead of a real one. Later in the decade the Serbs used deception positions with great success against U.S. airpower in the Kosovo war. However, the dummy positions constructed by the Iraqis were so transparently phony that no one attacked them. Several times I drove up on devastated artillery batteries with guns overturned and trucks burned out. A kilometer away would be a dummy battery, pristine and untouched.

Once the last elements of the Eastern Coalition Forces passed through us, there was nothing to do but wait and see what developed. We were ostensibly in reserve, but I couldn't conceive of a circumstance in which we would be needed. If the Iraqis had tried to fight for Kuwait City, we might have been needed, because historically city fighting always incurs a lot of casualties. But the Iraqis were either running or surrendering in droves, so I didn't see Kuwait City becoming a Middle East version of Stalingrad.

So while the eastern division advanced, the SANG brigade sat and waited. The only Saudi guardsmen north of us were the artillery battalion. On the day the allies reached Kuwait City, Colonel Noble decided to ride up and visit them. Seeing that we were all straining at the leash to go to Kuwait City (and no doubt sensing that our brigade's major part in the war had already been played), he relented on his "no-one-forward-of-the-brigade-limit-of-advance" policy and let me and about a dozen other American advisors accompany him. The Marines had defeated a counterattack at Kuwait airport, and the Eastern Coalition Forces had encountered only spotty and half-hearted resistance. Coalition forces were poised outside the city, and we drove north eagerly in order to see the liberation of Kuwait first-hand.

The difference between the clean and well-maintained highway of 1 August and the wreck before me now was striking. The road had been all but destroyed for the first ten kilometers or so inside Kuwait. There was trash and refuse everywhere (on top of everything else, the Iraqis were major litterbugs). The pall of the oil fires added to the general dinginess of the scene as we moved north. We passed through numerous logistical trains elements of the eastern division forces and a few mechanically broken down Saudi M60 tanks, with their crews beside them calmly awaiting recovery. What struck me as I drove north was the relative absence of knocked-out enemy vehicles on or around the main highway. There were some, but they stood individually or in small groups. There was nothing to indicate that a large armored column had been attacked near the road coming south from Ahmadi. We had been told this was the case during the last night of the Khafji battle. I remembered advising Colonel Noble to break off the attack and establish a hasty defense. It made me wonder where the wreckage of the 5th Mechanized Division was. All that worry about the Iraqi second-echelon forces joining the Khafji battle and all those air strikes diverted and now where were the results? I began to suspect that the whole thing was just a phantom. There never had been that huge armored column, and we had bombed a lot of nothing. Noble had been right all along. There were as many broken-down vehicles as knocked-out ones. (The Iraqis' old maintenance habits were coming to the fore again.) We passed school buses bringing Iraqi prisoners south, the faces of the prisoners displaying a mixture of bewilderment and relief. At no time did I see an Iraqi prisoner show defiance. They were all just happy to be out of it. The school buses lent a weird touch: enemy soldiers as truant children being taken to detention.

It was coming up to Ahmadi that we first began running into joyous groups of Kuwaiti citizens. Cars traveled up and down the highway honking and weaving in and out of military convoys. Coalition forces had already entered the city, and now a huge carnival atmosphere enveloped the place, along with the oil smoke. A carload of young women, with Sheik Al Sabah's picture taped to the front of the car, which was festooned with American flags, waved us down. I thought it might be some sort of emergency, but as soon as we got out the women swarmed all over us, hugging us and ululating in the Arab woman's cry of victory. One especially pretty girl who couldn't have been more than twenty years old seized me in a bear hug and gave me a long and passionate lip lock that Donna would not have approved of one bit. The girls asked us to come home with them and promised us even more substantial shows of gratitude, but we begged off on that and contented ourselves with signing our names on their Kuwaiti flag. They drove off honking and happy and probably looking for younger and more willing GIs.

We stopped several more times as people flagged us down, but each time it was just to shake hands or have our picture taken. Families crowded themselves around us and had their relatives snap the picture. A few even pressed babies into our hands so they could have a picture of us holding the child. Somewhere in Kuwait there must be about a dozen pictures of me standing among various families, grinning like an idiot. We offered to hand out MREs, but no one was starving; in fact, all of them tried to offer us some small sweet or other that had survived Iraqi confiscation. Arab hospitality even in the worst of adversity. We learned just to honk and wave to the groups by the road as we approached Kuwait City; otherwise, it would have taken all day to get there.

Moving into the city, we could see that there were abandoned Iraqi positions everywhere. The standard of camouflage for these positions was as bad as the ones we had seen in southern Kuwait, and they could be seen from a long distance. They appeared to be made out of cinder blocks and sandbags. One even sat in the middle of an over-pass across the Ahmadi highway. Most had abandoned weapons and ammunition in them. I remembered the tiled trenches and could only shake my head in wonderment. After six months to prepare a defense, this was the best the Iraqis could do? It was utterly pathetic. The positions stood out as clearly as panel targets on a tank gunnery range. Half of them didn't even have fields of fire to cover the obsta-cles they were emplaced to protect. The Iraqis had done well to aban-don these defenses.

As we made our way into the city, we saw armed Kuwaiti resis-tance fighters and U.S. Special Forces troops at many of the intersec-tions. Even more people were out on the streets, going nowhere in particular, just milling around and waving American and Kuwaiti flags. I saw some Kuwaiti resistance fighters pushing several men down the sidewalk, kicking and punching the men as an angry crowd of people followed along behind them. I guess these were some of the collaborators we had heard about on the news. Oh well, you back the wrong horse, you pay the price. The city had numerous buildings either afire or already burned out, and the streets were scattered with wrecked and abandoned vehicles. There were no lights to speak of. All of Kuwait City was bathed in a dark overcast twilight from the oil fires. Numerous cars and trucks drove around, and their headlights gave the scene a strangely lit quality. It was very noisy with all the horns honking and the small-arms fire. We inched along slowly, mainly because of people stopping us and shaking our hands but also because of celebrating Kuwaitis who kept whizzing out of side streets in cars, honking and waving flags. The farther we got into the city, the more we could see that numerous buildings had been deliberately destroyed and set alight. More of Saddam's scorched earth policy, to despoil what he couldn't possess. I decided to go and see the Sheraton, to bring my odyssey full circle, if you will. We crept along the first ring road and eventually got to the traffic circle I had watched from my hotel room in what seemed a lifetime ago.

The Sheraton was gutted. The Iraqis had set it on fire, then parked a tank in front of it and shelled it repeatedly. I pulled my truck up in front of it and got out to stare at the devastation. Carloads of people honking their horns sped by, but I hardly noticed them. It was 2 August. The invasion seemed ages ago, but it had been only eight months. It was a strange and emotional moment for me. I didn't get weepy; I just sat there with a big lump in my throat and a twisted feeling in my stomach. Then I remembered the champagne in my cooler and thought that if there was ever a time, this was it. The bottle had been bounced around, and half was lost when I opened it, but I offered a toast and had a long swallow in front of the gutted hotel. It was as pure and sweet a moment of victory as I have ever felt in my life.

More trucks and cars passed the hotel, and there was a lot of firing into the air. I ducked reflexively at the noise, but no one was shooting at Americans in Kuwait City that day, at least on purpose. Some of the hotel staff was sitting on the steps, and a few of them remembered me. The Prince Charles admirer had departed Kuwait in October, and the hotel had been used as Iraqi officers' billeting. I gave the staff some MREs and a five-gallon can of fuel, then started back to my truck. I stopped once more and looked at the hotel. Remembering the nice place it had been before, this scene seemed such a damned shame.

A truck drove by me as I was getting into my vehicle, and a Caucasian woman waved at me from the back and yelled, "Are you an American?" I was startled and replied that I was and asked who she was. She started to answer but the truck pulled away. Intrigued, I followed them to the large park close to the Sheraton where I caught up with them as they were getting out of their vehicle. I could spot the young woman easily among the Arabs; she was in her mid- to late twenties, auburn haired and pretty. She looked disheveled but happy as she told me her story. Her name was Cathy and she was from Oregon and had been working in Kuwait City. When the invasion came she stayed with Kuwaiti friends and began assisting the resistance almost as soon as it was organized. I was surprised that she had not volunteered to be repatriated with the other western women and children in late August. She told me she wouldn't have felt right leaving her Kuwaiti friends. For sheer adventure, her story beat mine cold. I listened in wonder for a few minutes as she described life on the run in occupied Kuwait. Cathy was a seriously gutsy young lady.

I offered to take her back through Saudi Arabia and get her on a plane home, but she said she wanted to stay with her friends for a few more days. She also declined my offers of food and water. She did ask if I would call her parents and tell them she was all right, which I cheerfully said I would do. Then she was off to join her friends, leaving me to reflect yet again how many extraordinary people I had met in the last few months.

The scene in the park was awe inspiring. Thousands of people thronged around, jumping up and down and waving. Most were Kuwaiti, but there were also many guest workers from various Asian nations who had been trapped in Kuwait for the entire crisis. The sky was darkening rapidly as the wind blew the thick clouds of oil smoke over the city. The only illumination came from car lights, fires, flashlights, and floodlights being powered by generators. The mood in the park was happy bordering on hysteria. Pictures of Saddam were being trampled and spat upon. Some Kuwaiti armored personnel carriers pulled up to the waterfront across the road and began firing their .50-caliber machine guns into the air, the red ribbons of tracer disappearing into the blackness. Everyone was cheering and shouting. Above it all came the cry again and again, *"Allah Akbar! Allah Akbar!"* God was indeed great.

The other advisors and I were parked near the large flagpole watching the crowd throng around us and generally enjoying ourselves. Some of the Asian guest workers were short of food, and we gave away all our MREs in short order. Some of the girls approached us shyly for pictures, and before we knew it we had a dozen of them clustered around us while someone brought out a camera to preserve the moment. I noticed some Kuwaitis trying to raise a large national flag on the flagpole. Unfortunately they couldn't, because the lanyard had been removed by the Iraqis. However, they were not to be deterred. Presently, a cherry picker truck crept its way through the crowd to us and the Kuwaitis went about raising their flag. It took them a while. The wind had picked up, and the men in the bucket were buffeted considerably. In addition, the side braces on the truck were broken, so it was top heavy. For a minute I thought it was going to tip over and squash a few people, but the guys in the bucket managed to tie the flag to the top of the pole. Streaming against the wind it was beautiful—red, white, and green against the black sky. Everyone in the park started cheering and making noise at an even greater intensity, and every vehicle's horn seemed to be honking. A spotlight shone on the flag. Suddenly a weapon near me discharged, then another, then seemingly hundreds. Tracers were streaking into the black sky in a wild show of pyrotechnics. Many of them came way too close to the guys in the cherry picker, who screamed in terror, but I don't think anyone but me noticed. The men weren't hit, but I have no doubt they had to change their pants after they got down.

The indiscriminate small-arms shooting was disconcerting. With so many bullets splashing around, it was only a matter of time before someone was hit by happy firing. It seemed as good a time as any to get out of Kuwait City. We were essentially tourists anyway, and nothing good could come from sticking around. A conversation with Colonel Noble on the radio confirmed this. Everyone was to meet on the highway south of Ahmadi and return to the brigade.

The sky was even blacker now and the wind was howling, adding dust storms to the already limited visibility. Cars and military vehicles zoomed all over the place, and the trip back was a nightmare. We were fortunate to have only one wreck (which practically totaled the vehicle but fortunately didn't seriously hurt anyone). When we got back, Colonel Noble forbade anyone else to go to Kuwait City. We would stay in contact with our artillery, but other than that we would stick to our own patch of southern Kuwait.

For the next few days we just hung around and waited to see what would happen. The line battalions didn't have much to do—they ran the border crossing station and escorted the odd prisoner-of-war convoy—but for the most part they just sat in their positions. The guys who had their work cut out for them belonged to the engineer company. They were in their glory. We were responsible for restoring the main road in the southern part of Kuwait, and the SANG engineers went at it with a will, filling in tank traps and fire ditches, removing barbed wire, and clearing minefields. Soon the main supply road within our sector was as good as we could make it without actual paving equipment. The engineers then went to work clearing minefields and destroying ammunition dumps farther afield from the actual main road.

We listened on the BBC about the successful meeting between General Schwarzkopf and other coalition leaders with the Iraqis and about the end of the war. It was a strange feeling. Our situation hadn't changed much, so the end of the war didn't have as much impact as I imagined it had in those units that had attacked the

Republican Guards. I didn't have any elated feeling of "I've survived it," because (except for a few instances during the Khafji fight) my life hadn't been in much danger. It was like a sudden, unexpected ending to a movie: "Show's over. . . . Bye." I had the vague feeling that there should be something else.

With the formal ending of hostilities, the traffic to Kuwait City increased tenfold: commercial and military trucks carrying all kinds of supplies, reporters, government officials from numerous nations, and U.S. military traffic of every stripe. There were a few bizarre incidents, such as when an American unit tried to take one of the knocked-out T-55s near Khafji as a "trophy." It was a piece of battlefield junk, but the Saudis got quite indignant about it. I could see their point; it was *their* piece of battlefield junk. They had knocked it out, so they felt a proprietary interest in it. I saw a lot of American units pass through dragging captured Iraqi vehicles. They now adorn the front entrances of headquarters buildings everywhere.

The sky was still black from the fires and the air quality was nasty. Many of us were coughing up black junk, and I wondered how long we would have to stay in Khafji. The artillery battalion returned a few days after the cease-fire, and soon all Saudi combat units had come back south. The MODA units traveled straight back to their barracks, but the King Abdul Aziz Brigade was told to remain on the border, reestablish border security, and prevent smuggling and uncontrolled border crossing from the Kingdom into Kuwait. They would have to do this until the regular border patrol and customs routine could be reestablished. The guardsmen were not happy with this news but took it like the good servants of the king they were.

The border duty was mostly boring—identifying abandoned weapons and ammunition sites, and monitoring the flow of people from Kuwait to Saudi Arabia. (The guardsmen limited themselves to checking other Arabs and third country nationals; Americans and other coalition members were just waved through.) The guardsmen did stop a few trucks trying to smuggle guns from Kuwait to Saudi Arabia (entrepreneurs trying to get rich quick on all the free rifles lying around Kuwait), but for the most part it was just a dull grind of patrolling and performing maintenance on equipment, and waiting for the word to go home. We were apprehensive that this border duty might drag on for months, but as it turned out we were there for only about three more weeks. At the end of March we received orders to return to Al Hofuf.

The convoy back was a memorable experience. The brigade had almost two thousand vehicles, and more than six hundred of them were V-150 armored cars. Each armored car was flying at least one large Saudi national flag with the sword on the green field and Arabic script proclaiming the greatness of God. The convoys started out in good order, but when we hit Jubayl all hell broke loose. Like horses smelling the barn, convoys picked up speed and vehicles passed one another. Saudi civilians who had become inured to the endless convoys of American troops went wild with delight at the sight of hometown boys. Cars wove in and out of our convoys, honking and waving; people leaned out the windows waving Saudi flags. The Saudi guardsmen waved and cheered, proud enough to burst. The reception we received driving through Jubayl and Dammam paled before the one that awaited the brigade at Al Hofuf. All the Saudi guardsmen's families were waiting for them and there was a huge celebration.

It was their moment, so all the advisors went to the big house in Al Hofuf and downloaded their vehicles. It was strange having so many people in a house I normally had to myself, but there was room for everyone. A truck from Riyadh brought our mail, and I had letters from everyone. Donna was back at her job and soon I would join her in Riyadh, where we would belatedly begin our life as a normal married couple. My parents were fine, and I had a few letters of congratulations from friends. The letter from the army I opened last. It contained the orders for my next assignment: the 10th Mountain Division at Fort Drum, New York. This was not my first choice, but what the hell. It was an infantry division, and being in upstate New York would be close to Donna's family in Toronto.

The brigade spent the next three months not doing much of anything. We went into Ramadan schedule soon after we returned from Khafji, and the remainder of my time in Saudi Arabia was spent mainly documenting the lessons learned from the war and helping with next year's training plan. Quinn and the Vinnellis fell right back into place. Except for the captured tanks in front of the brigade headquarters, you might have thought the Gulf War had never happened. Eventually I turned the brigade team over to Major Tidler and went to Riyadh to outprocess.

The last night in Saudi Arabia, I lay next to Donna and listened to the muezzin in the distance. The tour hadn't worked out so badly. I'd definitely had my share of adventure. Now I was in for another adventure, parenthood. At least Fort Drum would be a nice, quiet assignment, just the place to start a family. After all, who ever heard of the 10th Mountain Division going anywhere?

With that lighthearted thought, I went to sleep. I was wrong, of course. My upcoming assignment to Fort Drum would see me deployed to Hurricane Andrew relief and Somalia, but that's another story.

POSTSCRIPT

CAMP DOHA KUWAIT, FEBRUARY 28, 2003

As I write this the build-up of forces in Kuwait continues and de-spite the hopeful talk of newscasters and politicians, war with Iraq looks all but certain. It has been an eventful dozen years since I stood in front of the burned-out Sheraton and marveled at having come full circle without so much as a scratch. Now we go through our scud drills in the headquarters, preparing for possible Iraqi chemical strikes as the force build up continues. (The more things change . . .)

As before, the weak-kneed and faint of heart are predicting disas-ter, and, as before, the troops phlegmatically shake their heads and continue their preparations. ("No blood for oil!"—yes, we've seen this movie before). Many of the people around me were deployed for Afghanistan before this and it is common to find men who have been away from their families for over a year. The full meaning of the old World War II deployment standard of "In it for the duration plus six months" is starting to come home to us. Everyone bitches, but no one truly complains. There is a great sense of mission and purpose around me. After all the months of waiting everyone just wants to "finish this asshole" and go home. I have never been prouder to be a member of the American Army. Soldiers are magnificent people.